The Obituary Book

The Obituary Book

ALDEN WHITMAN

Chief Obituary Writer of
The New York Times

STEIN AND DAY/*Publishers*/New York

CONTENTS

6   CONTENTS

THE ART OF THE OBITUARY

EVERY DAY IN the world 146,000 persons die. In the United States alone there is one death every sixteen and a half seconds for a total of 5,236 a day. And in New York City the number who die each day is 250. But even on the best of days, when newspapers can allot generous space, only a minuscule portion of those who have died are wept by others than relatives and friends. Death, the cliché assures us, is the great leveler; but it obviously levels some a great deal more than others.

In these circumstances, one's chances of leaving a memorial in print are slim. There are, however, some simple rules (but not necessarily infallible ones) for obtaining post mortem inches of type. The chiefest of these is to be either unassailably famous or utterly infamous: either way a man has established a public name, and editors will feel bound to write about him. One is better off, of course, if his celebrity rests on solid foundation—if he's been a President of the United States, the first to transplant a human heart, winner of a Nobel Prize, outstanding in the arts; has contributed singularly to the public weal, has been a surpassing entertainment star, or a captain of finance or industry. Nonetheless, it is not necessary to do anything useful to be famous, as witness the Duchess of Windsor or Barbara Hutton.

As for infamy, the more majestic the scale the better the obit, for scoundrels are inherently interesting as epitomizing one aspect of the Walter Mitty in all of us. The rule is, don't be a piker. Lizzie Borden wasn't; nor was Al Capone; nor Legs Diamond; nor Interior Secretary Albert B. Fall; nor Ivar Kreuger. It's the middle achievers who get short shrift: Bernard Goldfine, Willie Sutton, Mickey Cohen.

There are also several minor orders of fame and infamy: authors of best sellers; chefs; opera divas; murky poets; sports personalities; judges; college presidents and professors; former Nazis who have cleansed themselves by building weaponry for the United States; former Communists who have purged themselves to the FBI; movie, radio, and television figures; generals and admirals; and philanthropists. These (and others like them) all hold perfectly legitimate occupations and are generally respected and thus likely to rate a good sendoff in print.

There is yet another category, and that is eccentricity. England nourishes her oddballs more than America does, but we have been known to esteem flagpole sitters, bosom friends of multiple cats and dogs, recluses, marathon dancers, and persons otherwise unschooled who know the story line of every opera or who can recite the list of Popes backward to St. Peter.

A final choice is to be controversial. This may be risky, for the praise one receives may be offset by the brickbats that are almost certain to come his way. Joe McCarthy was indeed controversial, but maybe it would be preferable to shun his obloquy. Mayor Daley? Spiro Agnew? Judge Julius Hoffman? Abbie Hoffman? The chances are that they will die with generous space, but not all the flowers will be sweet.

Just as there are rules for gaining obituary recognition, there are ways for guaranteeing against it. The poor, those who work in an occupation not high on the prevailing scale of social values, or who belong to one of the lesser regarded ethnic groups, or have never previously been in the news for good or ill, are unlikely to make it in death. Some blacks, of course, do these days, but they have to be exceptionally well known.

Alas, in obituaries, as in other news areas, the notion still prevails that "names make news." Never very logical or defensible, the concept persists in bedazzling most editors and writers—and readers, too, who have been conditioned to accept the idea by the very writers and editors who proclaim it. This reciprocal feedback explains why the taxi driver, the construction worker, the housewife and mother, tend to be ignored in death.

By and large, death is the least well reported of news events despite the fact that the obit page is the most widely read in most newspapers. This is because an obituary is so often thought of as the recording of a death rather than as a recapitulation of a life. This is certainly how it was on *The New York Times* until five and a half years ago.

Previously, it had been *The Times*'s practice to print a matter-of-fact and rather brief account of a person's life. Containing few quotes or flashes of perception, these obits were as dreary to read as an entry in *Who's Who*. In this respect they were not much different from obits that appeared—and still do—in most American papers, where the practice was—and still is—to hand out obits to young reporters (to teach them a sense of discipline in writing), to rewrite men for knocking out in an idle moment, or to older reporters spinning out the days to retirement. Save for local notables, most papers relied—and still do—on matter supplied in advance or on an immediate basis by The Associated Press or United Press International. The result has been dull writing, or, even worse, puffery.

Generally speaking, there are three kinds of obituaries in most big-city papers: those of a paragraph or two that record the passing of persons deemed of slight prominence or interest either locally or from afar; those of up to a column in length that deal with men and women of greater apparent eminence or accomplishment; and those running up to four full pages (reserved in *The Times* for Presidents of the United States) that recount lives whose significance is believed to merit extensive treatment. The first two kinds of obits are, in *The Times*'s practice, ordinarily supplied by the wire services or the bureaus or produced on day or night rewrite. Most of the longer ones are hand-crafted in advance, although there are occasions when one has to be written with an eye on the clock. The explanation for this is quite simple: it is impossible to anticipate every big death.

How does the obit writer choose whom to do and in what order? The first priority goes to Presidents and former Presidents of the United States and other illustrious officials and world statesmen. It would be an embarrassment to be caught wanting upon the death of such obvious personages. After that, age claims the next priority: a ninety-year-old is more likely to die than a fifty-year-old. And within the age priority, the obit writer has a subpriority that is based on a person's prominence, complexity, and perhaps the availability of materials about him. Cutting across all this, of course, is a person's state of health; an ailing man or woman has to be done at the moment.

In general, though, I try to keep to advances on those whose careers and lifeworks are substantially behind them and on whom, therefore, little updating is required at the moment of death.

This is probably as good a point as any to say a word about the nature of an obituary, especially a long one. It is (or should be) the recital of the main features of a life and the person who led it; it should be constructed as a whole and written with grace, capturing, ideally, its subject's unique flavor. An obit is a form of biography, of course, yet it is not a biography, which is ordinarily quite detailed and which usually takes a point of view. A good obit should not be a partisan document. Indeed, it ought to be as dispassionate and as many-sided as possible, telling what the person thought of himself, what his friends thought, and what his critics had to contribute. This is not so easy as it sounds, because any obit writer inevitably comes to like some subjects better than others. The trick is not to let this show.

The fundamental resource of the obituarist is his newspaper's morgue, a file of clippings from newspapers and magazines in which his subject is mentioned. The richer the morgue the easier the research task. *The Times* has a superb morgue, the harvest of clippings over many years.

After winnowing out the useful clips, I ordinarily turn to our Editorial Reference Library, which is unusually well stocked with biographical material not only from standard reference works but also with books on an astonishing variety of subjects from aardvarks to Zeitgeist. Lacking success there, I use the New York Public Library and other special libraries, in which the city abounds. There is virtually nothing in print that one can't find out if he looks hard enough and is willing to spend the time. There are also, thank God, usually academic experts at the other end of a telephone who are happy to share their recondite researches with a less erudite reporter.

The Times itself, moreover, contains an enviable collection of men and women with special knowledge. There are at least two scholars of Chinese, one of Japanese, a bridge expert, a chess wizard, a clutch of music, movie, dance, and art experts, a couple of economists, several physicians, men with experience in every country in the world, a staff of foreign correspondents on active duty, national reporters and a Washington Bureau. There is nothing Barmecidal about the feast of brains for the picking on *The Times*. Indeed, some excellent obits have been written by these experts out of their special competence.

A further resource, in which *The Times* is a pioneer, is the interview with a small number of likely obituary subjects, men and women who can add substantially to the writer's understanding of them and their careers. This is an enormously important avenue to knowledge, for these interviews can add an extra dimension to the finished obit—a sense of intimacy with the man or woman whose life is being portrayed.

Aren't such interviews ghoulish, both for the interviewer and the subject? In the four years or so that I have been doing them, I must say that I have never felt like an undertaker; nor, so far as I can discern, have I been so regarded. Only the young are immortal. Elderly people have reconciled themselves to mortality and are thus often willing to look back over their lives with a mixture of pride, candor, detachment, and even amusement.

I discovered this in my first interview in 1966—that with former President Harry S Truman in Independence, Missouri. It was 8 A.M. on a bitterly cold late winter day when the sprightly, eighty-one-year-old Mr. Truman stepped out of his car and, cane in hand, entered the private wing of the Harry S Truman Library. Inside, he greeted me with a professional handclasp, and took me to his office. After chatting about his daughter Margaret, whom I had met on several occasions, Mr. Truman swung around in his former White House chair, fixed me through his rimless spectacles and announced in his characteristic Missouri twang, "I know why you're here, and I want to help you all I can."

Our conversation ranged freely over the controversial incidents of his Presidency. He became, I believe, fascinated with the idea of talking for history, as it were, for he spent most of the day with me, including a visit to his barber in Kansas City.

Since then I have talked to more than thirty persons around the world, acquiring background material and quotations that have been incorporated in their obits. I have been turned down by remarkably few persons, among them Bernard Law Montgomery of World War II fame and Edmund Wilson, who said he was too busy being a critic to be bothered. Some others have been hesitant at first; but, having acquiesced, seem to have enjoyed themselves.

One of these was Sir Anthony Eden, British Prime Minister during the murky Suez Canal crisis of 1956, now Lord Avon. At first His Lordship was adamant. "I have never given a private interview," he wrote me. In London in 1967 I pressed him by telephone. Pleasantly, he said no again, until I had the wit to say, "But, sir, this is not an interview for now, but for the future." "Oh," he replied, brightening, "you mean it's for when I'm dead." "Well, that's the short of it," I said. "In that case," he continued, "do come and have tea with me at the House of Lords." The result was a behind-the-scenes recapitulation of the Suez business as well as some glimpses into his private self.

Another notable with whom I was lucky was Samuel Beckett. The Irish novelist and playwright, who lives in Paris, has a reputation for disliking to reveal himself. I wrote him. No answer. I phoned him. No, he had absolutely nothing to say about his writing or himself. He hesitated a moment and I thought he was about to hang up. Then, "So long as you are in Paris, I'll have a drink with you and you can get an impression of me, but that is all." We arranged to meet at the Closerie des Lilas. Sitting at a table there, the conversation began uncertainly— the weather, his affection for the Closerie, his unhappy visit to New York. After about ten minutes he stopped the chat abruptly, and I was thinking of a graceful way to leave. "All right," he said suddenly, "I am here, you are here, ask me anything you want." Grabbing a menu (and then another and another), I scribbled furiously as Mr. Beckett unwound in reminiscence and comment.

The only person who has asked for questions in advance and who has submitted written replies is Vladimir Nabokov. But after handing me his responses, all meticulously typed, the author of *Lolita* and *Ada* fell to talking most of an afternoon about himself, his adventures in

America, and his work. A jolly man who seemingly cannot resist a pun or a joke, he appeared to relax as the sun streamed into the Montreux-Palace Hotel, in Montreux on the shore of Lac Leman, where he is a permanent guest. At one point, I inquired about the pronunciation of his surname. It set him off, with gales of laughter, into a recital, complete with facial twistings, of the variety of ways it is mispronounced, and ended with a brief tutorial session in how to say nah-BOAK-off in proper Russian.

On another occasion, Henry Miller, whose voice has never lost its Brooklynese, recalled for me the circumstances under which he wrote the *Tropic* books and spoke candidly of his love affairs and the inspiration for his erotic watercolors.

And François Mauriac, taking me on a tour of his home near Bordeaux, reflected on the sources of his sensibilities in his Roman Catholic upbringing and the manner in which he tried to express himself in his novels and essays.

I have a recollection, too, of Graham Greene meeting me at the door of his Paris flat and saying, "Oh, so you're the young man who's come to write my obituary, are you?" And then of an engaging conversation about his novels and entertainments. And of the diminutive Marc Chagall, padding about his Essex House suite in carpet slippers, talking about his conceptions of the world and his art. And of Conrad Aiken, elephantine and lumbering, rumbling his discontents that fame had overlooked him. And of Dean Acheson, sitting bolt upright in an easy chair in his Georgetown home, discussing patricianly his Cold War dealings with the Russians.

From these conversations—all the more frank and open because the person knows that what he says is not for immediate quotation—emerges some of the best material. The task is to distill it and integrate it with information from other sources into a finished article. It is never, for me at least, an easy job, and I have the greatest respect for my colleagues from whose nimble fingers prose flows as water from the rock smote by Moses.

From what has been published—from my first piece in 1964 to that on Alexander Kerensky who died in June 1970—I have chosen the thirty-seven obits that comprise this book. I have selected those that please me, without altering them in afterthought. Some are better than others; some seem creaky to me now; some read along damned well.

In publishing them, I wish to thank *The New York Times* for generous permission to reprint articles that first appeared in its pages. I recognize with pleasure my debt to Clifton Daniel, an associate editor of *The Times*, who approved my first obit trip to Europe in 1967 and a global trip in 1969. I have the deepest sense of gratitude to Abe Rosenthal, the managing editor of *The Times*, who gave me the opportunity to write obits when he was metropolitan editor, and to Arthur Gelb, the present metropolitan editor, who has paid me the compliment of his confidence by leaving me virtually to my own devices. I am grateful, too, to Harrison E. Salisbury, an assistant managing editor, who has lent me some of his knowledge at moments when I needed it badly.

Every obit in this book has been put together with the help of many hands and brains—those of Albin Krebs, my distinguished fellow obit writer; Mrs. Gloria Saffron, our devoted copy editor; and other colleagues I have consulted over the years, among them Michael Hopkins, Roberto Medina, Leonard Krisow, and Gerald Satterwhite of the Morgue; Gray Peart and Mona McCormick of the Editorial Reference Library; Linda Amster, Linda Lake, Barbara Bennett, and Judith Greenfeld of Editorial Research; and Samuel Solovitz, head night copy boy, who has been justly described as the heart and soul of the City Room.

And not least my wife Joan, the hoop that holds the staves of my life together. To her truly belongs this book.

July 4, 1970   ALDEN WHITMAN

The
Obituary
Book

J. B. S. HALDANE

J. B. S. Haldane died in India on December 1, 1964, at the age of seventy-two. The British geneticist and writer was an extraordinary person—a practicing scientist who was also a practicing humanist. I found this combination estimable, and it was difficult to know when to stop writing about the man who harbored it.

FACIALLY, Professor Haldane resembled Rudyard Kipling; epigrammatically, he took after George Bernard Shaw; politically, he followed Karl Marx; but in science he was indubitably John Burdon Sanderson Haldane.

Biologist, biochemist, geneticist, and sage of science in general, Professor Haldane was a daring experimenter, with himself as his own chief rabbit. "It is difficult," he once said by way of explanation, "to be sure how a rabbit feels at any time. Indeed, many rabbits make no serious attempt to cooperate with scientists."

He was, moreover, an indefatigable writer about science for the layman.

He made lasting contributions in human physiology by developing a simple treatment for tetanus (lockjaw), by laying the groundwork for high-pressure oxygen therapy and surgery, and by pioneering the principles of the heart-lung machine now widely used in heart and brain surgery.

In genetics, he was the first to discover linkage in mammals, to map the human chromosome, and to measure the mutation rate of a human gene. He also contributed to studies in human physical endurance and defenses against mustard gas, and he demonstrated the importance, in terms of survival, of deep bomb shelters in wartime.

Equally notable were his indirect contributions as a stimulant and teacher for more than forty years in Britain and in India. His students and his colleagues regarded his mind as luminous and lucid and his ideas as suggestive and succinct. Honored and decorated, he became a philosopher of the life sciences, shaping new pathways for biology and genetics and pointing to new directions for research in evolution.

In this respect, Professor Haldane counted human inequality as a blessing. "I believe that any satisfactory political and economic system must be based on the recognition of human inequality," he said in one of his last public lectures. He explained that "as our understanding of genetics increases, we shall, I believe, see that that society is freest in which opportunity for acting according to one's genotype [hereditary make-up] is maximized."

This appeal for the recognition of innate diversity could well have stemmed from Professor Haldane's own life. He was born and reared in a British society that refused to be confined by the establishment. Individualism, even eccentricity, was its hallmark.

Of Scottish ancestry, Professor Haldane was born at Oxford on November 5, 1892, the son of Dr. John Scott Haldane, a physiologist and mining expert who developed the decompression method used to avoid "the bends" in divers.

His sister was Naomi Mitchison, a novelist; his uncle was Viscount Haldane, once Lord Chancellor under a Labor government. Professor Haldane attended Eton and New College, Oxford, taking his degree in the classics.

He learned science by apprenticeship, assisting his father from the age of eight onward until he began formal research in 1910. His career was interrupted by World War I, which he fought as a member of the Black Watch. He was wounded and gassed twice (it was after this experience that he became an expert on mustard, chlorine, and other gases) and was demobilized as a captain in 1919.

After the war, he became a fellow of New College, and from 1922 to 1932 he was a reader in biochemistry at Cambridge.

There he was the center of a cause célèbre. He was dismissed for "gross immorality" in 1925 after being named corespondent in an undefended divorce suit involving Charlotte Franken, a writer. Supported by G. K. Chesterton, Bertrand Russell, W. L. George, and other notables, Professor Haldane won a reversal of his ouster and established the precedent that the private life of a Cambridge professor was to be considered as having nothing to do with his work at the institution. Miss Franken and the professor were married shortly after his vindication.

After a year as visiting professor at the University of California, in 1932, a year in which he was elected a Fellow of the Royal Society, he returned to Britain as a professor, first of physiology, then of biometry, at London University, where he remained until 1957, when he left Britain for India in a huff over the presence of American troops on British soil.

Departing London for Calcutta, near where he later set up a laboratory and home, Professor Haldane said: "I want to live in a free country where there are no foreign troops based all over the place; yes, I do mean Americans."

He became an Indian citizen, wore Indian garb, fasted on occasion in the manner of Gandhi, and lived quietly with his second wife, the former Helen Spurway, a science colleague he married in 1945 after Miss Franken divorced him. There were no children by either marriage.

As a scientist, Professor Haldane believed in finding out things for himself. To study fatigue, he once shut himself for long periods in a tight chamber, the air charged with carbon dioxide. Early in his career, he poisoned himself by swallowing bicarbonate of soda and hydrochloric acid, and found that ammonium chloride could cure convulsions in children. At one restless point in his life, in 1927, he underwent a blood-transfusion test in which blood was transferred from one part of his body to another.

In trying to find a cure for diabetes, he allowed himself to be put into a diabetic coma and then operated on without anesthetic so other doctors could carry out tests on him.

Professor Haldane was a burly, tweedy, shaggy man with a remarkably large head. Describing himself in 1940 he wrote: "I measure 6 feet 1 inch, weigh 245 pounds; and enjoy swimming and mountain walking. I am bald and blue-eyed, with a clipped mustache; a moderate drinker and a heavy smoker. I can read eleven languages and make public speeches in three, but am unmusical. I am a fairly competent public speaker."

He might have added that he also liked to tweak Americans. "The trouble with your school system," he once remarked to an interviewer in New York, "is based on its failure to recognize that children differ from one another. Every child receives the same training—an obvious error. In itself it is an indication of your genetical ignorance."

Professor Haldane's serious shafts were usually directed to upholding the concept of a pluralistic genetic society in which science would be man's servant. "It is easier to alter the social organization than to alter human beings," he said.

In a Shavian aphoristic manner, he observed that "the genetic heaven must be a place in which there is room for all sorts of people, each best at something or other."

"There is not any perfect man except in relation to tasks and environment," he insisted, contending that "a feebleminded strong man would give a better account of himself in the Darwinian natural struggle for existence than a physically weak intellectual."

Arguing the virtues of diversity with a homely example, he once remarked: "You cannot have a successful marriage unless the wife is better than the husband at some things. For example, I cannot cook or play the piano like my wife, but, on the other hand, she is not as good a mathematician as I am. Mutual respect is what you want all through society."

From this he concluded that "the society that enjoys the greatest amount of liberty is the one that permits and respects the greatest amount of polymorphism," or variety in human forms.

Outlining his genetic and social credo, he said: "I do not believe in uniformity. I think the more individuals in the world the better. If there is one lesson man can learn from the animals, it is just this: You have all sorts of dogs—shepherd dogs, wolfhounds, Newfoundland dogs, dachshunds, terriers, and St. Bernards.

"Would anyone think of producing only one species of dog and call it the perfect dog, eliminating all the others? What makes human life amusing is getting all these varieties of dogs into one family. And the hope for humanity is that that sort of a thing should go on, not only among dogs, but among human beings as well.

"If we have any lesson to learn from animal and plant genetics, it is that there is not any one best type in the species. On the contrary, we have various environments and various species to fit into them."

Professor Haldane wanted man to control science for his own benefit. "While man does not yet know how to control his own evolution," he once asserted, "it behooves us to begin thinking about what we should do when the time does come, as it probably will, when this knowledge becomes available to us.

"If we had discussed in advance what we should do with nuclear energy long before we knew how to use it, we might have agreed in advance not to use it in atomic bombs and would have gone a long way toward solving the problem we face today."

Early in his career, Professor Haldane developed scorn for Nazi racial tenets. "The doctrine of the equality of man, although clearly untrue as generally stated, has this much truth—that on a knowledge of their ancestry we cannot yet say one man will and another man will not be capable of reaching a given cultural standard."

This conviction, plus the climate of opinion in liberal circles in Britain in the 1930's, plus his own reading in Marx, Lenin, and especially Engels, drew the scientist toward sympathy with the British Communist Party.

In the middle thirties he announced that he was a Marxist, a description he applied to himself also in 1964. He joined the British party in 1942, served on the editorial board of the *London Daily Worker* until 1949 and wrote numerous articles for that paper and the *Daily Worker* in New York, mostly on scientific subjects. He cooled toward official Communism as time went on and declined to accept the biological notion of Professor Trofim D. Lysenko, the Soviet biologist, that characteristics produced by environment can become hereditary. He left the party toward the end of the 1940's.

As a Communist writer, Professor Haldane could make outrageous remarks with an apparent straight face, as when he wrote that Lenin had cured him of gastritis.

"I had it for about fifteen years," he said, "until I read Lenin and other writers, who showed me what was wrong with our society and how to cure it. Since then I have needed no magnesia."

Although he insisted that Marxism contained a working hypothesis for scientific research and application—a view he expounded at some length in *The Marxist Philosophy and the Sciences* in 1938—he was by no means a dogmatist, nor did he quote patristic utterances.

Professor Haldane had a certain amount of wry humor about himself. "I cannot deny the possibility, but at no time in my life has my personal survival seemed to me a probable contingency," he once said. And toward the close of his life, after he had been operated on for a particularly painful cancer, he wrote a doggerel in which he said, "My final word, before I'm done / Is 'Cancer can be rather fun.'" Then he added, "I know that cancer often kills. But so do cars and sleeping pills." He titled his verse "Cancer's a Funny Thing."

Professor Haldane held many academic honors. In addition to being a Fellow of the Royal Society, he was a corresponding member of the Société de Biologie, the Deutsche Akademie der Wissenschaften, the National Institutes of Sciences of India, the Royal Danish Academy of Sciences, and an honorary member of the Moscow Academy of Sciences.

He held honorary degrees from Oxford, the Universities of Paris, Edinburgh and Groningen. He wore the Darwin Medal of the Royal Society, the Darwin-Wallace Commemorative Medal of the Linnaean Society, and the Kimber Medal of the United States National Academy of Sciences. He was also made a Chevalier of the Legion of Honor in 1937 for his scientific services to France.

At his death he was head of the Genetics and Biometry Laboratory of the government of Orissa, India.

In addition to numerous papers in scientific journals, Professor Haldane's principal books were: *Daedalus* (1924), *Callinicus* (1925), *Pos-*

sible Worlds (1927), *Animal Biology* (with J. S. Huxley, 1927), *Science and Ethics* (1928), *Enzymes* (1930), *The Inequality of Man* (1932), *The Causes of Evolution* (1933), *Fact and Faith* (1934), *Heredity and Politics* (1938), *Science and Everyday Life* (1939), *New Paths on Genetics* (1941), *Science Advances* (1947), and *The Biochemistry of Genetics* (1953).

T. S. ELIOT

T. S. Eliot died in London on January 4, 1965, at the age of seventy-six. This obit was written on deadline. Luckily, I was able to draw on my recollections of the poet; for in company with other Harvard students I had taken tea with him almost weekly when he was in residence in Cambridge, Massachusetts, in the spring of 1930.

>   This is the way the world ends
>   This is the way the world ends
>   This is the way the world ends
>   Not with a bang but a whimper.*

THESE FOUR lines by Thomas Stearns Eliot, written as the conclusion to *The Hollow Men* in 1925, are probably the most quoted lines of any twentieth-century poet writing in English. They are also the essence of Eliot as he established his reputation as a poet of post-World War I disillusion and despair.

They were written by an expatriate from St. Louis, a graduate of Harvard College, who had chosen to live in London and who was working as a bank clerk.

The bang and the whimper, together with *The Waste Land* published three years earlier, established Eliot as a major poet. From there he went on to mellowness, fame, financial independence, and a Nobel Prize in 1948, but he always remained, in the layman's view, the poet of gray melancholy.

This persisted despite notable literary criticism that established new pathways in the field and despite two plays of considerable merit, *The Cocktail Party* and *Murder in the Cathedral*. These, while not of flaming hue, were not yet gray.

Cursed though he might be with that reputation, Eliot's early poems did not represent the more mature conclusions of his later years about the state of mankind and the world as put forth in *The Four Quartets*— or his delicious sense of humor, which included himself.

One example of his ability to see himself as something less than magisterial was expressed in this poem:

> How unpleasant to meet Mr Eliot!
> With his features of clerical cut,
> And his brow so grim
> And his mouth so prim
> And his conversation, so nicely
> Restricted to What Precisely
> And If and Perhaps and But . . .

Whereas Eliot began his seminal *The Waste Land* with the line "April is the cruellest month" and ended it 434 lines later with "Shantih shantih shantih," his more seasoned reflections included these lines from *Four Quartets*:

> . . . And right action is freedom
> From past and future also.
> For most of us, this is the aim
> Never here to be realised;
> Who are only undefeated
> Because we have gone on trying;
> We, content at the last
> If our temporal reversion nourish
> (Not too far from the yew-tree)
> The life of significant soil.

Not only did Eliot shift his philosophic outlook, but his poetic accents also became almost conversational, verging on the informal.

In his later years he had an office in London in the publishing house of Faber & Faber, of which he was a director. There he carried on his business, writing letters and articles, somewhat like the clerkish type he resembled.

In appearance he was then, as he was in early life, a most unlikely figure for a poet. He lacked flamboyance or oddity in dress or manner, and there was nothing of the romantic about him. He carried no auras, cast no arresting eye, and wore his heart, as nearly as could be observed, in its proper anatomical place. Indeed, he was a rather stooped man of about six feet who had a somewhat prim demeanor.

His habits of work were equally "unpoetic," for he eschewed bars and cafes for the pleasant and bourgeois comforts of an office with padded chairs and a well-lighted desk.

Talking of his work habits, he once said:

"A great deal of my new play, *The Elder Statesman,* was produced in pencil and paper, very roughly. Then I typed it myself first before my wife got to work on it. In typing myself I make alterations, very considerable ones. But whether I write or type, composition of any length, a play for example, means for me regular hours, say ten to one. I found that three hours a day is about all I can do of actual composing. I could do the polish perhaps later."

Eliot's dress was a model of the London man of business. He wore a bowler and often carried a tightly rolled umbrella. His accent, which started out as pure American Middle West, did undergo changes, becoming over the years quite British U.

The U was complete and unfeigned. "I am," he once said stoutly, "an Anglo-Catholic in religion, a classicist in literature, and a royalist in politics." Even so, his ascetic austerity drew the line at gin rummy, which he delighted to play of an evening. He also kept a signed photograph of Groucho Marx, cigar protuberant, in his study at home.

These touches lend credence to Eliot's attempts in later years to soften some aspects of his credo. His religious beliefs, he asserted, remained unchanged, and he was still in favor of monarchy in all countries having a monarch, but the term "classicism" was no longer so important to him.

The poet was born on September 26, 1888, into a family of some privilege that had a good background in the intellectual, religious, and business life of New England. After a year at Milton (Massachusetts) Academy, he entered Harvard in 1906 in the class that included Walter Lippmann, Heywood Broun, John Reed, and Stuart Chase. He completed his undergraduate work in three years and took a master of arts degree in his fourth.

Although he never took his doctorate, he completed the dissertation in 1916. It was titled *Experience and Objects of Knowledge in the Philosophy of F. H. Bradley.* This thinker's monist view of personality greatly influenced Eliot's poetic sensibility, reinforcing his themes of human isolation in guilt.

His Harvard classmates recall that he dressed with the studied carelessness of a British gentleman, smoked a pipe, and liked to be left alone. This aspect of Eliot was hardly altered when he returned to Harvard in the 1930's for a half year as a sort of poet in residence.

In that sojourn he lived in an undergraduate house near the Charles River and entertained students at least once a week at teas. The tea was always brewed, and he poured with great delicacy, his long and tabescent fingers clasping the handle of the silver teapot. The quality of his tea, the excellence of the college-provided petits fours, and the rippling flow of his conversation drew overflow crowds of students, who sat on chairs, on the floor, and on windowsills.

At these functions, Eliot was shy and patient with the halting undergraduates, and he must have suffered many fools, but such was his courtesy that he never showed it openly. He just sat and talked, reclining in a high-backed cloth chair, puffing and relighting his pipe, crossing and uncrossing his tweed-covered legs.

Eliot was an omnivorous and retentive reader. He consumed philosophy, languages, and letters, and this lent his poetry an erudition and scholarship unmatched in this century. Indeed, he carried scholarship so far as to footnote *The Waste Land* as though it were a thesis for a doctorate. He was also able, because of his extensive reading, to converse (and hold reasoned views) on a range of subjects from Shakespeare to Karl Marx.

His views and his expression of them were usually pungent.

"No one can go very far in the discerning enjoyment of poetry," he once remarked, "who is incapable of enjoying any poetry other than that of his own time and place. It is in fact a part of the function of education to help us to escape—not from our own time, for we are bound by that—but from the intellectual and emotional limitations of our own time."

He had a strong dislike for most teaching of poetry, and he once recalled that he had been turned against Shakespeare in his youth by didactical instructors.

"I took a dislike to *Julius Caesar* which lasted, I am sorry to say, until I saw the film of Marlon Brando and John Gielgud, and a dislike to *The Merchant of Venice* which persists to this day.

"It may be that a few plays and poems must be sacrificed [in school] in order that we learn that English literature exists and that an ordinary acquaintance with it is desirable."

Eliot believed, moreover, that "unless a teacher is a person who reads poetry for enjoyment he or she cannot stimulate pupils to enjoy it." Pursuing this theme, he once described how teachers of literature should go about it: "My Ideal Teacher will teach the prescribed classics of literature as history, as part of history which every educated person should know something about, whether he likes it or not; and then should lead some of the pupils to enjoyment, and the rest at least to the point of recognizing that there are other persons who do enjoy it. And he will introduce the pupils to contemporary poetry by exciting enjoyment; enjoyment first and understanding second."

Eliot, however, was not one to minimize the difficulties of understanding poetic complexities or achieving empathy with its mood and feeling. "The reader of a poem," he admonished, "should take at least as much trouble as a barrister reading a decision on a complicated case."

In 1915, Eliot became a teacher in the Highgate School in London, and the next year went to work in Lloyds Bank, Ltd. Hints of this commercial experience, of which he rarely complained, although the work must have been tedious, peep unexpectedly out of his poetry. For instance, A *Cooking Egg* contains these lines:

> We two shall lie together, lapt
> In a five per cent. Exchequer Bond.

Eliot's association with the "little" magazines—those voices of protest against the establishment—began when he was assistant editor of *Egoist* from 1917 to 1919.

He established *The Criterion*, a literary publication that never had a circulation exceeding 900. Later he was a working editor for Faber & Faber.

The first poem that started Eliot's reputation was *The Love Song of J. Alfred Prufrock* in 1917. In it he assumed the pose of a fastidious, world-weary, young-old man, aging into ironic wit. The poem is full of exquisitely precise surrealist images and rhythms, but it also has some everyday metaphors. Part of it goes:

> I grow old . . . I grow old . . .
> I shall wear the bottoms of my trousers rolled.
> Shall I part my hair behind? Do I dare to eat a peach?
> Shall I wear white flannel trousers, and walk upon the beach?

Eliot's strictures on applying concentrated efforts to the understanding of poetry could well apply to his next major poem, *The Waste Land*. Heavily influenced by Ezra Pound (it was in fact dedicated to that other poet of obscurity), *The Waste Land* was an expression of gigantic frustration and despair. But it made his reputation, although its author conceded in later years that he wrote it "simply to relieve my own feelings."

The poem, a series of somewhat blurred visions, centers on an imaginary waste region, the home of the Fisher King, a little-known figure in mythology, who is sexually impotent. Writing on *The Waste Land*, Helen Gardner, an authority on Eliot's writings, noted: "The sense of boredom and horror behind both the beauty and ugliness is expressed by juxtaposition of the beautiful and the ugly." In another reference, Miss Gardner wrote of Eliot's "union of the common and the formal, the colloquial and the remote, the precise and the suggestive."

Those critical of Eliot's writing accused him of obscurity for its own sake. They found his verses full of coy and precious little mannerisms. They accused him of loading down his writing with obscure code references that could not possibly be known except to a few intimate friends such as Pound. Unless you knew that Eliot called Pound "Mop" and that Pound called Eliot "Possum" you couldn't possibly know what they were getting at, these critics asserted.

After *The Waste Land*, Eliot's development was tortured and hesitant, but was clearly marked. His interest in the spiritual development of man rather than in his spiritual inadequacies grew after his early period, when he poked more or less good-natured fun at the church in such works as *The Hippopotamus*. He sees the haloed hippo ascending into heaven:

> Blood of the Lamb shall wash him clean
> And him shall heavenly arms unfold,
> Among the saints he shall be seen
> Performing on a harp of gold.

> He shall be washed as white as snow,
> By all the martyr'd virgins kist,
> While the True Church remains below
> Wrapt in the old miasmal mist.

In one of his poetry readings at Columbia University, Eliot recited *The Hippopotamus*. "It doesn't seem shocking to anybody now, I think, as it did all those years ago." He discussed his comparison between the hippopotamus and the church:

> . . . the True Church need never stir
> To gather in its dividends.

He recalled: "A good many years after I had written those lines I became a church warden and we were wondering how to keep the church going on the collections. So one lives and learns."

Eliot was regarded as an important literary critic as well as a poet. Much of his criticism was first published in literary reviews or delivered from the lecture platform. His first critical book, *The Sacred Wood*, was published in 1920.

This book and much of Eliot's subsequent criticism introduced certain types of writing to the intelligent reading public with accompanying evaluation that heightened interest in important writers who were not so well known.

It is possible that Eliot is most widely known through his drama *Murder in the Cathedral*, which was often produced in the United States and was made into a motion picture. It is a grim, sardonic account of the murder of Thomas à Becket, Archbishop of Canterbury, in 1170. An opera, *Assassinio Nella Cattedrale*, written by Ildebrando Pizzetti, was based on the Eliot drama and enjoyed a critical success.

Two of Eliot's plays enjoyed critical success in London and New York. *The Cocktail Party*, published in 1954, was a story of deeply religious experience told against a background of highly literate and amusing British people. *The Confidential Clerk* told of bastardy and general unhappiness.

In his lighter moments (and there were many) Eliot was an unabashed aelurophile. He kept cats at home, bestowing upon them such names as Man in White Spats; he also wrote a book of poems called *Old Possum's Book of Practical Cats*; and in his dry, cadenced voice he read the verses on the platform and for recordings.

These lines from *The Naming of Cats* illustrate Eliot's profound insight into the narcissistic world of the feline:

> But I tell you, a cat needs a name that's particular,
> A name that's peculiar, and more dignified,
> Else how can he keep up his tail perpendicular,
> Or spread out his whiskers, or cherish his pride?
> Of names of this kind, I can give you a quorum,
> Such as Munkustrap, Quaxo, or Coricopat,
> Such as Bombalurina, or else Jellylorum—
> Names that never belong to more than one cat.
> But above and beyond there's still one name left over,
> And that is the name that you never will guess;
> The name that no human research can discover—
> BUT THE CAT HIMSELF KNOWS, and will never confess.
> When you notice a cat in profound meditation,
> The reason, I tell you, is always the same:
> His mind is engaged in rapt contemplation
> Of the thought, of the thought, of the thought of his name:
> His ineffable effable
> Effanineffable
> Deep and inscrutable singular Name.

In 1927, Eliot became the first important American man of letters since Henry James to become a British subject. He said at the time:

"Here I am, making a living, enjoying my friends here. I don't want to feel like being a squatter. I might as well take full responsibility."

In 1949, King George VI conferred the Order of Merit on the poet. This is one of Britain's highest awards, and no more than twenty-four persons may hold it at one time.

Eliot returned to his native country many times, and in 1948 resided in Princeton, where he worked at the Institute for Advance Study. In 1950, he gave the first Theodore Spencer Memorial Lecture at Harvard on "Poetry and Drama." He lectured frequently and gave readings of his poems in New York and throughout the country.

In London, Eliot lived in a comfortable, modern apartment in Chelsea overlooking the Thames. In 1915, he married Miss Vivienne Haigh-Wood, who died in 1947. They had no children.

In January 1957, Eliot married Miss Valerie Fletcher, his private secretary. He was then sixty-eight years old and his bride about thirty.

MARTIN BUBER

Martin Buber died in Jerusalem on June 13, 1965, at the age of eighty-seven. One of the great thinkers of this century, he developed a philosophy of religion with profound consequences for both Jewish and Christian theology. His obituary was written on deadline, and it was one of my first experiences in becoming an instant expert on abstruse matters.

MARTIN BUBER was a Jewish religious philosopher of magisterial proportions whose views on the uniqueness of human and divine relationships had a fertilizing effect on the Christian world.

His philosophy of personalism was an amalgam of religious mysticism, Old Testament inspiration, modern psychology, and earthy common sense. It contended that man could achieve an intimate relationship with God through an intimate interrelationship with his fellow man; and that each man's relationship with God and a fellow man was distinct.

He strove for a meeting, "a dialogue," between man and God, with man as "I" and God as "Thou." This concept was developed in his major philosophic work, *I and Thou.*

Professor Buber's views were influential not only among Jews, but also among Protestant theologians. He impressed Reinhold Niebuhr as "the greatest living Jewish philosopher," and he was an inspiration in Dr. Niebuhr's thinking as well as in that of Paul Tillich, another leading Protestant theologian.

By his emphasis on dialogue Professor Buber was regarded as one of the pioneer bridge builders between Judaism and Christianity. In this respect, his views accented the nonformal aspects of religion as contrasted to theological systems. Religion for Professor Buber was experience, not dogma. He doubted that man was made to conform with canon law, or with elaborately worked out plans for existence. On the contrary, Professor Buber's credo stressed individual responsibility.

A story that was told to illustrate this point concerned an aged pious man, Rabbi Susya, who became fearful as death drew near. His friends chided him, "What! Are you afraid that you'll be reproached that you weren't Moses?" "No," the rabbi replied, "that I was not Susya."

The responsibility to be oneself means, in Professor Buber's view, that there is no rigid fate; that man, by contention with the forces about him, has the possibility of improving his chances for happiness. In fact, according to Professor Buber, man has an obligation to achieve an identity, to refuse to abdicate his will before the monolithic power of party, corporation, or state.

Professor Buber pointed to the duality of things—love and justice, freedom and order, good and evil; but he did not suggest a happy middle way between them.

"According to the logical conception of truth," he once explained, "only one of two contraries can be true, but in the reality of life as one lives it they are inseparable.

"I have occasionally described my standpoint to my friends as the 'narrow ridge.' I wanted by this to express that I did not rest on the broad upland of a system that includes a series of sure statements about the absolute, but on a narrow, rocky ridge between the gulfs, where there is only the certainty of meeting what remains undisclosed."

Professor Buber suggested two forms of relationships for man—an I-it relationship and an I-thou. The first is impersonal and imperfect.

An example of the I-it relationship would be where one person treats another as a machine; or when lovers find only a projection of themselves in each other.

In religious matters, the I-it is expressed when man abstracts God, or regards him as out of reach, or builds theological systems in which God is remote, or considers God too vast. Professor Buber, however, did not deny that God was the great mystery of the Old Testament, but he insisted that he was also personal.

"Of course," Professor Buber wrote, "He [God] is the Mysterium Tremendum that appears and overthrows, but he is also the mystery of the self-evident, nearer to me than my I."

The I-Thou of Professor Buber's thinking stands for the kind of dialogue—love or even hate—in which two persons face and accept each other as truly human. There is in such a dialogue, he argued, a fusion of choosing and being chosen, of action and reaction, that engages man's highest qualities.

I-Thou meetings, he explained, are "strange, lyric and dramatic episodes, seductive and magical, but tearing us away to dangerous extremes . . . shattering security."

The I-Thou relationship, because it strips away pretension, permits man to meet with himself, Professor Buber said. And, ultimately, it brings man into contact with God, whom Professor Buber called the "Eternal Thou."

This supreme confrontation has been described by Professor Maurice S. Friedman of Sarah Lawrence College, one of the leading interpreters of Buberism. It is "perhaps best understood," Dr. Friedman wrote in his *Martin Buber: The Life of Dialogue,* "from the nature of the demand which one person makes on another if the two of them really meet. If you are to meet me, you must become as much of a person as I am. In order to remain open to God [man] must change his whole being."

Believing that man's earthly chore is to realize his distinctiveness through the dialogue process, Professor Buber opposed both rigid individualism and collectivism. His social ideal was a small community unit somewhat like the kibbutzim of rural Israel.

Professor Buber also looked at Scripture in a special way. The Bible, in his view, was neither an infallible guide to conduct nor a mere collection of legends, but a dialogue between Israel as Thou and God as I.

Because of this interpretation and because Professor Buber was casual in his observance of Talmudic law, many Orthodox rabbis looked upon him as a heretic. As for Reform Jews, some of them also criticized Professor Buber because they thought he had made too much of the metaphysical Hasidic sect, from which he drew many of his ideas.

Many Jews also were dismayed by the application that Professor Buber made of his beliefs in calling for an improvement of Arab-Israeli relations. This attitude rested on his assertion that "the love of God is unreal unless it is crowned with love for one's fellow men."

Professor Buber was a small plump man with a large paunch. He was bald with a fringe of hair that hung down to meet the luxurious growth of a mustache and beard that virtually concealed the entire lower part of his face. When he walked he took rapid short waddling-like steps but nonetheless moved with a sort of delicate grace.

He lived in an old Arab stone house with red tile roof and garden in the Talbieh section of Jerusalem, which before Israel's independence was the quarter of the wealthy Arab merchants. His house had belonged to an Arab Christian family who left Jerusalem shortly before the war broke out in 1948. He lived simply in the book-crammed house with his study and bedroom on the ground floor. The furniture was old and dark and heavy and looked as if it had been brought with him from Vienna when he came to Palestine in 1938.

For several years he had not been active outside his home because of advancing age and periodic spells of ill health. But he loved to have visitors and to talk endlessly. When a caller phoned he would hear a click and then the quick sharp one-word response: "Buber."

When receiving visitors in his study, Professor Buber, who dressed informally, got angry with anyone who tried to ask him personal anecdotal questions, insisting that his private life was just that.

In conversation he would rest his interlocked fingers on his paunch and then move them to his forehead as he meditated about his response. He weighed every word and when he finally answered it would be in a very slow, low voice that seemd tinged by melancholy.

On his eighty-fifth birthday in 1963, some three hundred students at Hebrew University staged a torchlight parade to his house to pay homage to him. They swarmed into his garden and he walked out on his verandah, his face wreathed in smiles. The students sang to him and he talked briefly to them as they listened in absolute silence; and then they all went into his house for cookies and soft drinks.

Six months later, he flew to Amsterdam to accept one of Europe's greatest prizes, the twenty-eight-thousand-dollar Erasmus award, presented for his contributions to the continent's spiritual unity.

Martin Buber was born in Vienna February 8, 1878, of middle-class parents who were divorced when he was three years of age. He spent much of his childhood in Lemberg, Galicia, with his grandfather Salomon Buber, a well-known Hebrew scholar.

While studying the Talmud with his grandfather, he also read poetry and novels and paid an occasional visit to neighboring towns where he met Hasidic rabbis, holy men who could lead a community united by its love of God and its veneration for a wise man.

When he was thirteen he began a drift away from formal Judaism, symbolized by his offering a bar mizvah synagogue talk on Friedrich von Schiller, the German poet-dramatist, rather than on a scriptural subject. Later he gave up the daily prayer ritual, but not without misgivings that almost led him to suicide because of what he said later was "a mysterious and overwhelming compulsion" to visualize the "limiting brink of time— or its limitlessness."

He was rescued, he said, by reading Immanuel Kant and perceiving, as a result, "an eternal far removed from the finite and the infinite."

He entered the University of Vienna at seventeen and studied philosophy and the history of art there and at the Universities of Berlin, Zürich, and Leipzig. He received a Ph.D. from Vienna in 1904, but he did not make use of the title.

It was at the University of Leipzig, in 1900, that he was caught up by Theodor Herzl's Zionism, in which he found not only a political movement that suited him but also a religious idea that helped to resolve his spiritual confusion.

In 1901 he became editor of *Die Welt*, the Zionist journal, and the following year he helped to found Judischer Verlag, a Jewish publishing house.

One of the writers for *Die Welt* was Paula Winkler, a brilliant, aristocratic Roman Catholic. She was converted to Judaism on their marriage and remained at his side for sixty years. In her own right, Mrs. Buber was a novelist under the name of Georg Munk.

Meanwhile, there was a split in Zionism. Professor Buber was one of those who believed that a spiritual revival was more urgent than political nationhood. Mr. Herzl favored a political solution. In the course of the division, Professor Buber dropped out of active Zionism and retired into solitude for five years.

He passed that time in remote Jewish villages in what was then Galicia (now Poland), living among the Hasidim and studying their literature and their zaddick, or holy men.

At the time this demotic Judaism was considered as bordering on the occult, but Professor Buber found in Hasidism an experience of direct communion with the Divine. He was also impressed by the joy, the ecstatic dance and the wordless song with which they worshiped.

The Hasidic folklore, in its simplicity, was likewise profound, he believed. One such story concerns the good Jew whose seemingly simple-minded son was set to herding sheep. On the Day of Atonement the boy, although unable to read the prayers, was brought to the synagogue.

It was a dark period, and Rabbi Israel ben Eliezer Baal-Shem, founder of the Hasidic sect, strove before the Ark and the congregation prayed for hours. The young shepherd also wanted to participate in the ceremonies, so he took a reed pipe from his pocket and began to play.

The congregation turned on him in horror, but not the rabbi, who rebuked them, saying, "The boy's song has pierced the clouds of the Evil One and carried our prayers directly to heaven."

Professor Buber collected a number of these tales; and with his publication of them they became a part of Jewish and European culture.

Returning from his retreat among the Hasidim, Professor Buber was active in Jewish journalism, editing from 1916 to 1924 *Der Jude,* a periodical of the German Jews. From 1926 to 1930, in concert with a Catholic and a Protestant, he edited the journal *Die Kreatur.*

At the same time he was professor of comparative religion at the University of Frankfurt, from 1923 to 1933. When the Nazis excluded Jewish students from institutions of higher learning in 1933, Professor Buber helped to set up adult education for them.

He himself was dismissed from his professorship. He spoke out, however, once lecturing on "The Power of the Spirit" in Berlin although he knew that two hundred S.S. men were in the audience. Utterly silenced in 1938, he went to Palestine, where he was professor of social philosophy at the Hebrew University until his retirement in 1951.

Professor Buber was a prodigious writer. More than seven hundred books and papers by him are listed in one "selected" bibliography. Many of them deal with aspects of the I-Thou philosophy. He was also a translator of renown. His rendering of the Old Testament into German, begun with the late Franz Rosenzweig, is considered by many as the best in existence.

In Israel, Professor Buber was no conformist. For example, he opposed the execution of Adolf Eichmann, the Nazi put to death by Israel for crimes against the Jews.

"For such crimes," he said at the time, "there is no penalty." He took the position that where the imagination cannot envision a suitable penalty for such horrendous crimes as Eichmann's, death was meaningless.

Professor Buber visited the United States in 1951. The lectures he delivered here were later published as *Eclipse of God* and *At the Turning*. He received an award from Union Theological Seminary and from Hebrew Union College in Cincinnati.

ADLAI E. STEVENSON

Adlai E. Stevenson died in London on July 14, 1965, at the age of sixty-five. My obit was written in sorrow and in haste for the next day's paper—sorrow because I had admired his grace as a public man and haste because his death was unexpected. Mr. Stevenson was a unique personality in American politics. With all his blind spots (these were elaborated in Portrait: Adlai E. Stevenson, of which I was senior author) he was among the most worthwhile of modern politicians.

ADLAI EWING STEVENSON was a rarity in American public life: a cultivated, urbane, witty, articulate politician whose popularity was untarnished by defeat and whose stature grew in diplomacy.

He graced the presidential campaigns of 1952 and 1956, and his eloquence and his wit won him the devoted admiration of millions of Americans.

In more than four years as the nation's chief spokesman at the United Nations, he gained the same sort of admiration from the world statesmen for his ready tongue, his sharp mind, and his patience in dealing with the grave issues that confront the world organization.

As chief United States delegate, with the rank of Ambassador, Mr. Stevenson was in the thick of debate and negotiations during the Bay of Pigs and Cuban missile crises, disarmament talks, upheavals in the Congo, the war in Vietnam, and the revolt in Santo Domingo.

One of Mr. Stevenson's greatest satisfactions was the signing in 1963 of the treaty banning all but underground testing of nuclear devices. He was a member of the United States delegation that traveled to Moscow to sign the document. Ironically, when he ran for the presidency in 1956, Mr. Stevenson suggested a world agreement to ban the testing of hydrogen bombs. It was attacked by the Republicans at the time as visionary, and it may have hurt his campaign.

During television coverage of Security Council debates, Mr. Stevenson's tanned, freckled, and balding head was a familiar sight as he sat at the Council's horeshoe-shaped table. He looked intent as he crouched over the table to listen to the remarks of another delegate. But he relaxed when it came his turn to speak. His words flowed easily and steadily in a voice that, for its precision and diction, reminded some of Ronald Colman, the movie actor.

His logic and his words could be coruscating, as when he was disputing Soviet spokesmen, or they could take wings of idealism, as when he was expounding the importance of the United Nations as the keeper of the world's peace.

However much Mr. Stevenson might berate the Soviet Union at the Council table, he refrained from banal personalities. The result was that he was on good social terms with the Soviet diplomats, as he was with those of other countries whose views he found more congenial.

Mr. Stevenson was appointed to his United Nations post in 1961 by President John F. Kennedy and reconfirmed in the job by President Lyndon B. Johnson. The appointment came in response not only to Mr. Stevenson's deep knowledge of foreign affairs but also the pressure from influential Democrats who had backed Mr. Stevenson for the presidential nomination in 1960.

Mr. Stevenson held Cabinet rank, but there were indications that his role as a policy maker was limited. In the Bay of Pigs crisis in 1961 he suffered grave embarrassment in Security Council debates because the White House had not briefed him truthfully on the United States involvement in the invasion of Cuba by Cuban exiles. It was a measure of his popularity in the diplomatic community that he recovered from that incident with little loss of prestige.

There was some hint that Mr. Stevenson was less than ecstatic about his United Nations responsibilities. "This job has been a terrible drill," he told Martin Mayer in an interview earlier this year for an article in *The New York Times Magazine.* "In my own life I've been accustomed to making policy," he continued. "I've sometimes been a little restless in this role of executing and articulating the policies of others.

"There is a disadvantage in being anywhere other than the seat of power. And every issue that comes to the U.N. has its antecedents before it gets here. The State Department has been involved in the negotiations, and now the situation has become insoluble, so it gets dumped onto us."

Mr. Stevenson also expressed the belief that he had become "an old and familiar face" at the United Nations headquarters building in New York. "You take on the coloration of your country, your country's face, and you become predictable," he said, adding: "You lose some of the rosy glow you brought with you. Apart from my taste for creative aspects, the time comes when you should bring in a fresh face and a new outlook."

Despite these reservations, Mr. Stevenson, with his Hamlet-like ability to state another proposition, said that "it's easy to reconcile a sense of duty with this job." He conceded that his decisions had "always come about more by circumstances and events than by conscious calculation."

As a diplomat, Mr. Stevenson put in punishing hours. Most days he was on the go from an appointment at 8:15 A.M. to well after midnight.

After an official working day, he would go on the cocktail-party-and-dinner circuit for the rest of the evening—social duties that his post required of him. In these he had a truly awesome stamina, for he was as eruditely charming late at night as he had been at breakfast.

A good part of Mr. Stevenson's charm rested in his ability to discuss himself without pomposity. Although he was badly beaten for the presidency by Dwight D. Eisenhower in 1952 and 1956, he was not bitter. Talking to a group of volunteers after his defeat in 1956, he said: "To you who are disappointed tonight, let me confess that I am too. . . . Be of good cheer and remember, my dear friends, that a wise man said: 'A merry heart doeth good like a medicine but a broken spirit dryeth the bones.' "

Mr. Stevenson, although he dressed well, was not happy as a fashion plate. As Governor of Illinois he preferred to work in his office in a brown tweed sports jacket, old trousers, and a striped shirt. His favorite footgear then was a pair of old golf shoes with the spikes removed.

His predilection for informal attire was not only a matter of personal comfort, but also an expression of the fact that, although he was well-to-do, he was not a conspicuous spender.

During his gubernatorial term, which began in 1949, he purchased only one new suit. A hole in his shoe, which was a trademark of his White House campaign in 1952, was another example of his frugality.

After his defeat in 1956 Mr. Stevenson practiced law and traveled extensively on business, visiting more than thirty countries. On one trip he spent three weeks in the Soviet Union and had a long conversation with the then Premier, Nikita S. Khrushchev.

In 1960 many liberals and intellectuals in the Democratic Party urged him to seek the presidential nomination. He was then, as he had been in 1952 and 1956, the idol of the eggheads, men and women who were not ashamed to confess to a college education and to ideas more profound than those ordinarily passed at the bridge table.

Professional politicians, however, were less enthusiastic, because he seemed reluctant to work with them and because they thought he talked over the heads of his audiences.

Mr. Stevenson vacillated, and it was not until the last minute that he agreed to let his name be placed before the convention. By then, it was too late. He got the applause of the gallery while Mr. Kennedy reaped the delegates' votes.

Some of Mr. Stevenson's ambivalence toward politics sprang from a feeling that glad-handing was a species of hokum. He expressed this sentiment to an old friend after one hard day of handshaking in the 1952 campaign in these words: "Perhaps the saddest part of all this is that a candidate must reach into a sea of hands, grasp one, not knowing whose it is, and say, 'I'm glad to meet you,' realizing that he hasn't and probably never will meet that man."

When he went into the 1952 campaign, Mr. Stevenson was virtually unknown nationally, but in the election he polled more than 27 million votes, a surprising figure. However, this won him only 89 electoral votes as General Eisenhower swamped him with nearly 34 million popular votes and 442 in the Electoral College.

The Democratic candidate emerged from the campaign with the grudging respect of many Republicans for the quality of his speeches— he wrote most of them himself—and for his good manners.

For all his politeness and his patrician birth and education, Mr. Stevenson became, after 1952, one of the hardest-hitting adversaries of the late Senator Joseph R. McCarthy, a Republican of Wisconsin, a notable exponent of jugular-vein politics.

Moreover, Mr. Stevenson turned into an articulate spokesman for internationalism and an active titular leader of his party.

To the shallowness of practical politics, he added a philosophy of liberalism that was almost Jeffersonian in its literate defense of the rights of the individual, its educated revulsion against mob-inflaming dema-goguery. "When demagoguery and deceit become a national political movement," he asserted, "we Americans are in trouble; not just Demo-crats, but all of us."

Genial, with a touch of shyness, this product of Princeton, Harvard, and Northwestern University seemed so out of place in practical politics that a more seasoned politician tutoring him for active campaigning re-called: "Godawmighty, we almost had to tear off the starched dickeys and the Homburg hat he used to wear."

Trained to the law and diplomacy, he was a realist at dealing with essential political compromise. But when moved deeply by principle he risked political sabotage and personal obloquy for his convictions.

Thus, during 1952, when he was asked why, in 1945, he had signed an affidavit speaking well of the reputation of Alger Hiss, later convicted of perjury, Mr. Stevenson replied: "I am a lawyer. I think that one of the most fundamental responsibilities, not only of every citizen, but particularly of lawyers, is to give testimony in a court of law, to give it honestly and willingly, and it will be a very unhappy day for Anglo-Saxon justice when a man, even a man in public life, is too timid to state what he knows and what he has heard about a defendant in a criminal trial for fear that defendant might be convicted. That would to me be the ultimate timidity."

On July 25, 1952, what was described as the first "open" Democratic National Convention in twenty years nominated Mr. Stevenson as its presidential candidate and Senator John J. Sparkman of Alabama as his running mate. They opposed General Eisenhower and the then Senator Richard M. Nixon of California.

Mr. Stevenson, then Governor of Illinois, had insisted repeatedly that he would "rather not" be President. He was quoted as having said that he was not fitted mentally, temperamentally, or physically for the office.

The Stevenson boom began in the spring of 1952, after he had visited President Harry S Truman in Washington. But keeping outwardly aloof from the scramble for convention delegates, he refused to identify himself as a candidate down to the moment the voting began.

In his acceptance speech to the convention the candidate told the cheering delegates: "Sacrifice, patience, understanding, and implacable purpose may be our lot for years to come. Let's face it. Let's talk sense to the American people."

His candor cost him many votes. On the question of who should receive the benefit of royalties from offshore oil deposits, he took his stand with President Truman that the federal government had "paramount rights" in the deposits. This cost him much support in Texas, Florida, and Virginia.

He refused to take a stand in favor of continuing discrimination against Negro citizens, which antagonized white supremacy elements in the Democratic Party in the South. At the same time his firm belief in states' rights and responsibilities cost him some Negro votes.

Among other issues that influenced the vote substantially were corruption in Washington, Communist infiltration, the Korean War, high taxes and the high cost of living, fear of inflation, and the growth of federal centralism. These were pressed by Republican campaigners.

But the greatest obstacle to Mr. Stevenson's success was the popularity of his opponent.

Analyses of the vote indicated that although labor had gone solidly for Mr. Stevenson and although he had retained much of the farm vote, he had lost the support of women voters and particularly the so-called independent voters of both sexes.

But the strength of Mr. Stevenson's candidacy was shown in the fact that under circumstances that should have produced an overwhelming Republican landslide—a popular candidate, popular issues, and an incumbent administration whose party had been in power for twenty years

—the Democratic candidate rolled up 3 million more votes than were received by President Truman in 1948 in his victory over Thomas A. Dewey.

With the 1952 election over, Mr. Stevenson took the role of opposition leader, although he admitted that he envied one man—the Governor of Illinois.

His first speech and a four-day visit to Washington rallied nearly all Democrats to his side. He received such an admiring welcome from the jubilant Republicans at the capital that political opponents jested that he could not have been feted more if his candidacy had been successful.

Part of the tribute arose because he took immediate steps to heal the wounds of the bitter phases of the campaign and did what he could to rally his fellow Democrats behind the incoming President.

During the visit, Mr. Stevenson met with Democratic leaders and mapped plans to unite the party in opposition. He also conferred with leaders of the Republican administration about his plans for a nonpolitical world tour, covering particularly the Far East.

On the five-month trip he talked with leading figures and studied conditions in Korea, Malaya, Burma, India, and the then Indochina, as well as in various European countries. He said the real purpose of his tour had been self-education.

Taking a vigorous part in the bitter congressional election campaign of 1954, he hammered in his speeches at the three principal issues of foreign policy, domestic economy, and internal security. This confirmed him as his party's chief spokesman. The Democratic victory in the elections made him the leading contender for the 1956 presidential nomination.

His attacks on the Republicans concentrated on the influence of Senator McCarthy. The Republican Party, he charged, had become "half McCarthy and half Eisenhower," and he accused Vice-President Nixon— the principal Republican campaigner—of preaching "McCarthyism in a white collar."

Mr. Nixon declared that Mr. Stevenson had "not changed since he testified for Alger Hiss," and he accused Mr. Stevenson of unconsciously having spread Communist propaganda.

After the election, Mr. Stevenson announced that he was returning to the private practice of law in Chicago. "I have done what I could for the Democratic Party for the past two years," he said, "and now I shall have to be less active and give more attention to my own affairs."

He still kept in touch with political and foreign affairs, however. In April 1955, after a long Democratic silence, he made a national radio address opposing the defense of the Nationalist Chinese islands of

Quemoy and Matsu. He also called for a joint declaration by the United States and its allies pledging united defense of Taiwan pending its final disposition.

Although Mr. Stevenson repeatedly refused to say whether he would be a candidate for the presidential nomination in 1956, he had won the support of the party's most influential leaders. However, many in the South who had opposed him in 1952 still did so.

In sharp contrast with his preconvention attitude of indifference toward the 1952 nomination, Mr. Stevenson jumped into the fight for the 1956 nomination by announcing his candidacy on November 15, 1955.

Moderation was the keynote of his campaign, particularly with respect to enforcement of the Supreme Court's decision abolishing racial segregation in public schools, but generally with respect to all issues, foreign and domestic.

Mr. Stevenson took an early lead in the race for the nomination. The support of political organizations in large-population states gave him an imposing list of delegate strength. However, he suffered setbacks in early 1956 state primaries, where Senator Estes Kefauver of Tennessee showed surprising popular support.

These reverses stimulated Mr. Stevenson to more aggressive tactics. Instead of holding aloof from the crowds, he began to make handshaking tours asking the voters for support. As the primaries continued, he began to fare better, and by May political observers seemed to agree that he had reversed the tide, which then appeared to be running in his direction.

Mr. Stevenson's campaign managers from the beginning claimed victory for him. They asserted that more delegates had been pledged to him than the majority necessary to nominate at the Democratic National Convention.

In 1952 Mr. Stevenson had surrounded himself largely with "amateurs," but in the 1956 campaign he put more emphasis on practical politics in choosing top aides at his Chicago campaign headquarters.

He pitched his early campaign speeches to a vigorous attack on President Eisenhower's foreign policy. Whenever possible he ignored his Democratic opponents for the nomination, and sought to draw the issue from the beginning as Stevenson versus Eisenhower.

In the election, he was defeated by a greater margin than in 1952, polling 26 million popular votes to more than 35.5 million by President Eisenhower. The Electoral College figures were 73 to 457.

Mr. Stevenson was born on February 5, 1900, in Los Angeles, where his father, Lewis Green Stevenson, was at the time an executive of Hearst newspapers, mining and ranching properties. His family roots went back to the pre-Revolutionary War period.

He was a grandson and namesake of a Vice-President of the United States—the Adlai Stevenson who held office in the second term of Grover Cleveland's administration. Through his mother, he was a fifth-generation Illinoisan, a grandson of Jesse Fell, who was the first to propose Abraham Lincoln for the presidency.

When Adlai was six years old, the family moved back to their home town of Bloomington, Illinois, where Mrs. Stevenson's family owned *The Daily Pantagraph*. Adlai's father later became State Secretary for Illinois and, from 1914 to 1917, served as chairman of the State Board of Pardons.

Mr. Stevenson went to the Choate Preparatory School, Wallingford, Connecticut, and Princeton University, from which he was graduated in 1922. He was managing editor of *The Daily Princetonian*.

After leaving Princeton, Mr. Stevenson went to Harvard Law School for two years. He got passing marks but was uninterested in his studies.

A legal case that evolved from the death of an uncle redistributed shares in *The Pantagraph* among members of the family. As a result Mr. Stevenson and his cousin, Davis C. Merwin, decided they would learn the newspaper business.

Mr. Stevenson spent a couple of years on the paper in various editorial posts, but by the time the courts had ruled that the Stevenson and Merwin families should have equal shares of ownership, his interest in becoming a newspaper editor had waned.

He decided to finish his law course and, having fallen a year behind his classmates, who already had been graduated from Harvard, he entered the law school of Northwestern University. He received his law degree in 1926.

Soon after his graduation, he settled in Chicago to practice law.

In December 1928, Mr. Stevenson married Ellen Borden of Chicago. Her father, a socialite and financier who made the first of several fortunes as a colleague of John Hertz in the Yellow Cab Company, later became active in mining in St. Louis.

The Stevensons were divorced in 1949. His wife was said to abhor politics and to have wished to devote herself to the world of art and literature. No other person and no scandal were involved in the legal proceedings, held in Las Vegas, Nevada. The couple had three sons, Adlai Ewing 3d, Borden, and John Fell.

Soon after the 1952 presidential boom started for Mr. Stevenson, he was approached by a would-be biographer. The man told the Governor he was going to write a book about him.

"I don't see how you are going to do it," Mr. Stevenson said. "My life has been hopelessly undramatic. I wasn't born in a log cabin. I didn't work my way through school nor did I rise from rags to riches, and there's no use trying to pretend I did. I'm not a Willkie and I don't claim to be a simple, barefoot La Salle Street lawyer. You might be able to write about some of my ancestors. They accomplished quite a lot at one time or another but you can't do anything much about me. At least, I'd hate to have to try it."

Actually, Mr. Stevenson had laid the groundwork for his political career by public service that began in 1933, when he first went to Washington as one of the many bright young lawyers President Franklin D. Roosevelt had summoned to help formulate the New Deal.

For two years, Mr. Stevenson was special counsel to the Agricultural Adjustment Administration, touring the country, holding hearings, and advising regional groups of farmers, ranchers, orchardists, and dairymen how to utilize the measure, and then returning to Washington to try to work out marketing agreements.

At the end of the two years he went back to private law practice in Chicago. He served as president for one term of the Chicago Council on Foreign Relations—a post in which he got considerable experience as an after-dinner speaker—and he also became Chicago chairman of the William Allen White Committee to Defend America by Aiding the Allies.

Mr. Stevenson brought people like Wendell Willkie, Carl Sandburg, and Dorothy Thompson to address meetings, one of which, in 1941, filled the Chicago Stadium. In the summer of that year the late Frank Knox, then Secretary of the Navy and a close friend of Mr. Stevenson's, telephoned.

Mr. Stevenson later quoted Mr. Knox as saying, "Everyone else around Washington has a lawyer and I guess I ought to have one too."

He was in Washington within a few days, starting to prepare legal machinery whereby the Navy, in case it became necessary, could take over the strikebound Kearny shipyards in New Jersey, then building essential warships. He continued to do similar legal work for the Navy Department until 1943, when he led a mission to Italy to plan occupation policies.

Later he served as an assistant to Secretaries of State Edward Stettinius and James Byrnes. He also was a representative to the San Francisco United Nations Conference, and then was an aide to the United States delegation in the United Nations General Assembly.

At the meeting of the General Assembly held in London in January 1946, Mr. Stevenson was senior adviser to the American delegation. He resigned after the session ended in March, but President Truman appointed him alternate delegate to the second session that fall.

Mr. Stevenson returned to Chicago in 1947. His friends backed him as a "cleanup" candidate against the Republican administration of Governor Dwight W. Green. Winning the backing of Jacob M. Arvey, chairman of the Cook County Democratic Committee, he was nominated for Governor. Paul Douglas, then professor of economics at Chicago University, was named for Senator.

The Democratic "cleanup" team swept into office, Mr. Stevenson defeating Mr. Green by 572,000 votes, while President Truman was nosing out Thomas E. Dewey in Illinois by a mere 34,000. The self-styled "amateur" in politics consecrated his government in an inaugural address to "plain talk, hard work, and prairie horse sense."

During his term in office Mr. Stevenson was credited with these accomplishments:

§He sent state policemen to stamp out commercial gambling downstate when local officials failed to act.

§He lopped off 1,300 nonworking politicians from the state payroll.

§He set up a merit system in the state police force that ended the system of politically preferential appointments.

§He increased state aid to school districts.

§He started a broad road-improvement program that included enforcement of truck weight limits, a higher gasoline tax, and increased truck licenses to pay construction costs.

§He overhauled the state's welfare program, placing it on a merit basis and forcing financially able relatives to pay for the care of patients.

§He streamlined the state government by pushing through seventy-eight reform measures.

§He converted the political State Commerce Commission, the utility rate-fixing agency, into a bipartisan body.

An attendant at the birth of the New Deal, Mr. Stevenson supported Mr. Truman's successor Fair Deal, but his differences with the administration on some phases of domestic policy were implicit in his own record in Illinois. The variance was evident in his stand on the cost of government, taxation, and negligence toward official irregularities and corruption.

"I think government should be as small in scope and as local in character as possible," he said on one occasion.

Mr. Stevenson was the author of seven books: *Major Campaign Speeches, 1952, Call to Greatness, What I Think, The New America, Friends and Enemies, Putting First Things First,* and *Looking Outward.*

LE CORBUSIER

Le Corbusier died on the French Riviera on August 27, 1965, at the age of seventy-seven. One of the most disputatious of modern architects (combativeness seems to be a trait of most of them), he had singular convictions and daring. These characteristics made him more than ordinarily interesting as an obit.

CHARLES-EDOUARD JEANNERT-GRIS, whose professional name was Le Corbusier, was as contentious in his manner as he was influential in his architectural ideas. "I am like a lightning conductor: I attract storms," he said.

Disputes swirled about him and his conceptions for more than forty years, and in them he was almost always a temperamental participant, for he regarded himself, especially in his later years, as beset by red tape, politics, and underappreciation.

Nevertheless, his influence was so enormous and so persuasive that there are few areas in modern building and city planning in which it is not reflected. Le Corbusier, according to Arthur Drexler of the Museum of Modern Art, was one of the three greats in modern architecture, the others being Ludwig Mies van der Rohe and Frank Lloyd Wright.

Le Corbusier's output was not large—fewer than one hundred buildings—yet it was distinctive. Among outstanding examples of his work are the Visual Arts Center at Harvard University in Cambridge, Massachusetts; the Ronchamp Chapel at Vosges, France; the capital buildings for the Punjab at Chandigarh, India; an apartment house at Marseilles and another in Berlin; a ten-story glass-walled office building in Moscow; a Salvation Army center in Paris, and the Ministry of Education building in Rio de Janeiro.

That structure, a honeycomb of sun-shading, breeze-admitting vanes at the windows, was widely copied in South America, notably in Brasilia and in other tropical countries. There are no examples of pure Le Corbusier in New York. The over-all conception of the United Nations

Secretariat Building, at 43d Street and the East River, was his, but the bold design was toned down, much to his annoyance. When the structure was finished, he complained: "A new skyscraper, which everyone calls the 'Le Corbusier Building,' has appeared in New York. L-C was stripped of all his rights, without conscience and without pity."

The Lever Building on Park Avenue, which appears to be built on stilts, also incorporates one of Le Corbusier's fundamental notions—that the massive bulk of a big building should be offset by placing it on uprights and that pedestrians should be allowed to pass underneath the main structure.

In his early days, before he saw New York, Le Corbusier praised American skyscrapers, but he took one look at the city's slab buildings and crowded canyons and announced: "Your skyscrapers are too small!"

"New York is the most beautiful manifestation of man's power, courage, enterprise, and force," he said in 1935, "but it is utterly lacking in order and harmony and the comforts of the spirit. The skyscrapers are little needles all crowded together. They should be great obelisks, far apart, so that the city would have space and light and order. Those are the things that men need just as much as they need bread or a place to sleep."

Not only was Manhattan a jungle of masonry, he said, but the Hudson and East Rivers were also hidden and New York Harbor was lost. Nonetheless, Le Corbusier liked some aspects of the United States.

He advised his fellow architects "lost in the sterile backwaters of their foliage, their pilasters, and the lead roofs" to look for inspiration to American grain elevators and silos and factories. These he considered "the magnificent first fruits of the new age."

In the years before World War II, Le Corbusier was an amiable man, with an atelier full of students who worked for him for nothing. He was vain then, but not difficult or bitter.

With the end of the war he expected many commissions from the French government to redesign bombed-out cities, but received only one—to plan an apartment house at Marseilles. Frustrated, he grew increasingly acidulous, aloof, and egocentric, and his knack for making enemies became almost a developed art.

Never a ready man with a franc, he also grew penurious, sometimes to the point where he felt he was being taken advantage of. This trait had been exhibited earlier in a long and complicated dispute with the Museum of Modern Art over the ownership of some items the museum displayed in one of its shows devoted to his work.

The architect was quick to see hostility toward him. Last April, for example, he was still berating his critics and reminding them of how mistaken they were. "For fifty years I have gotten kicks in the rear," he said. "And now Le Corbusier has become Le Corbusier. They are worried about what he's doing. They keep track of his projects. What a laugh! I have given them plenty of grief, too. I have taught them that architecture is the play of forms and of volume in light. They didn't know this."

When he first enunciated his architectural credo he was equally didactic. "Architecture has nothing to do with the various 'styles,'" he said in the 1920's. "The styles are to architecture what a feather is on a woman's head; it is something pretty, though not always, and never anything more. Architecture has graver ends. . . . Mass and surface are the elements by which it manifests itself."

Structure, Le Corbusier went on, is what makes a building beautiful, and he singled out the "great primary forms"—cubes, cones, spheres, cylinders, and pyramids. These, he said, are always beautiful, and what can be reduced to these basic shapes is good architecture.

Le Corbusier was a slight man, and a slim one in his younger days. His face was long and pale; his lips were thin, and his hair was slicked back without a part over a high forehead. According to the painter Fernand Léger, he was "a very odd specimen" who went bicycling in a derby hat and a dark sack suit. The architect was known to his intimates then and later as Corbu, although he often referred to himself in the third person.

He was at one time a constant smoker. "I used to smoke cigarettes, pipes, and cigars all day long," he said once. "I had my suits made with a special pocket to hold a box of 250 kitchen matches; I used up a box a day. In 1942 I quit smoking because a friend said I couldn't. I put my sixty pipes in a drawer and have never smoked since. Almost every night I dream that a friend is offering me a cigar. I do not accept it, even in the dream."

In later years Le Corbusier put on weight and looked rather stocky and bourgeois in a double-breasted suit. He also took to being solemn. Describing his work habits, he said last spring: "The birth of a project is for me like the birth of a little dog or a child. There is a long period of gestation; there is a lot of work in the subconscious before I make the first sketch. That lasts for months. One fine morning the project has taken form without my knowing it. Each problem provokes in me this interior meditation. I don't say to my collaborators, 'Here's a problem; do your best to solve it.' I seek the solution myself, closed up in a room three meters by three meters."

The architect was not exaggerating the extent of his working space at his whitewashed studio at 35 rue de Sèvres in Paris. It was behind an old wooden door at the top of a winding staircase, and on the door was a big "Keep Out" sign. Dominating the cramped room was a big photograph of children playing on the roof of the Marseilles apartment house that he had designed.

This building, like so many of his creations, was controversial. Completed in 1952, it is made of blocks of raw concrete on which the marks of the form boards were left visible. Traditionalists denounced it, and a hardware supplier refused to sell locks or hinges for it for fear of tarnishing the company name. However, the tenants liked the seventeen-story building, and Walter Gropius, the architect, declared: "Any architect who does not find this building beautiful had better lay down his pencil."

In the theories of Le Corbusier, the notion of "machine" has an important place. Just as he considered that, in relation to printing, "the picture is a machine of emotion," so he was the inventor of the phrase "a house is a machine to live in," and it reflected his iconoclastic, experimental attitudes. Some critics thought it also represented a too austere and even inhuman view of man.

Yet Le Corbusier had always represented himself as the pioneer of an essentially gracious architecture. Thus, in order of importance, he ranked the "raw materials" of the urbanist: the sky, trees, iron, cement; he wished to bring man the "essential joys" to which all have right—the sun, space, verdure.

From this state of mind stem his principles of architecture: primal importance of the site; its exposure to the sun; the support wall, made useless by the steel framework and replaced by a glass sheet; the street belongs to the pedestrian (automobile and rail traffic go underground or overhead); construction on piles (the house is healthier and the ground disencumbered); pure air, cleansed of the toxic fumes of the city and obtained from a system of ventilation incorporated in the building, etc.

On such principles Le Corbusier, an enthusiastic town planner, drew up plans for Paris, Antwerp, Algiers, Buenos Aires, Montevideo, and towns in India.

His masterpiece was his predominant share in making Chandigarh, the new city built from scratch on the plains of the Punjab, India, from 1951 to 1957. In this great work, sponsored by Prime Minister Jawaharlal Nehru, Le Corbusier softened the rigidity of some of his characteristic forms. He bowed to the Indians' objection that their lack of elevator technicians precluded skyscraper construction. Chandigarh is a sprawling bungalow city. The buildings for which he was primarily responsible— the government center at its heart—contained numerous innovations to cope with India's scorching sun, and were built in undecorated, rough-finished concrete for reasons of economy.

Charles-Edouard Jeanneret-Gris was born October 6, 1887, in La Chaux-de-Fonds, Switzerland. His father was an enameler of watch faces.

After studying at the School of Fine Arts of his native town from thirteen to eighteen, being apprenticed to an engraver from 1905, he studied in the ateliers of several eminent architects in Vienna, Paris, and Berlin, though he never earned a degree.

His first experimental buildings were erected in La Chaux for his father and for well-to-do watch manufacturers. He moved to Paris in 1917, where he at first could find no architectural work and managed a factory while painting in his spare time.

From 1920 to 1925 he wrote a series of articles in the magazine *L'Esprit Nouveau* that expressed his architectural philosophy and made him famous.

He was co-founder with the painter Amédée Ozenfant of this magazine, which propagated "purist" theories. Derived from cubism, it was the aim of "purism," which preached plastic severity, to react against the tendency to decoration, which at that time certain cubists seemed to be slipping into.

One important result was to establish his identity under the name Le Corbusier. He had chosen the pseudonym, the family name of his maternal grandmother, to keep his identity as architectural propagandist separate from that as aspiring painter. But Le Corbusier the architect eclipsed Jeanneret the artist.

A tireless international lecturer, he was also a trenchant writer. He originated the dictum that design should proceed "from within to without; the exterior is the result of an interior." He also wrote of New York and Chicago as "mighty storms, tornadoes, cataclysms, they are so utterly devoid of harmony."

The titles of the works in which Le Corbusier expressed his ideas reflect his humanistic modernism: *A House—A Palace* (1928), *The Radiant City* (1935), *When Cathedrals Were White* (1937) and *The House of Men* (1942).

Le Corbusier formed an architectural firm with his cousin, Pierre Jeanneret, in 1924. Within a few years, he was involved in a bitter controversy over his plan for the League of Nations building in Geneva.

It was preferred over all others by a majority of the architectural jury, but was ruled out on the technicality that the papers were written not in the China ink specified by the contest rules, but in printer's ink.

A series of appeals brought Le Corbusier a consolation prize, and again his plan was recommended by an architects' jury. But a final committee of ambassadors rejected his plan and commissioned four other architects to collaborate on a new design. Le Corbusier sued, but the League's palace was duly built in monumental style.

The architect received several commissions after World War II when Europe badly needed rebuilding. His plan was adopted for the reconstruction of La Pallice, the port of La Rochelle. His Maison Radieuse, a seventeen-story apartment house on stilts at Nantes Rezé, Marseilles, was constructed after difficulties with planning authorities and a suit by the Society for the Protection of Esthetic Beauty in France.

Le Corbusier's all-concrete chapel to replace a church destroyed by the war in the tiny town of Ronchamp, in the Vosges Mountains, caused a stir in 1955. The building had not a single straight line; its walls sloped inward or outward and the ceiling seemed to sag. The strange, swelling roof with flared eaves was designed to catch the winds and create organ tones. It swept down to a spout intended to carry rainwater to a tank.

Instead of the usual formal windows, it had a series of irregular openings, no two of the same dimensions, with stained glass of Le Corbusier's own design. Many critics thought it the most humane and personal of all his creations.

In 1930, Le Corbusier married Yvonne Gallis, a Monégasque. She was reputed to be a splendid cook and a calming influence on her volatile husband, although she was not enthusiastic over the walls of glass he built into their Paris apartment.

"I am tearing my hair out by the roots! All this light is driving me crazy!" she said shortly after they were wed, but she put up with it nonetheless.

ALBERT SCHWEITZER

Dr. Albert Schweitzer died at Lambaréné, Gabon, on September 4, 1965, at the age of ninety. He had wrought two monuments to himself—a system of ethics elaborating the principle of Reverence for Life and a jungle hospital compound in the Republic of Gabon. He was a world-celebrated figure, and my obit sought to explore the man and his accomplishments in some depth and with more candor than some of his disciples liked.

THE CONCEPT of man's ultimate redemption through beneficent activity—the theme of Part II of Goethe's *Faust*, a metaphysical poem much admired by Albert Schweitzer—threads through this extraordinary man's long, complex, and sometimes curious life. With Faust himself he could join in saying:

> This sphere of earthly soil
> Still gives us room for lofty doing.
> Astounding plans e'en now are brewing:
> I feel new strength for bolder toil . . .
> The Deed is everything, the Glory naught.

"You must give some time to your fellow man," Schweitzer counseled in paraphrase. "Even if it's a little thing, do something for those who have need of a man's help, something for which you get no pay but the privilege of doing it."

Also like Goethe, on whose life and works he was an expert, Schweitzer came near to being a comprehensive man. He was, among other things, a theologian, musicologist, organ technician, physician and surgeon, missionary, philosopher of ethics, lecturer, writer, as well as the builder and chief force of the famous hospital complex at Lambaréné, in Gabon, the former French Equatorial Africa.

To a marked degree Schweitzer was an eclectic. Franco-German, yet cosmopolitan in culture, he drew deeply from the music and mysticism of the eighteenth century, especially Bach, Goethe and Kant. At the same time, he was a child of the nineteenth century, accepting its creature comforts yet rejecting its complacent attitudes toward progress. In line with the twentieth century he sought to put religion on a rational footing and to accept the advances of science; yet he was a foe to materialism and to the century's criteria for personal success.

As a person, Schweitzer was an equally curious mixture. Widely honored with degrees, citations, scrolls, medals, special stamps, even the Nobel Prize for Peace in 1952, he seemed oblivious to panoply. He did not preen himself, nor utter cosmic statements at the drop of a cause. Instead, he seemed to many observers a simple, almost rustic man who dressed in rumpled clothing, suffered fools gladly, stated fundamental verities patiently and paternally, and worked unobtrusively. In this respect, he was undoubtedly made more of by cultists than he was willing to make of himself, although he was by no means a man with a weak ego.

Some of his more ardent admirers insisted that he was a jungle saint, even a modern Christ. But Schweitzer would have none of this adulation; he was quite satisfied that his own spiritual life was its own reward, that works redeemed him.

He took the search for the good life seriously. For him it had profound religious implications. "Anyone can rescue his human life," he once said, "who seizes every opportunity of being a man by means of personal action, however unpretending, for the good of fellow men who need the help of a fellow man." He sought to exemplify the idea that man, through good works, can be in the world and in God at one and the same time.

For all his self-abnegation, Schweitzer had a bristly character, at least in his later years, a formidable sense of his own importance to Lambaréné, and a do-good paternalism toward Africans that smacked more of the nineteenth than the twentieth century. For example, John Gunther got a dressing-down from Schweitzer for writing that he resembled Buffalo Bill and also, perhaps, for implying that he did not know what was going on in nationalist Africa.

If Schweitzer was thin-skinned to criticism from irreverent journalists, he heard little of it at Lambaréné, where his proprietorship was unquestioned. Not only did he design the station, but he also helped build it with his own hands. His co-workers were quite familiar with the businesslike and sometimes grumpy and brusque Schweitzer in a solar hat who hurried along the construction of a building by gingering up the native craftsmen with a sharp: "Allez-vous OPP! Allez-vous OPP-opp. Hupp, upp, OPP!"

When Schweitzer was in residence at Lambaréné, virtually nothing was done without consulting him. Once, for instance, he all but halted the station's work when he received a letter from a Norwegian child seeking a feather from Parisfal, his pet pelican. He insisted on seeing to it personally that the youngster got a prompt and touching reply from his own pen before work was permitted to resume. His autocracy, however, was more noticeable as his years advanced and as his medical assistants grew less awesome of him.

Schweitzer regarded most native Africans as children, as primitives. It was said that he had scarcely ever talked with an adult African on adult terms. He had little but contempt for the nationalist movement, for his attitudes were firmly grounded in nineteenth-century benevolence. Although thousands of Africans called him "le grand docteur," others plastered his village with signs, "Schweitzer, go home!"

"At this stage," Schweitzer said in 1963, "Africans have little need for advanced training. They need very elementary schools run along the old missionary plan, with the Africans going to school for a few hours every day and then going back to the fields. Agriculture, not science or industrialization, is their greatest need."

His attitude was sharply expressed in a story he liked to tell of his orange trees. "I let the Africans pick all the fruit they want," he said. "You see, the good Lord has protected the trees. He made the Africans too lazy to pick them bare." Although Schweitzer's views on Africa were sadly out of date, he did what no man had done before him— healed thousands and welded world attention on Africa's many plights. A jungle saint he may not have been; a jungle pioneer he surely was.

Whatever Schweitzer's personal idiosyncrasies, he constructed a profound and enduring ethical system expressed in the principle *Ehrfurcht vor dem Leben*, or Reverence for Life. It is conceivably the only philosophical concept ever to spring to life amid a herd of hippopotamuses.

As Schweitzer recounted this climactic incident, he had been baffled in getting an answer to the question, Is it at all possible to find a real and permanent foundation in thought for a theory of the universe that shall be both ethical and affirmative of the world and life? The answer came in a flash of mystic illumination in September 1915, as he was steaming up the Ogooué River in Africa.

Late in the third day of his journey he was on deck thinking and writing. "At the very moment when, at sunset, we were making our way through a herd of hippopotamuses, there flashed upon my mind, unforeseen and unsought, the phrase 'Reverence for Life.'"

"The iron door had yielded," he went on, "the path in the thicket had become visible. Now I had my way to the idea in which world-

and life-affirmation and ethics are contained side by side! Now I knew
that the world-view of ethical world- and life-affirmation, together with
its ideal of civilization, is founded in thought."

Schweitzer's ethical system, elucidated at length in *The Philosophy of
Civilization*, is boundless in its domain and in its demands. He sum-
marized it once by saying: "A man is ethical only when life, as such,
is sacred to him, that of plants and animals as that of his fellow men,
and when he devotes himself helpfully to all life that is in need of
help."

"Let me give you a definition of ethics," he wrote on another occasion. "It is good to maintain and further life; it is bad to damage and
destroy life. And this ethic, profound, universal, has the significance of
a religion. It *is* religion."

Called upon to be specific about Reverence for Life, he explained
that the concept "does not allow the scholar to love for science alone,
even if he is very useful to the community in so doing. It does not permit the artist," he continued, "to exist only for his art, even if it gives
the inspiration to many by its means. It refuses to let the businessman
imagine that he fulfills all legitimate demands in the course of his
business activity. It demands from all that they should sacrifice a portion of their own lives for others."

Schweitzer earnestly sought to live his philosophy, which for him
was a creedal guide to action. He was genuinely proud of his medical
and missionary station at Lambaréné. He had scratched it out from the
jungle beginning in 1913; he had designed it; he had worked as an
artisan in constructing many of its buildings; and, although the station
was many times beset by adversities that would have discouraged a less
dedicated man, it had grown at his death to more than seventy buildings, 350 beds and a leper village of two hundred.

The compound was staffed by five unpaid physicians, seven nurses,
and thirteen volunteer helpers. Visitors who equated cleanliness, tidi-
ness, and medicine were horrified by the station, for every patient was
encouraged to bring one or two members of his family to cook for him
in the ditches beside the wards. Babies, even in the leper enclave,
dropped toys into dust of the unpaved streets and then popped the play-
things into their mouths. Noisome animals wandered in and out of the
compound, including Schweitzer's pet parrot (which was not taught to
talk because that would lower its dignity) and a hippopotamus that
once invaded the vegetable garden.

Lambaréné resembled not so much a hospital as a native village
where physicians cared for the sick. Actually, Schweitzer preferred (and

planned) it in this fashion on the ground that the natives would shun an elaborate, shiny, and impersonal institution.

The compound even lacked electricity, except for the operating and dental rooms, and members of the staff read by kerosene lamp. It, of course, had no telephone or radio or airstrip.

Schweitzer's view that "simple people need simple healing methods," however it might have outraged medical sophisticates, won for Lambaréné a tremendous measure of native confidence. Thousands flocked there; thousands responded to Schweitzer's sermons as well as to his scalpel; for he believed that the good shepherd saves not only the animal but also his soul.

Lambaréné was suffused with Reverence for Life to what some critics thought was an exaggerated degree. Mosquitoes were not swatted, nor pests and insects doused with chemicals; they were left alone, and humans put up with them. Indeed, building was often brought to a halt lest nests of ants be killed or disturbed. On the other hand, patients received splendid medical care; and few seemed to suffer greatly from the compound's lack of spit and polish.

Schweitzer's accomplishments are recognized even by his most caustic critics. One of them, Gerald McKnight, wrote in his book *Verdict on Schweitzer*: "The temptation for Schweitzer to see Lambaréné as a place cut off from the world, in which he can preserve its original forms and so reject any theory of treatment or life other than his own, is understandable when one considers the enormous achievement he has attained in his own lifetime. He came to the Ogooué in 1913 when horses drew the buses of London and leprosy was considered an incurable scourge. Housed originally in the grounds of a mission, he chose to leave this comparative sanctuary for the unknown and forbidding regions of the jungle nearby.

"No doubt a wish to have absolute dominion over his hospital drove him to this course, linked with the inner purpose which had brought him to Africa, but it was none the less heroic. Today, the hospital has grown, entirely under his hand and direction, into a sizable colony where between 500 and 600 people live in reasonable comfort. No greater tribute to his abilities as a conqueror of the jungle need be cited than the fact—regarded locally as something of a miracle—of his own survival."

Schweitzer came to French Equatorial Africa as a tall, handsome, broadly powerful young man with a shock of rich, black hair, enormous mustaches, and a look of piercing determination in his bold eyes. The years thinned and grayed his hair (without making it less unruly); age seamed his face, shrank his frame, made him appear bandy-legged; time softened his eyes, made them less severe; but determination to make his life an "argument" for his ethical creed was as firm at ninety as it was on his thirtieth birthday, the day he decided to devote the rest of his life to the natives of Africa as a physician. Schweitzer's arrival at this decision was calculated, a step in a quest for a faith to live by. It was a search that had haunted him, driven him, since childhood.

Albert Schweitzer was born at Kaysersberg, Haute Alsace (now Haut-Rhin), on January 14, 1875, just two months after Germany had annexed the province from war-prostrate France. During that year, his father, a Lutheran pastor, moved with his wife and eldest son to the neighboring village of Günsbach among the foothills of the Vosges. It was to this picture-book Franco-German village and its vineyards that Schweitzer was invariably to return in between periods of self-imposed exile in Africa.

As a child, he was frail and an indifferent student in everything but music, for which he showed the interest of a prodigy. He began to play the church organ at eight, when his feet barely reached the pedals. At the age of eighteen he entered the University of Strasbourg as a student in theology, philosophy, and musical theory. By this time he had also studied the organ briefly in Paris under the legendary Charles-Marie Widor, who was so impressed with his pupil's talents that he taught him then and later without fee. Indeed, Schweitzer became a notable organist, especially in the works of Bach, and his recitals in Europe helped to finance his medical work in Africa.

Schweitzer's university life was interrupted by a year of compulsory military service in 1894, a period that proved crucial to his religious thinking and to his life's vocation. The moment of awakening came as he was reading Matthew 10 and 11 in Greek, chapters that contain Jesus's injunctions to his apostles, among them the one that commands, "Heal the sick, cleanse the lepers, raise the dead, cast out devils: freely ye have received, freely give," and the verse that urges men, "Take my yoke upon you, and learn from me; for I am meek and lowly in heart: and ye shall find rest unto your souls."

Schweitzer was struck not only by the application of these verses to himself, but even more by the over-all content of the two chapters as expressed in Jesus's assertion that "the kingdom of heaven is at hand." These chapters started a chain of thought that resulted in *The Quest for the Historical Jesus*. Published in 1910, it at once established Schweitzer as an eminent, if controversial, theologian whose explosive ideas had a profound influence on contemporary religious thinking.

Schweitzer depicted Jesus as a child of his times who shared the eschatological ideas of late Judaism and who looked for an immediate end of the world. Jesus, Schweitzer contended, believed himself the Messiah who would rule in a new kingdom of God when the end came; at first Jesus believed that his Messianic reign would begin before his disciples returned from the teaching mission commanded of them in Matthew 10. When the world's end did not occur, according to Schweitzer's view, Jesus concluded that he must undergo an atoning sacrifice, and that the great transformation would take place on the cross. This, too, failed; hence, Schweitzer argued, the despairing cry, "My God, my God, why hast thou forsaken me?"

"The Jesus of Nazareth . . . who founded the kingdom of Heaven upon earth, and died to give his work the final consecration, never had any existence," Schweitzer wrote. "He is a figure designed by rationalism, endowed with life by liberalism and clothed by modern theology in an historical garb."

Schweitzer maintained, nonetheless, that Jesus's concepts are eternal. "In reality, that which is eternal in the words of Jesus is due to the very fact that they are based on an eschatological world-view, and contain the expression of a mind for which the contemporary world with its historical and social circumstances no longer had any existence. They are appropriate, therefore, to any world, for in every world they raise the man who dares to meet their challenge, and does not turn them and twist them into meaninglessness, above his world and time, making him inwardly free, so that he is fitted to be, in his own world and in his own time, a simple channel of the power of Jesus."

Meantime, as these beliefs were maturing in Schweitzer's mind, he continued his student life at Strasbourg and fixed with great precision the course of his future. In 1896, at the age of twenty-one, he pledged himself that he would give the following nine years to science and art and then devote himself to the service of suffering humanity.

In those years he completed his doctoral thesis in philosophy, a study of Immanuel Kant's views on religion; studied the organ, again with Widor in Paris; won his doctorate in theology; was ordained a curate; taught theology and became principal of the faculty at Strasbourg; wrote The Mystery of the Kingdom of God; and, at Widor's urging, completed a study of the life and art of Johann Sebastian Bach.

The English version, J. S. Bach, is a two-volume translation of the German text, itself an entire reworking of the first version written in French. It approaches Bach as a musician-poet and concentrates on his chorales, cantatas, and Passion music. Schweitzer presents Bach as a religious mystic, as cosmic as the forces of nature. Bach, he said, was chiefly a church composer. As such, and as a Lutheran, "it is precisely to the chorale that the work of Bach owes its greatness."

"The chorale not only puts in his possession the treasury of Protestant music," Schweitzer wrote, "but also opens to him the riches of the Middle Ages and of the sacred Latin music from which the chorale itself came.

"From whatever direction he is considered Bach is, then, the last word in an artistic evolution which was prepared in the Middle Ages, freed and activated by the Reformation, and arrives at its full expression in the eighteenth century."

Turning to Bach's nonchurch music, Schweitzer said: "The Brandenburg concertos are the purest product of Bach's polyphonic style. We really seem to see before us what the philosophy of all ages conceives as the fundamental mystery of things—that self-unfolding of the idea in which it creates its own opposite in order to overcome it, and so on and on until it finally returns to itself, having meanwhile traversed the whole of existence."

Bach's *Well-Tempered Clavier* also drew Schweitzer's warmest praise. "Joy, sorrow, tears, lamentation, laughter," he wrote, "to all of these it gives voice, but in such a way that we are transported from the world of unrest to a world of peace, and see reality in a new way, as if we were sitting by a mountain lake and contemplating hills and woods and clouds in the tranquil and fathomless water."

Schweitzer's probing conception of Bach created a sensation in its time, and it still remains a classic study, not only for the detailed instructions it provides for the playing of Bach but also for its challenging esthetic.

As a virtuoso of the organ, Schweitzer brought to his playing, especially of Bach, a scholarship that was infused with romanticism, in which the printed note was sometimes ignored while the composer's pictorial poetry and symbolism were accentuated.

True to his pledge, Schweitzer turned from music and theology to service to others. On October 13, 1905, he posted letters from Paris to his parents and friends saying that at the start of the winter term he would become a medical student to prepare himself for the life of a physician in French Equatorial Africa.

This decision, protested vigorously by his friends, was, like so many others in his life, the product of religious meditation. He had pondered the meaning of the parable of Dives and Lazarus and its application to his times, and he had concluded that Dives represented opulent Europe, and Lazarus, with his open sores, the sick and helpless of Africa.

Explaining his decision later in more mundane terms, Schweitzer said: "I wanted to be a doctor that I might be able to work without having to talk. For years I had been giving myself out in words. This new form of activity I could not represent to myself as talking about the religion of love, but only as an actual putting it into practice."

For seven years, from 1906 until he received his M.D. degree in February 1913, Schweitzer studied medicine, but he did not entirely cut himself off from his other worlds. Attending the University of Strasbourg, he still served as curate at St. Nicholas, concertized on the organ, conducted a heavy correspondence, and examined Pauline ideas, especially that of dying and being born again "in Jesus Christ." It resulted in a book, *Paul and His Interpreters*, published in English in 1912.

That same year he resigned his curateship and his posts at the university and married Hélène Bresslau, the daughter of a well-known Strasbourg historian. A scholar herself, she became a trained nurse in order to share her husband's life in Africa.

On Good Friday 1913, the couple set sail from Bordeaux for Africa, where Schweitzer established a hospital on the grounds of the Lambaréné station of the Paris Missionary Society. The society, wary of Schweitzer's unorthodox religious views, had barred him from preaching at the station, but agreed to accept his medical skills.

Lambaréné, on the Ogooué River a few miles from the Equator, is in the steaming jungle. Its climate is among the world's worst, with fiercely hot days, clammy nights, and seasonal torrents of rain. The natives have all the usual diseases, plus Hansen's disease (leprosy), dysentery, elephantiasis, sleeping sickness, malaria, yellow fever, and animal wounds.

From the first, when Schweitzer's hospital was a broken-down hen coop, natives flocked by foot, by improvised stretcher, by dugout canoe to Lambaréné for medical attention.

He had barely started to clear the jungle when World War I broke out. He and his wife (they were German citizens) were interned as prisoners of war for four months, then released to continue the work of the hospital. In this time and the succeeding months he started to write the two-volume *The Philosophy of Civilization*, his masterwork in ethics, which was published in 1923. It is a historical review of ethical thought leading to his own original contribution of Reverence for Life as an effective basis for a civilized world.

Schweitzer's book (and other writings as well) disputed the theory that human progress toward civilization was inevitable. He disagreed sharply with Aristotle that man's knowledge of right and wrong would surely lead him to make the right choices. He maintained, instead, that man must rationally formulate an ethical creed and then strive to put it into practice. In Reverence for Life, he concluded, "knowledge passes over into experience."

In 1917 the Schweitzers were returned to France and later to Alsace. To support himself and to carry on the work at Lambaréné, Schweitzer joined the medical staff of the Strasbourg Hospital, preached, gave lectures and organ recitals, traveled, and wrote. He returned to Africa alone in 1925, his wife and daughter, Rhena, who was born in 1919, remaining in Europe.

In the almost eight years of his absence, the jungle had reclaimed the hospital grounds, and the buildings had to be rebuilt. This was no sooner under way than Schweitzer fell ill, an epidemic of dysentery broke out, and a famine set in. The epidemic prompted Schweitzer to move his hospital to a larger site two miles up the Ogooué, where expansion was possible and where gardens and orchards could be planted. Two physicians had arrived from Europe, and to them and to two nurses he turned over all medical responsibilities for a year and a half while he supervised and helped to fell trees, clear ground, and construct buildings. The main hospital room and the dispensary were complete when he departed for Europe in midsummer 1927.

He returned to Lambaréné in 1929 and remained for two years, establishing a pattern of work in Africa and sojourns in Europe during which he lectured, wrote and concertized to raise funds for his hospital. On one of these occasions, in 1949, he visited the United States and lectured on Goethe at a conference in Aspen, Colorado.

Hundreds flocked to hear him and to importune him. On one occasion a group of tourists pulled him away from the dinner table to get an explanation of his ethics. He responded with remarkable courtesy for about twenty minutes until one questioner prodded him for a specific application of Reverence for Life. "Reverence for Life," Schweitzer replied, "means my answering your kind inquiries; it also means your reverence for my dinner hour." The tourists got the point and he returned to his meal.

On his trips to Europe, Schweitzer invariably made his headquarters at his home in Günsbach, which was expanded until it was also a leave and rest center for the hospital staff. Of an afternoon, Schweitzer could often be seen leaving his home to slip over to the church to play Bach. (He played Bach at Lambaréné, too, on pianos specially lined with zinc to prevent rot.) He not only played throughout Europe, but he also repaired church organs and kept up a ceaseless study of music.

Schweitzer received many honorary degrees and recognition from a number of governments and learned societies. He was made an honorary member of the British Order of Merit in 1955. He was elected to the French Academy in 1951.

After his wife died in 1957, Schweitzer was almost continually in Lambaréné. He celebrated his ninetieth birthday there in 1965 as hundreds of Africans, Europeans, and Americans gathered to wish him well. Among the messages he received was one from President Lyndon B. Johnson. "In your commitment to truth and service," the President cabled, "you have touched and deepened the lives of millions you have never met."

FATHER˙DIVINE

Father Divine died September 10, 1965, in a mansion on his Peace Mission Cult's seventy-three-acre estate outside Philadelphia. A man who inspired enormous devotion among his followers, whose aspirations and wants he somehow fulfilled, Father Divine was more a sociological than a religious phenomenon. His cult, which recognized no racial distinctions, practiced a crude communion of goods in which there was food and work for all. If Father Divine's exhortations seem unsophisticated, it must be remembered that his disciples valued statements of certitude above subtle logic.

FATHER DIVINE's height was five feet two inches, and his customary dress was a carefully tailored five-hundred-dollar silk suit. He was bald and paunchy. His face was round and cherubic. His eyes were soft and doelike. His rhetoric was replete with malapropisms, and many of his sentences seemed virtually unintelligible.

However, to thousands who looked upon him and heard him speak, Father Divine was God Almighty, who had arrived full grown on earth in a puff of smoke (he once gave the date as "the time of Abraham") to divulge a creed of peace, communal living, celibacy, honesty, and racial equality.

The movement was called the Kingdom of Peace, but for all its spiritual aspects it was most decidedly of this world.

Although the Kingdom of Peace's absolute ruler accepted such trappings of wealth as Rolls-Royce limousines and freedom from material want, and of divinity as the reverence of his followers in the United States, Europe, Africa, and Australia, he did not specifically declare that he was God.

"I don't have to say I'm God, and I don't have to say I'm not God," he once remarked. "I said there are thousands of people call me God. Millions of them. And there are millions of them call me the

Devil, and I don't say I am God, and I don't say I am the Devil. But I produce God and shake the earth with it."

This disclaimer apart, Father Divine accepted without apparent qualm the assertion of his followers that he was God. On the walls of the movement's missions and houses (they were once called "Heavens") the banners read "Father Divine is God."

In his correspondence and in his weekly newspaper, *New Day*, references to Father Divine were always capitalized; and there was an implication of divinity in the words he used to sign his letters. These subscriptions read:

"This leaves me well, healthy, joyful, peaceful, lively, loving, successful, prosperous and happy in spirit, body and mind and in every organ, muscle, sinew, joint, limb, vein and bone, and in every atom, fiber and cell of my bodily form."

As for defining God, Father Divine said:

"God is not only personified and materialized. He is repersonified and rematerialized. He rematerialized and He rematerialates. He rematerialates and He is rematerializatable. He repersonificates and He repersonifitizes."

In practice, Father Divine fostered a mass cooperative, a primitive communism, based on the Last Supper. The banquet table, often laden with as many as fifty different viands, was a religious symbol.

There were songs and impromptu sermons, but no formal service, no Scriptural reading and no clergy. "Peace, it's wonderful" was the theme preached at the movement's meetings; and "peace" rather than "hello" and "goodbye" was the word of greeting and departure for members of the Kingdom.

Father Divine promulgated a belief that those who joined his Kingdom entered upon a new life, and this accounted for his followers' discarding their family names for such cognomens as Peaceful Samuel, Victory Love, Miss Charity, Holy Quietness, and Positive Love.

Along with a change of name (which was not mandatory) there was a change of conduct (which was mandatory). Father Divine did not permit his followers to smoke tobacco, drink liquor, or use cosmetics; he banned the use of obscene language; he barred attendance at the movies and at stage plays and he interdicted the acceptance of gifts or tips.

Moreover, Father Divine ruled out undue mixing of the sexes as an evil of the flesh, but he did countenance spiritual marriage, citing his own second marriage as an example. This occurred in 1946, when he married Miss Edna Rose Ritchings, a twenty-one-year-old Canadian stenographer.

Miss Ritchings, whose name in the Kingdom of Peace was Sweet Angel, was married to Father Divine secretly in Washington. The event was disclosed three months later at a Lucullan banquet at Woodmont, the Kingdom's thirty-two-room manor house, in Lower Merion Township, near Philadelphia.

Introducing his wife as "the Spotless Virgin Bride," Father Divine explained that they were united "in name only" because "God is not married."

More significant from a doctrinal point of view, Father Divine announced that he had transferred the spirit of his first wife, a Negro, into the person of his second, a white—and he proclaimed that they were one and the same. Thereupon, perhaps looking to his own eventual bodily disappearance from the earth, he said that henceforth his spirit would be possessed by Mother Divine.

The byword in the Kingdom of Peace was, "Father will provide." Judging from the chants of "Thank you, Father, thank you" and the murmurs of "Amen, brother," Father Divine did provide both spiritually and materially, for he handed out not only grace and equality, but also food and lodging.

Rooms at Kingdom hotels and missions cost as little as five dollars a week, with meals at about thirty-five cents apiece. Indigent followers slept and ate free. The low-cost service originated in the Depression years, and it undoubtedly helped to attract followers. The price of a meal then was a nickel.

Countering the material benefits of the Kingdom of Peace was the fact that those admitted to it placed their money and property at the Kingdom's disposal. Father Divine, however, was said not to have held any property in his own name, nor did he have a bank account. The movement's riches were compounded from the donations of its members.

Some real estate was owned outright by Palace Mission, Inc., a subdivision of the Kingdom of Peace. The title to other properties was held in the names of followers, with some parcels having as many as five hundred owners. Woodmont, the movement's showpiece, was called "The Country Seat of the World." Father Divine took up residence there in 1942 after departing what he regarded as an ungrateful New York and leaving behind scores of process servers acting for fallen-away disciples.

More than seventy-five estates or hotels of varying degrees of opulence were included in the United States realm of the Kingdom of Peace. In Philadelphia, these included the Tracy and Lorraine Hotels. There was also the Fairmount Hotel in Jersey City, and a large estate overlooking the Hudson River, at Krum Elbow in New York. Married couples living in these hotels and estates were separated.

These estates were the outgrowth of the "Heavens," the first of which was established at Sayville, L.I., in 1919. The eight-room house was purchased by "Major J. Devine"; it was the only property ever held in Father Divine's name.

The Sayville establishment is modest by comparison with that in Gladwyne, Lower Merion, with its tennis courts and outdoor swimming pool and its twenty-two-karat-gold dinner services, its silver tea services, rosewood furniture, and Oriental rugs.

His movement grew rapidly in the nineteen-thirties and forties when Father Divine was speaking frequently and voluminously. *New Day*, his weekly, was full of his speeches, sermons, and interviews on topical events.

Since 1955, however, the newspaper has been devoted almost entirely to reprints of earlier talks. Explaining this, one of his aides said recently:

"Father has said everything there is to say about everything."

Among the things about which Father Divine "said everything" was atomic energy. "I am the author and the finisher of atomic energy. I have harnessed it," he announced in 1945 when the United States dropped the first atom bomb on Hiroshima.

He propounded the secret of personality by saying:

"The individual is the personification of that which expresses personification. Therefore he comes to be personally the expression of that which was impersonal, and he is the personal expression of it and the personification of the prepersonification of God Almighty! Peace, it's wonderful!"

Of his Kingdom of Peace, he remarked:

"This is an impersonal Movement and it is not bound to an organization. It is enveloping the world the same as the light of civilization from the Christian movement. It does not belong to Me alone as a Person any more than the light of civilization belongs to an individual. It is impersonal by nature, impersonal in its characteristics and impersonal in its activities."

Although Father Divine insisted on enveloping his corporeal history (and his age) in mystery, there is some evidence that he was born George Baker in 1877 on Hutchinson's Island in the Savannah River in Georgia.

From childhood he worked around Georgia and, later, Maryland, at odd jobs for fifty cents a day.

Just before the turn of the century, he lived in East Baltimore, and was preaching in little Sunday schools around town. In 1907, he became "The Messenger," a disciple to Sam Morris, a Pennsylvania Negro who was trying to sell the idea that he was "Father Jehovia."

Two years later George Baker switched over to John Hickerson's "Live Ever, Die Never" group. Then he returned to Valdosta in Georgia to promote himself along these lines.

Official Valdosta, somewhat irritated, booked Mr. Baker as "John Doe, alias God," and tried him as a public nuisance. The choice of leaving Georgia or going to an insane asylum was given him. He quit Georgia in February 1914.

He headed then for New York. In 1915 a few Valdosta followers served and supported him in a rundown house on West 40th Street. As a sideline to his godly activities, he was their employment agent; he got them jobs as cooks, valets, waiters, and laundry help.

About this time he began to encourage his followers to believe that they could never die while they believed in him. When one of them came down with something likely to be fatal, Father Divine—then just "Major J. Devine"—would turn the follower out of the "Heaven." Dropped in some nearby flat, these unfortunates would be picked up by a city hospital, and would eventually go to potter's field.

Then Father Divine could truthfully say, "No one dies in My House," and his followers spread this word, to his advantage.

In 1931 the following had grown so large and was so noisy at the Sayville feasts, especially on weekends, that the police haled Father Divine before Justice Lewis J. Smith as a public nuisance. On November 16, the justice sentenced him to six months in jail and fined him five hundred dollars.

Four days later the justice died of a heart attack.

Father Divine was quoted as saying then: "I hated to do it!"

In recent years, Father Divine was seldom seen in public, and there were frequent reports that he had died. Five years ago he was admitted for a week to Bryn Mawr Hospital. The diagnosis was diabetic coma. Hospital records then listed him as Frederick Devoe and put his age at eighty. Whether this was his name or whether it was Baker was uncertain. All that his associates would say was:

"George Baker is the name given him by his enemies."

BLANCHE W. KNOPF

Blanche W. Knopf died in New York on June 4, 1966, at the age of seventy-one. The wife of Alfred A. Knopf, she was a figure in her own right in the book publishing world. It isn't often that a wife outshines her husband at his own game, but there was no doubt of it in Mrs. Knopf's case—she made the firm and graciously permitted Alfred to take the bows.

IN THE clubby man's world that is book publishing, Blanche Wolf Knopf was a feminine presence that commandeered respect. She asked no dispensation for being a woman, and she gave none. She insisted on being known as Blanche W. Knopf, not Mrs. Alfred A.; and she insisted equally on claiming for her own the authors she brought to the company. Her alertness and perspicacity in courting these writers and her driving energy as an executive contributed immensely to the success of the house of Knopf.

Although Mr. Knopf often personified the publishing enterprise to the public, close associates were aware of Mrs. Knopf's true role. Robert Nathan, the novelist and a long-time friend of the couple, summed it up this way:

"Alfred is terrifically majestic. He and Blanche are like Jupiter and Juno. He is the ultimate, she the penultimate, but in her own right just as ultimate."

For fifty years Mrs. Knopf had virtually no other life but book publishing. "The world of books is the world I know. I would not change it for any other," she once said. With her husband she helped found the company in 1915. From 1921 to 1957 she was vice-president and a director of Alfred A. Knopf, Inc., and president and director thereafter.

To the company she gave not only a sharp knowledge of belles-lettres but also an acquired intimacy with typography, paper, ink, and printing. Mrs. Knopf, moreover, was responsible for the famous Borzoi imprint on Knopf books. When it was devised in 1916 she was fond of the looks of borzois (Russian wolfhounds) and proposed that a drawing of one be used as a colophon.

"I bought a couple of them [borzois] later and grew to despise them," she said a few years ago. "They were cowardly, stupid, disloyal, and full of self-pity, and they kept running away. I wish I'd picked a better dog for our imprint."

Subsequently, Mrs. Knopf turned to Yorkshire terriers as pets.

The Knopfs initially made their reputation by publishing European authors and by presenting their books in attractive bindings and jackets. In the company's first years Mrs. Knopf was frequently in charge of the office while her husband traveled in search of authors. W. H. Hudson's *Green Mansions* was one of their early ventures, and its success helped to establish the Borzoi imprint, which was buttressed in the 1920's by such writers as Thomas Mann, Sigrid Undset, Katherine Mansfield, Knut Hamsun, Willa Cather, H. L. Mencken, and Clarence Day.

Starting in the thirties, Mrs. Knopf was often in Europe or South America in quest of authors. She was fluent in French and spoke Italian and Spanish, and, by reason of her Austrian background, had a large measure of Continental charm. These attributes, plus a sound knowledge of letters, helped her to win writers for the Knopf list.

In the forties she paid several visits to Latin America, obtaining the manuscripts of such highly regarded writers as Eduardo Mallea, Jorge Amado, Germán Arciniega, and Gilberto Freyre. Mrs. Knopf was regarded as being in charge of this field of the publisher's activities. Moreover, after World War II, she also directed the British and European aspects of the business.

Among the British writers that she signed up over the years were Hammond Innes, Elizabeth Bowen, Ivy Compton-Burnett, Muriel Spark, Angela Thirkell, and Alan Sillitoe. André Gide was one of her French discoveries, as were Jules Romains, Jean-Paul Sartre, Albert Camus, and Simone de Beauvoir.

In 1938 she persuaded Sigmund Freud to give Knopf his *Moses and Monotheism*, a book that helped spread the psychoanalyst's popular fame in the United States. Other of her European writers were Ilya Ehrenburg and Mikhail A. Sholokhov.

For her authors who wrote in foreign languages Mrs. Knopf arranged for translations into English, and her impeccable supervision of this delicate task helped to win her the writers' gratitude and loyalty. Between writer and publisher were steadfast personal friendships.

Mrs. Knopf's foreign list was peopled with intellectuals; but in the United States she was responsible for publishing authors of the hard-boiled school—Dashiell Hammett, James M. Cain, and Raymond Chandler—as well as the more gentle Mr. Nathan.

Mrs. Knopf was considered generous with authors—more so than her husband. Only recently, for example, she paid Virgil Thomson, the composer and critic, ten thousand dollars for his memoirs—a sizable advance in the publishing business.

In addition to her financial liberality, she devoted many hours to her authors' personal problems. "Blanche was always wet-nursing her writers," a friend recalled, "seeing them through family crises, advising them on doctors and dentists, taking them to lunch and helping them meet people they wanted to know. She has a natural sensitivity to literary people, and she enjoyed taking some part in their lives."

Mrs. Knopf tended to be reticent about herself. "I don't think a lady publisher is any different than a man publisher," she told an interviewer with some asperity. "And I don't see anything interesting about her. I'll talk about my books and my authors, yes. But me? I should say not."

Her authors, however, felt there was something special about her. Mr. Nathan, in a poem in her honor, called Mrs. Knopf the "soul" of the publishing company. Mr. Mann said that she "combines all the charm of the fair sex with an admirable energy and capacity in the realm of social and cultural activity."

"A man and his wife do not become Siamese twins, bent on identical pursuits and craving the same foods, friends, and diversions," Mrs. Knopf remarked in an interview in 1933. She might well have been describing her own marriage, for she and her husband were almost exact opposites in traits and tastes.

Mrs. Knopf was petite and chic; she was once plump, but for the last thirty-five years of her life weighed about a hundred pounds. Her face was longish, her eyes were gray-green beneath gently arched eyebrows; her hair was brown with a hint of red. She dressed very fashionably in Christian Dior creations, and, at the office, she sometimes wore a carmine scarf over the shoulders of a dress. Mr. Knopf is a large man, and he is addicted to purple shirts and loud neckwear.

Mrs. Knopf was widely known for her literary teas, at which she stimulated conversation with adroit questions and spent most of her time listening. "With Alfred," a friend said, "you are in the presence of a monologuist. He likes to pontificate, not to exchange ideas."

Reared by French and German governesses, Mrs. Knopf was thoroughly sophisticated and courteous but quite unsentimental. "Alfred knows a lot about the world, but he's not really worldly," an associate said. "He's courteous, but more or less as an afterthought, and he's sentimental, in a nineteenth-century way."

Mrs. Knopf disliked to age. She felt it virtually impossible, for example, to conceive of herself as a grandmother, and she declined to bask in that role. "Blanche wouldn't think of taking the kids to the circus, but that was one of Alfred's delights," a family friend said. "It wasn't lack of affection on Blanche's part; it was just that she couldn't stand being a grandmother."

In a number of other respects the Knopfs differed completely. Mrs. Knopf was not interested in haute cuisine and vintage wines (Mr. Knopf's loves) but preferred plain cooking and bourbon whiskey. She liked living in New York City, walking to work, reading serious fiction and being active in liberal causes. "Alfred's a country man, a seigneur, who likes to ride in his Rolls-Royce," another friend said. "He isn't likely to read his own authors from cover to cover unless they're historians. Politically, he's a Tory."

The Knopfs, though, shared a knowledge of, and fondness for, music and opera, with Mr. Knopf leaning to classics of the nineteenth century and earlier, and Mrs. Knopf favoring more modern composers. Their musical friends included George Gershwin, Artur Rubinstein, Yehudi Menuhin, Jascha Heifetz, and Dame Myra Hess. Mrs. Knopf named one of her dogs Jascha for Mr. Heifetz.

Mrs. Knopf often referred to herself as "the charwoman of the firm," and there was no question of her full devotion to it. She worked at a carved mahogany desk in a red-carpeted office at 501 Madison Avenue, a brief walk from her apartment on West 55th Street. She was tireless in going over manuscripts, editing book jacket material, and keeping the Knopf editorial staff on its toes. Mrs. Knopf "sometimes works secretaries until they are exhausted and then remorsefully sends them on paid leave," according to a Geoffrey Hellman article on Mr. Knopf in 1948 in the New Yorker.

Mr. Hellman depicted Mrs. Knopf as "hunchy." An aide recently called her "intuitive." "If you give her a piece of jacket copy to read," this aide explained, "she may return it, saying simply that she doesn't like it. She couldn't tell you why. On the other hand, if she likes it, she couldn't tell you why, either."

Even during her final years when she was ill and could scarcely see, she came regularly to the office and put in a workday that appalled her associates. She refused medication most of the time lest it dull her senses and her mental acuity.

Mrs. Knopf was born in New York in 1894, the daughter of Julius and Bertha Wolf. She attended the Gardner School here, but was largely privately educated. She met Alfred Knopf about 1911, when he was an undergraduate at Columbia College, and encouraged him in his ambition to become a publisher. The couple were married April 4, 1916. They had one son, Alfred Jr., who was vice-president of the publishing company until he resigned a few years ago to found Atheneum Publishers.

Mrs. Knopf was honored by two foreign governments. She was named a Chevalier of the Legion of Honor in 1949 (and later an Officer) for her support of French literature in the United States. For her interest in Brazilian letters she was, in 1950, made a Cavaleiro of the Brazilian National Order of the Southern Cross. Two years later she was promoted to the rank of Officer.

JEAN ARP

Jean Arp died in Basel, Switzerland, on June 7, 1966, at the age of seventy-eight. The French abstract sculptor and painter was one of the founders of the Dada movement in art. Known for the exceptional simplicity and clarity of his shapes, he helped decorate the Paris headquarters of the United Nations Educational, Scientific, and Cultural Organization. An artist is always a challenge to a writer: Are you telling what he is really all about? Luckily, Arp had defined himself quite well.

Alfred H. Barr, Jr., of the Museum of Modern Art in New York once described Jean Arp as "a one-man laboratory for the discovery of new forms." It was an apt summary, for Arp was a tireless innovator of abstract forms. But he did not care for other kinds, "especially," he remarked, "these naked men, women, and children in stone or bronze who untiringly dance, chase butterflies, shoot arrows, hold out apples, blow the flute."

On a visit to New York in 1948, his first to the United States, he illustrated his own attitude toward form with a piece of popcorn. "I begin with something like this," he explained, holding the kernel between his fingers. "I see just what expression it takes and develop that. Now this little bump here looks like a branch. Turn it around and we have a head, or a flower. But I don't want a head, a branch, or a flower, so I mold it a bit—or I may throw it away."

The last phrase, with its implication of disdain, did not appear to fit Arp, whose politeness and lack of pretension were renowned even when he was battling the conventional in art.

His sense of gentleness came to the surface, for example, when he stated his beliefs in this fashion: "Art is a fruit growing out of man like the fruit out of a plant, like the child out of the mother."

Many of his sculptures were distinctive for their smoothness. Some thought they resembled clouds on the verge of forming into recognizable objects, so that the eye read into them a shape they did not quite have in objective fact.

Arp's sculpture influenced many contemporary painters and sculptors. His forms were also widely copied in the decorative and commercial arts, and they can be recognized today in such things as swimming pools, book design, and advertising layouts. The copies, however, most often lacked the lyrical sense that infused the original creation.

Much of Arp's significance came from his leadership in the Dada and surrealist movements in modern art. With Hugo Ball and Tristan Tzara, he was a member of the original Dada group that in 1916 turned Zurich's Cabaret Voltaire into a headquarters for the subversion of all that was most respectable in European art and culture.

The word "Dada," according to art historians, was taken at random from a French-German dictionary. Its literal meaning then was "hobby horse."

In art, according to critics, Dadaism has come to be synonymous with calculated nonsense or a revolt against rigidities of expression.

For a half century Arp, in a copious outflowing of sculptures, collages, constructions, poems, and critical ruminations, remained loyal to the passions generated by the Dada ideology, yet his work was not doctrinaire. Indeed, his immaculate white marble carvings embodied wit, nuance, and elegance. The female torso was Arp's dominant sculptural theme, but in his hands its abstract rigor took on an almost erotic delicacy and fantasy.

Important as Arp's sculptures were, it was in the collage medium that he achieved his most striking originality. His torn-paper collages (he called them papiers déchirés) gave to modern art the strategies of pictorial improvisation and chance composition that have since become a standard procedure.

At the time of his large retrospective exhibition at the Museum of Modern Art in 1958, the artist said of these works: "I believe they represent the transition from abstract painting to 'liberated painting,' as I should like to call the new American painting."

Although he had in mind his influence on abstract expressionism, his point holds true for the underlying methods of pop art, color-field painting, and similar recent developments.

The third important segment of Arp's work is his constructed (and sometimes painted) reliefs. These occupy a middle ground between his sculptures, with their amorphousness, and his torn-paper collages. In the constructed form, cut-out pieces of painted wood are mounted on a panel. Among the best known are "Table," "Anchors," "Navel," and "Overturned Shoe with Two Heels Under a Black Vault."

Jean Arp was born Hans Arp on September 16, 1887, in Strasbourg, Alsace, which was then under German rule. In his early life he called himself "Hans" but he switched to "Jean" later on. However, he still used "Hans" when he wrote in German.

Educated at the lycée in Strasbourg, he quit school without graduating. He visited Paris in 1904, studied for two years in Weimar, Germany, then returned to Paris for study at the Académie Julian. His idiosyncratic style began to develop in 1909, when he went to live in solitude in Weggis, Switzerland, and sought to fashion for himself an impersonal, nonobjective style in painting. His works were first exhibited in Lucerne in 1911.

About that time he made the acquaintance of Wassily Kandinsky, whose abstract improvisation he fancied. He then became associated with that Russian painter, Franz Marc, and Paul Klee in an expressionist group that exhibited in Munich and Berlin in 1912 and 1913.

In World War I Arp lived in neutral Switzerland, and it was there in 1915 that he exhibited wall tapestries and drawings that were completely rectangular, geometric forms. Two years later, however, he began to devise the curvilinear, biomorphic forms that characterized so much of his later sculpture. He drew his initial inspiration for these fluid forms from the roots, broken branches, and stones he saw on the shores of Lake Maggiore.

In the early twenties Arp tended to surrealism, a schismatic outgrowth of Dadaism, and his first one-man show was at the Galérie Surréaliste in Paris in 1927.

Many of Arp's best-known sculptures were executed during the thirties. He used bronze, stone, and plaster. He also made woodcuts for books, a project he turned to in the fifties, and designed rugs and em' broideries. In addition, he wrote lyric poetry, mostly in German.

Arp's works are to be found in museums in New York, Paris, London, Zurich, Basel, Rome, Stockholm, Philadelphia, and San Francisco as well as in private collections.

In 1921 he married Sophie Henriette Gertrude Taeuber, who was also an artist. She died in 1943. So great was her husband's grief that he was unable to work for a long time and considered taking religious orders in the Roman Catholic Church, of which he was a communicant.

Throughout his life Arp, despite his apparent avoidance of nature, was deeply concerned by man's relationship to it. "If the human being loses contact with nature," he once said, "if there are no longer any trees, it is the end of the world. Machines, sputniks, I find them horrible, ridiculous. The human being has become presumptuous."

SHERMAN BILLINGSLEY

Sherman Billingsley died in New York on October 4, 1966, at the age of sixty-six. A host for more than thirty-six years to hundreds of social, theatrical, political, and business personalities at his Stork Club, he was the city's boniface extraordinary—a high-class speakeasy operator who kept his tone in the years after Prohibition was repealed. An arbiter of the after-dark set, he was an ornament to those who could afford him.

To THE GO-GO society of the nineteen-sixties, the Stork Club and Sherman Billingsley were as square and as outdated as the fox trot and the waltz. Yet to cafe society, that society's forebear in the thirties and forties, both the club and its host were symbols of eminent social status.

Where but in the Stork Club could one see Brenda Frazier, the city's loveliest debutante? Or H. L. Mencken with George Jean Nathan and Eugene O'Neill? Or Grace Kelly? Or Madame Chiang Kai-shek? Or the Duke and Duchess of Windsor? Or Andrei Gromyko? Or J. Edgar Hoover, Walter Winchell, and Leonard Lyons, not to mention the Ernest Hemingways?

"I have consorted with princes and nobility; the elite of the world have graced my tables. This is a place unique unto itself; no other place in the world can duplicate it," Mr. Billingsley said when he was "Sherm" to the personalities who trooped to what Mr. Winchell called "the New Yorkiest place in town."

Mr. Winchell, along with other newspaper gossip columnists, helped to create the popularity of the Stork Club and the legend of Mr. Billingsley by mentioning both with great frequency.

Mr. Billingsley had a number of tiffs with his celebrated guests, some of whom he barred temporarily from the club for what he called "misbehavior." Jackie Gleason, the television performer, was among these, as were Elliott Roosevelt, a son of President Franklin D. Roosevelt, and the late Humphrey Bogart.

There was some suspicion that Mr. Billingsley, with his keen sense of publicity, refused admittance to these celebrities for the sake of newspaper space. But some who could not get past the red velvet rope were so stricken that they turned in their gold club keys and never tried to patch up their differences with Mr. Billingsley, who was actually quite a mild-mannered man.

Mr. Billingsley was delighted to serve as host to the famous, and he provided them with their own room, the Cub Room. Regular patrons could be assured of their tables there, and among the steady customers were James A. Farley, Bernard M. Baruch, Gene Tunney, Joe DiMaggio, Dorothy Lamour, Helen Hayes, and Ethel Merman.

Of the Stork Club, an observer wrote:

"The show consists of common people looking at celebrities and the celebrities looking at themselves in the mirrors—and they all sit popeyed in admiration."

Mr. Billingsley was assiduous in promoting that success formula. He employed two crews of press agents, one in the daytime and the other at night. He bestowed gifts on even the humblest guest—lipsticks and flacons of perfume for the women, whiskey or champagne for the men. It was excellent business while it lasted, for his yearly intake was said to exceed $3 million in the club's best years.

Even so, Mr. Billingsley worked sixteen hours a day at his job. He called himself managing director of the club, asserting that it was owned by his wife, Hazel. His attitude toward the club employees was paternal, and he bitterly resented their joining unions in the hope of improving their wages and working conditions.

Mr. Billingsley also had his troubles with Josephine Baker, the Negro entertainer, in 1951. She charged that she was discriminated against at the Stork when she was not served with what she considered reasonable promptitude. Civil rights pickets marched outside the club in protest, but no evidence of discrimination was found after a city investigation.

Ordinarily, Mr. Billingsley was soft-spoken and suave, although his speech seemed to some overstudded with such Westernisms as "golly." His regionalism, however, was basically genuine, for John Sherman Billingsley was born in Enid, Oklahoma, a village of three hundred persons, on March 10, 1900.

His schooling ended after fourth grade, and his first earnings, according to Jerome Beatty in the American Magazine, came from the sale of discarded whiskey bottles to bootleggers in the dry state of Oklahoma.

When Sherman was twelve, he moved to Anadarko, Oklahoma, where he worked with his elder brothers in their chain of cigar and drug stores. Later, while still in his teens, he went to Detroit and became proprietor of three neighborhood grocery stores.

These proved profitable enough to provide him with five thousand dollars, with which he came to New York in 1923 and purchased a drug store in the Bronx. That pharmacy, according to students of Mr. Billingsley's life, dispensed whiskey on prescription and was so expert at it that the young man soon owned a chain of twenty such drug stores in the Bronx and neighboring Westchester County.

Never one to squander his earnings, Mr. Billingsley invested in real estate and even built a number of apartment and private houses. A two-block residential street just south of the Bronx campus of New York University—Billingsley Terrace—is still evidence of his realty ventures of the twenties.

The first Stork Club opened on West 58th Street in 1929. "It was the first speakeasy that had a carpet on the floor and a canopy out front," Mr. Billingsley recalled.

His ambition, he said, was to operate "a nice place where people can come for a good time and where I can bring my family any time without their seeing anything I wouldn't like them to see."

The West 58th Street club was closed by Prohibition agents, but it reappeared by 1932 without noticeable difficulty at Park Avenue and 51st Street. With the repeal of Prohibition in late 1933, he re-established the club at 3 East 53rd Street, where it remained until it was closed for good on October 5, 1965.

ELIZABETH ARDEN

Elizabeth Arden (Mrs. Elizabeth N. Graham) died in New York on October 9, 1966, at an undetermined age. The queen of the beauty industry built a multimillion-dollar business in salons, cosmetics, and clothes from an original stake of less than one thousand dollars. Over a span of fifty years the chairman of the board and president of Elizabeth Arden, Inc., managed her company with the same assiduity that she operated her race-horse affairs; and with the same success. For her acumen and her oddities, she was an obituarist's dream.

FLORENCE NIGHTINGALE GRAHAM made her fame and fortune from rich women and fast horses. In achieving glistening success she treated her women like horses and her horses like women. Both gave every appearance of loving her pampering.

Her women craved that mystical thing called beauty, and Mrs. Graham, under the name Elizabeth Arden, convinced them that they could attain it if they permitted themselves to be steamed, rolled, bathed in wax, massaged, and showered in one of her more than fifty sumptuous salons. The billion-dollar beauty business, which Elizabeth Arden helped create, gave her an income in the millions.

She was a sociological and historical phenomenon. "Arden made the cosmetic industry," an observer said recently. "She is the mother of the treatment business."

Also adding to her income were Maine Chance Farm horses that she raced under the name Mrs. Elizabeth N. Graham. Her thoroughbreds included Jet Pilot, which won the Kentucky Derby of 1947. Mrs. Graham encouraged her horses by addressing them in baby talk—she called them "my darlings"—feeding them special clover ("It's their spinach"), piping music into their fly-free stalls, seeing to it that they were massaged and conditioned with Elizabeth Arden creams and lotions, and keeping them in clean, tastefully decorated stables.

Mrs. Graham liked only handsome horses (those flunking her beauty test were quickly sold off), and she insisted that her jockeys spare the whip and that her trainers not overexert the animals. Nonetheless, she was serious about horses and she seemed to enjoy the confidence of many of them.

Elizabeth Arden was also serious about women, and she enjoyed the friendship of hundreds who were wealthy and highly placed socially. They constituted the bulk of the trade at her major temples of glamour and at her two beauty-restorative resorts, both called Maine Chance Farm.

The fifty big salons are in the principal cities and resorts of the United States, Canada, Mexico, Peru, Europe, and Australia. The New York salon occupies eleven of twelve floors at 691 Fifth Avenue, near 54th Street. Like every other major Arden salon, it is entered through a bright red door.

In Paris, the Arden salon is on the Place Vendôme, a few steps from the Ritz. It is managed by Miss Arden's sister, Vicomtesse Henri de Maublanc, and it employs a countess to handle its press relations. The salon's socially distinguished clients have included, of course, the Duchess of Windsor, and others have been Princess Charles d'Arenberg, Olivia de Haviland, and the Begum Aga Khan.

In addition to these salons, Elizabeth Arden operated about fifty establishments throughout the world for facials and hairdressing. These are elegant but less elaborate than the full-treatment salons.

Moreover, Elizabeth Arden manufactured about three hundred scented cosmetics products sold in department stores and pharmacies around the globe. The best seller over the years has been Arden's Velva Moisture Film, a lotion available in a number of shades that is applied before make-up.

Through her clients in the beauty business and her friendships in the horse world, Mrs. Graham became prominent in society. She gave many parties, some at her duplex apartment on Fifth Avenue. For many years she was a patroness of the annual luncheon and fashion show for the benefit of the American Women's Voluntary Services; she sponsored the annual Blue Grass Ball (named for one of her perfumes) for the New York Travelers Aid Society; she was active in the Friends of the Philharmonic and in obtaining financial support for the American Symphony Orchestra directed by Leopold Stokowski.

In whichever of her worlds Mrs. Graham was present, she appeared as comely, fragile, fluttery, and ageless. But although she stood only a little over five feet tall and was slender, she was about as fragile as a football tackle; and anyone who mistook her wispiness for indecision quickly discovered that she had a will of steel and the power to execute it.

She was, however, undeniably ageless, a circumstance that she accentuated by concealing her birth date. A company spokesman said it was December 31, 1884, but others were certain it was 1880. Whatever it may have been, Mrs. Graham, in her sixties and seventies, looked twenty years younger, even on close inspection of her face. Moreover, her hair never grayed publicly, but remained mostly a beige-blond. "I can't see any reason why any woman should ever have to have gray hair," she told a gray-haired reporter in 1965. This was just one reflection of Mrs. Graham's vanity and her uncompromising belief that youthfulness was somehow an important ingredient of beauty.

Mrs. Graham lived suffused in pink. Early in her business career she came to the conclusion that it was the most flattering color in the spectrum, and she never changed her mind about its power to make drab subjects glow in its reflected warmth. She dressed mostly in pink or its variations (once in a great while she wore blue or beige), and she once doused her hair in a pink rinse.

The intensity of her pink changed with the fashions. Some seasons it was a bright cherry pink and some seasons it might have undertones of lavender. When ethereal complexions were in fancy a few years ago, Elizabeth Arden pink was as pale as the dawn's early light.

Pink also dominated the décor of Mrs. Graham's Manhattan residence, her apartment adjoining the Surf Club at Miami Beach, her cottages at the Belmont and Saratoga race tracks, and her living quarters at Maine Chance Farm, Lexington, Kentucky. Pink was in evidence, too, in her twelfth-century gothic castle in Ballymore Eustace, twenty miles outside Dublin. The castle is part of a 507-acre estate for horses and cattle.

Pink, in addition, was the signature color of the jars and covers for Elizabeth Arden products. She once halted production on a jar because the color was not exactly right. The step cost $100,000, but she regarded that as a trifle. Even Elizabeth Arden press releases were mimeographed on pink paper. Unaccountably, they arrived at newspaper offices in plain brown envelopes.

Although Elizabeth Arden subscribed to the notion that cosmetics make the woman, she did not neglect the role of smart clothes. Negligees, lingerie, and day and evening costumes were offered for sale in her salons. She had several designers over the years, including Antonio del Castillo, Oscar de la Renta, and Ferdinando Sarmi. The custom and ready-made collections were considered elegant for women verging on middle age.

Miss Arden herself was always well dressed, in either a trim suit or a gently flowing gown. She invariably wore diamonds, a pearl necklace, and earrings. The scent of Mémoire Chérie, an Arden perfume, was rarely absent; nor was a handbag, a small alligator one, which she carried even in her own living room.

The chief ingredients of beauty, in Miss Arden's view, were a clean skin, natural make-up, a slim waistline and a simple hairdo. In her later years she condoned rather flamboyant eye make-up, but she was adamantly against close-cropped hairdos. "If you read the papers, you will notice that no girl with short hair has made an advantageous marriage lately," she remarked in 1950. "So what's the sense of looking like a shaved bulldog?"

Born near Toronto of Scotch-English parents, Florence Graham grew into a young woman of ambition who migrated to New York in 1908 in search of a more active life than Toronto provided. She got a job with Eleanor Adair, a beauty specialist, learned massage, and looked into the elementary formulas for cosmetics.

Miss Graham, as she was then, entered the beauty business at an opportune moment. Only hoydens used rouge and lipstick. The respectable women employed, in moderation, talcum powder and some rose water and glycerin; but in the new freedom that was then beginning, they yearned for ladylike beauty aids. Miss Graham capitalized on that situation by helping to create and popularize creams, lotions, and oils—and salons at fashionable addresses in which they could be professionally applied.

Leaving Adair's by 1910, Flo Graham went into business with Elizabeth Hubbard in a salon in a brownstone at 509 Fifth Avenue. The partners, both strong-minded, drifted apart, and Miss Graham carried on alone. At first she decided to change her corporate name to Florence Nightingale and then she hit upon Elizabeth Arden. The "Elizabeth" derived from Miss Hubbard and the "Arden" from Tennyson's *Enoch Arden*, Miss Graham's favorite poem at the moment.

Shortly afterward, Miss Graham became Mrs. Graham in the belief that a married woman inspired more confidence in her customers. (Over the years she answered both to "Miss Arden" and to "Mrs. Graham," although she generally reserved the latter name for her racing activities.)

From the outset Elizabeth Arden prospered. The owner, then as later, was certain that her point of view in any situation was the right one. When chemists told her that a fluffy face cream—"like whipped cream"—was an impossibility, she autocratically disagreed. And, of course, she was right.

A. F. Swanson, a chemist with Stillwell & Gladding, was the man who produced the light cream, called Cream Amoretta, in 1914. Ardena Skin Tonic, an astringent lotion, was devised next. These two products were the basis of the Arden fortune, which was also, in the early days, augmented by the addition of rouge and eye shadow.

In 1915 Miss Arden moved up Fifth Avenue and opened a wholesale department to produce and sell her expanding line to department and drug stores around the world. She moved into 691 Fifth Avenue in 1930.

From 1915 to 1934 the Arden wholesale division was managed by Thomas Jenkins Lewis, Miss Graham's first husband and a man with a flair for advertising and salesmanship. When they were divorced, Mr. Lewis, who had not been permitted to own stock in Arden, went to work for Helena Rubinstein, Elizabeth Arden's archrival in the beauty field. (There was a second marriage, in 1942, to Prince Michael Evlanoff; it ended in divorce thirteen months later.)

Miss Arden was a hard taskmaster. She demanded perfection from her employees, not all of whom were capable of rendering it. But those who did remained on the payroll for decades. Those who did not meet the Arden standards were dismissed out of hand.

Creating cosmetics was an Arden specialty. She tried them all on herself—and on her employees. But the final decisions were made by Miss Arden, whose passion for detail was legendary. This extended to every phase of her business—the color of the package, the wording or mood of an advertisement, the naming of a perfume.

By and large Elizabeth Arden's salons catered to women forty years of age and older. For them a basic day at her New York salon included exercise, steam cabinet, and massage, shampoo, set, and restyling, manicure, pedicure, facial, make-up, and lunch. All this, done in a setting of eighteenth-century French and Regency décor, cost about fifty dollars—without tips, which might readily run 20 percent.

The Maine Chance Farm in Mount Vernon, Maine, was open from June to September; the other, near Phoenix, was open in the winter only.

A week's restorative course cost about $750, exclusive of tips. For this sum a client lived in a combination of Byzantine luxury and Spartan spareness.

A number of distinguished women were guests at a Maine Chance Farm, including Mrs. Dwight D. Eisenhower, Mrs. Barry Goldwater, Clare Boothe Luce, Perle Mesta, Beatrice Lillie, and Gwen Cafritz, a Washington social leader.

Mrs. Graham became acquainted with race horses through her devotion to society. Mrs. Graham's stable did very well indeed into the early 1960's; but the sale of Gun Bow in December 1963 marked the beginning of the decline of Maine Chance Farm. Its name has not figured in big races in recent years. The stable's total earnings from 1943 through last September 30 were $4,711,437, according to the *Daily Telegraph*, the racing newspaper.

When her horses won (which was perfection), she was open-handed with the jockeys. For example, Eric Guerin, Jet Pilot's rider in the Derby, was rewarded with 20 percent of the $92,160 purse, double the usual fee. Giving it gave Mrs. Graham pleasure.

S. S. KRESGE

S. S. Kresge died near Mountainhome, Pennsylvania, on October 18, 1966, at the age of ninety-nine. The founder of the S. S. Kresge Company's network of stores in the United States, Puerto Rico and Canada made millions out of dimes. A frugal genius, he was an American success story that was all the more interesting for his quirkiness.

BY COMBINING a genius for merchandising, a delight in hard work, and a passion for frugality, Sebastian Spering Kresge accumulated a fortune in the hundreds of millions of dollars from a chain of 5- and 10-cent stores and, later, of variety-department and discount stores. He was among the earliest and most vigorous practitioners of the chain-store principle, having obtained the idea from Frank W. Woolworth, whom he met as a traveling tinware salesman.

Starting with one store in Detroit in 1899, he lived to see his S. S. Kresge Company become the second-largest variety chain in the country (after F. W. Woolworth) with annual sales in 1966 of more than $851 million through 918 outlets in the United States, Puerto Rico, and Canada. The company employed more than forty-two thousand people.

Despite his personal parsimony, Mr. Kresge proved a generous philanthropist, especially through the Kresge Foundation, which he set up in 1924 "to help human progress through benefactions of whatever name or nature." He made an initial contribution of $1.3 million to the fund and, in all, he gave it securities with a book value of $65 million at the time of the donation.

Mr. Kresge was a foundation trustee until June 1966, by which time its net worth was $175 million and its grants had totaled $70 million. Among its gifts were $10 million to the Newark (New Jersey) Museum; $3 million for a medical research building at the University of Michigan at Ann Arbor; $1.75 million to the same institution for the Kresge Hearing Research Institute; $1.5 million to Michigan State University for the Kresge Art Center at East Lansing; $1.5 million to Northwestern University; $1 million to Wayne University in Detroit; $2 million to Harvard for Kresge Hall at the Harvard Business School; $1.5 to the Massachusetts Institute of Technology for a campus and religious center in Cambridge, Massachusetts; and $400,000 to Columbia University.

In addition, the foundation was an active supporter of the Methodist Children's Home near Detroit and of hospitals and medical research in the fields of cancer and multiple sclerosis.

Through the foundation and out of his own pocket, Mr. Kresge contributed more than $1 million to the Anti-Saloon League, which fought for the adoption of the Eighteenth Amendment and for its rigorous enforcement. His personal benefactions also included the Young Men's Christian Association, the Methodist Church, of which he was a member, and a number of other churches.

Mr. Kresge was as stanchly opposed to nicotine as he was to spirituous beverages. He once said that he "made it a rule never to give a dollar to any church the pastor of which used tobacco." Much of his opposition to smoking and drinking was based on his feeling that they were wasteful of a man's energy and money. He himself was a teetotaler and a nonsmoker. Moreover, on the ground that it was a frivolity, he declined to play cards.

Although Mr. Kresge eventually had millions of dollars at his disposal, he never attained proficiency in the art of spending money on himself and those close to him. The necessities and habits of his boyhood on a Pennsylvania farm and his youth as a teacher for twenty-two dollars a month, plus the personal economies he practiced in the early years of building his chain-store empire, left an ineradicable mark.

He used a pair of shoes, for example, until they were thoroughly worn out. When the soles got thin, he lined them with paper. He dressed inexpensively in plain suits, and they were threadbare by the time he tossed them out. Once in the mid-nineteen-twenties when he was living in New York and employing a valet, he noticed that the man pressed a suit for him every day. "Don't press them so often," Mr. Kresge told him. "Don't you realize they'll wear out soon if you do."

At about the same time, when he was fifty-eight, some friends persuaded him to take up golf. He played three rounds, passing most of his time hunting balls he drove off the fairway, and then decided the game was not for him because, he said, he could not afford to lose a golf ball.

One of the few diversions that Mr. Kresge enjoyed was motoring. His first car was an air-cooled Franklin, which, according to a close associate, "he ran until the wheels fell off." In the twenties he drove a Packard to the limit of its life expectancy; and in his later years he also picked his automobiles for their durability rather than their chrome.

A pinch-purse attitude also had a part in the breakup of two of Mr. Kresge's marriages. He was divorced in 1924 by his first wife, the former Miss Anna E. Harvey, whom he had married in 1897. One of her complaints was his personal stinginess. This, too, was among the complaints of his second wife, the former Miss Doris Mercer, whom he married in 1924, when she was thirty-one and he was fifty-six. This wife divorced him in 1928 after a series of charges and countercharges, including the keeping of a love nest, that made Mr. Kresge's name a headline word in New York. His third and final marriage was more tranquil. This was to the former Mrs. Clara K. Swaine, whom he married in October 1928. She was thirty-five at the time and he was sixty-one. The union lasted until his death.

Paradoxically, Mr. Kresge was open-handed in his two divorce settlements. His first wife and their five children received a reported $10 million; his second wife received an estimated total of $3 million.

A generous spirit also marked Mr. Kresge's dealings with his associates and employees. By the time he retired as president of his company in 1925, there were thirteen of his management team who were millionaires. And from the very start of his enterprise he gave Kresge workers paid sick leave, paid holidays, profit-sharing, bonuses, and pensions on retirement.

In the early years of the expansion of his chain Mr. Kresge spent much of his time visiting his stores and selecting sites for new ones. A gnomelike man with a round face, benign smile and a stocky figure and stubby hands, "S.S.," as he was known, was a familiar sight in his red-front stores. He insisted on knowing every store manager and his family personally and on shaking hands, in a friendly fashion, with the clerks, whom he was wont to engage in fatherly conversation. One of Mr. Kresge's great assets, it was said, was an ability to pick competent employees and to inspire them to loyalty and productive toil.

Mr. Kresge was genuinely good at homilies and the homey touch. Until the death of his mother in 1940 at the age of 100, each Kresge store displayed a photograph of her at her son's order.

Mr. Kresge ascribed his own success as a merchant to industry and thrift. "I think I was successful because I was willing to work, because I saved and because I heeded good advice," he once said. "I worked— and I didn't work only eight hours a day, but sometimes eighteen hours. When one starts at the bottom and learns to scrape, then everything becomes easy."

Mr. Kresge toiled from his earliest years. He was born at Bald Mount, Pennsylvania, near Scranton, on July 31, 1867, the son of Sebastian Kresge and Catherine Kunkle Kresge, farmer folk of Swiss ancestry.

When he was barely five, Sebastian was assigned his share of farm chores. He attended rural schools, then Fairview Academy at Brodheadsville, Pennsylvania, and, finally, the Eastman Business College at Poughkeepsie, New York. Sebastian was so eager for schooling that he struck a bargain with his father: if the father would finance him through business college, he would give his father all his earnings until he was twenty-one.

These consisted mostly of the twenty-two dollars a month received for teaching in Gower's School, Monroe County, Pennsylvania, and his pay as a deliveryman and clerk in a Scranton grocery store. The only money he kept for himself was derived from beekeeping, a hobby he maintained in adult life. "My bees," he said later, "always reminded me that hard work, thrift, sobriety, and an earnest struggle to live an upright Christian life are the first rungs of the ladder of success."

It was in a hardware store in Scranton in 1889 that he began to develop his talent for merchanting. One of the impressions that he derived from his experience was what he considered the evil resulting from a small merchant's granting too much credit. He saw that housewives tended to overorder simply because they did not have to pay cash and that the merchant's own bills, as a result, often lagged. Later Mr. Kresge insisted on cash trading in his stores.

His industry gave Mr. Kresge his first chance to display his business acumen. His bookkeeping work sometimes left him with time on his hands. Because he hated to be idle, he tried to make himself useful at odd jobs; and on his own he repaired, polished, and sold a pile of rusty, second-hand stoves.

This feat impressed his employer and won him a job as a traveling salesman for W. B. Bertels Sons & Co. of Wilkes-Barre, Pennsylvania, for which he sold hardware and tinware in New England and the North Central States. One of his customers was Frank Woolworth, who had founded dime stores in 1875. He obtained a Woolworth order for nineteen gross of articles, one gross for each of the Woolworth stores then in existence. The order impressed Mr. Kresge with the tremendous potential of the chain-store business. He liked it because it was a cash transaction and thus encouraged thrift. He also saw the value of central purchasing for the owner of the chain, a practice that Kresge stores adopted in order to maximize profits.

When he had saved eight thousand dollars from his earnings during eight years as a salesman, he resolved to go into business for himself. He had met John G. McCrory, who was then operating a chain of six bazaar stores and two 5- and 10-cent stores. In February, 1897, Mr. Kresge joined Mr. McCrory in opening 5- and 10-cent stores in Memphis and Detroit, Mr. Kresge being half-owner of the two stores. Within two years Mr. Kresge was manager and then sole owner of the Detroit store. In 1900 Mr. Kresge organized, with his brother-in-law, Charles J. Wilson, Kresge & Wilson to operate the Detroit store and another in Port Huron, Michigan. Business was so brisk that Mr. Kresge was encouraged to open stores in other key cities. By 1907 he had bought out Mr. Wilson, changed the company name to S. S. Kresge, and was operating stores in Detroit, Port Huron, Toledo, Pittsburgh, Cleveland, Columbus, Indianapolis, and Chicago. His stores, then as now, were situated in heavily trafficked areas and appealed to the bargain hunter. Mr. Kresge had a reputation for entrepreneurial daring in opening stores and making them succeed as a personal challenge.

When the business went public in 1912 with a capitalization of $7 million, there were eighty-five stores. The company was reincorporated in 1916 under the same name, but with a capitalization of $12 million. Mr. Kresge was president of the company from 1907 to 1925 and chairman of the board from 1913 to June 1966. There were 307 stores in 1925, when he left the presidency; and in the late twenties Kresge stock was selling at close to nine hundred dollars a share.

The heyday of the strictly 5- and 10-cent stores was in the years before 1920. The Kresge Company, for example, made much of the fact that nothing in its stores cost more than a dime; and there was a seemingly endless variety of things that could be purchased at that price or less, ranging from hairpins and false hair to wood-handled scrub brushes and bench vises.

With the inflation that set in after World War I, the number of things that could be profitably sold for a dime or under dwindled. As a result, Kresge added the Green Front Store to its Red Front line. The new shops proclaimed items for sale at twenty-five cents to a dollar. And these, too, prospered.

Still later, after World War II, Kresge's expanded into the discount and variety-department store business and offered for sale items priced in the hundreds of dollars. Company stores also, of course, still retailed many less expensive articles.

In addition to his corporate activity with Kresge's, the merchant was president for many years of the Kresge Realty Company, which had extensive holdings. In 1925 he also purchased a large interest in Stern Brothers, a New York department store now owned by the Allied Stores Corporation; an interest in the Fair, a Chicago department store now operated by Montgomery Ward & Co.; and an interest in Kresge-Newark, Inc., a Newark department store.

From 1899 to 1924 Mr. Kresge lived in Detroit. In the following four years he was in New York. There, to please his second wife, he professed an interest in music and opera and took to living on what, for him, was a munificent scale, with an apartment on Park Avenue. It did not last, however; and when he married for the third time he divided his time between a quiet twenty-six-acre estate at Mountainhome, Pennsylvania, not far from where he was born, and a winter home in Miami Beach.

Mr. Kresge remained active in the affairs of his company into his nineties. He was not, however, much in the public limelight after 1940. Of his children only the eldest, Stanley S., went into the dime-store business. On his father's retirement in 1966, he became chairman of the board. The other children were Howard C.; Mrs. H (Ruth) Nugent Head; Mrs. Charles S. (Catherine) Dewey Jr.; and Mrs. John (Anne) Watling.

Mr. Kresge held several honorary degrees, among them a D.B.A. from Albion College; a D.H.L. from Dickinson College and LL.D.'s from Wayne University and Michigan State University. He also received a citation for distinguished service from the University of Michigan.

Throughout his life Mr. Kresge insisted that the first steps in life were the most important. "If you are asking me what I think about life and its teachings," he once said, "I will answer you by saying that success is at the bottom of the ladder, and not at the top. I mean by that, everything depends on the beginning at the bottom."

WALDO FRANK

Waldo Frank died on January 10, 1967, on Cape Cod, his home for many years. He was seventy-seven. A writer of social commitment and pronounced liberal views, he played an important role in the development of American letters in the early years of this century. His criticisms of our culture remained remarkably fresh, a circumstance that gave him in death an extraordinary contemporaneity.

To be praised and feted abroad as a major writer and to be ranked at home as a minor one was the curious lot of Waldo David Frank.

In Latin America his name for many years evokes recognition in literate circles as a sensitive writer about the United States scene and as a perceptive friend of Hispanic culture. In the United States, on the other hand, it conveyed an author of turgidly earnest mystical novels, cultural criticism, and tracts. The paradox of this was that the bulk of Mr. Frank's work dealt with United States, not Latin, life and society.

Among United States readers Mr. Frank was most often associated with the artistic and literary upsurge of the 1910's and 1920's, when American literati were loudly abandoning the corseted gentility of Victorianism. This was symbolized by the seven arts, a magazine with a lower-case title that Mr. Frank helped to found and edit.

He was also known for two rather mystic parables in novel form, *The Death and Birth of David Markand*, published in 1934, and *The Bridegroom Cometh*, issued in 1938.

In addition, Mr. Frank was frequently in the news as a supporter of various liberal causes ranging from the Scottsboro boys in the 1930's to the Fair Play for Cuba Committee of the 1960's.

As a Hispanicist Mr. Frank was called "a literary ambassador to Latin America." He was, according to Van Wyck Brooks, the literary historian, "at home with Spaniard, mestizo, and Indian alike, loving their dances, their religion, the form of their minds." Three of his books were usually cited as demonstrating the acuity of his insights. One was *Virgin Spain*, which established his influence in Latin America when it was first published in 1926; the second was *South American Journey*, issued in 1943; and the third was *Birth of a World: Bolivar in Terms of His Peoples*, a biography of the South American liberator commissioned by the Venezuelan government and published in 1951.

Mr. Frank was distressed by the duality of his reputation and inclined to feel that Americans were too culturally debased to appreciate him. "I have an audience here, and it grows," he said, referring to the United States. "But the growth is slow. But if the fault were wholly mine, then how explain the success of my books in Latin America . . . ? May it not be the fault of the industrial revolution, of the exchange we have effected that places temporary well-being, temporary satisfactions, above salvation, above the relationship of man to the infinite, which is the theme of all my books, and which is understandable to people not too marked, too regimented by industry, by forces that have destroyed to so great an extent, to an extent you probably don't realize, the dignity, the divinity of man."

He believed that Americans had been "victimized" into accepting a puerile and second-rate culture. "So far our democracy is not functional," he asserted, adding in sputtering tones: "From reason we have drifted downward toward emptiness, the belief in salvation lost, the conception of wholeness lost. Not far up this street [Broadway] there is a big electric sign that spells out the words Amusement Palace. Do you know what this Amusement Palace offers? Pinball machines! Come in, come in, forget yourself for ten minutes watching the little balls run the tracks of a pinball machine. And that is amusement! It is a profanation of the word. Amusement—the muses: the spirits of history, of great tragedy, of religion. Amusement palace—pinball machines!"

For his part, Mr. Frank strove to show Americans the cosmic dimensions of man's essence. These, he believed, could be achieved through personal commitment to ideals and fulfillment of one's inner capacities. It seemed at times as if Mr. Frank were harking back to a Jeffersonian pastoralism, but he insisted that the Machine (and he invariably used the capital letter) could and should be man's servant.

As foes of mass-produced culture he held up Thoreau, Whitman, and Mark Twain. These writers, he said, had a vision of the wholeness of man, a metaphysical concept with which Mr. Frank was much occupied. "Man," he argued, "may be said to live horizontally and perpendicularly. His horizontal life consists of his social, economic, and class relations. His perpendicular life is the direct flow of his blood and spirit. In the whole man . . . the horizontal and the perpendicular are interfused; they are qualities organically present in each other, and divisible only for purposes of definition."

Whitman seemed to Mr. Frank to approach his ideal. "The living core and marrow of his work," he declared, "is the mystical revelation of God and Cosmos within the self, and the active incarnation of this selfhood in the American republic."

Although Mr. Frank was scathing of the state of American civilization as "sleazy," he had faith in its future. "There is a bloom within our land which Europe lacks," he proclaimed, "a generosity and the faith and will which flower from it."

Mr. Frank's almost religious fervor for a society perfused by free, whole, and cultured individuals often boggled his readers on account of his murky prose style. Typical is this paragraph explaining his philosophy of man:

"The universal, of course, metaphysically, is a Norm. But a man may know his relation with the Cosmic and yet, through the very depth this gives him of relation to men, feel and be isolated on the surface of human intercourse. He must link his cosmic connection with the social."

Even a friendly critic, Lewis Mumford, said that Mr. Frank "demands vital efforts on the part of his reader." Less sympathetically, Charles Poore of *The New York Times* called Mr. Frank's prose "woolly rhetoric."

In his most active years Mr. Frank kept regular office hours at his typewriter, turning out two thousand finished words a day. These included a newspaper column for Latin American papers and for the Spanish-language press in this country.

He was a short, stocky man with dark hair and a dark mustache who was given to wearing tweedy clothes. Away from the typewriter he was genial and sociable; some friends, however, thought him arrogant at times, or at least intellectually snobbish toward people in the mass.

His manner in conversation was intense, even nervous, and he was inclined to talk as he wrote—in somewhat mystical terms. He was also a sensitive performer on the cello, and he liked to swim and sail—two hobbies that were tailored to his life at Truro, on Cape Cod.

Waldo Frank was born August 25, 1889, in Long Branch, New Jersey, the son of Julius J. and Helene Rosenberg Frank. A gifted youth, he took both his bachelor of arts and his master's degrees at Yale in 1911. He was elected to Phi Beta Kappa, the honor society, and he contributed drama criticism to the New Haven *Courier-Journal*.

After college Mr. Frank worked in New York, dividing two years between the *Evening Post* and *The New York Times*. Following a year in Germany and France, he returned to New York to devote his life to writing. His early fictional themes related to the unconscious self and social and psychological discords of temperaments in conflict with their environments. These themes, in one guise or another, also recurred in some of his later novels.

In 1916 Mr. Frank was a founder, with James Oppenheim, the poet, of a remarkable literary magazine, *the seven arts*. It was pocket-size and it lasted a little more than a year, but it published virtually all the "new" authors who were then on the threshold of great reputations. With Van Wyck Brooks as his co-editor, Mr. Frank opened the magazine's columns to Sherwood Anderson, Robert Frost, Floyd Dell, Theodore Dreiser, Carl Sandburg, D. H. Lawrence, John Dos Passos, Amy Lowell, Walter Lippmann, Max Eastman, Randolph Bourne, John Dewey, Romain Rolland, Padraic Colum, and Eugene O'Neill.

The journal was "a bonfire burning in a depressing gray fog," its admirers said. But, the bonfire was too bright, for the magazine's opposition to World War I brought about its demise.

One of what Mr. Frank called "the great moments in my life" came in 1919 in Pueblo, Colorado, where he had stopped off between trains.

"I always like to poke around cities," he recalled. "I was told that one of the sights of the place was a big steel plant outside the town, so I got on a bus to ride out there. Sharing the bus were a group of Mexican laborers and women; I had never seen Mexicans before.

"The steel plant was a great modern building, high against the sky, and across the road from it was an adobe village where my fellow passengers lived.

"It came to me that these men and women had something to tell me, that they were different from the men and women that I had always known, that they had roots very deep in the earth, that they knew a quiet, a wholeness that I did not know.

"Two years later I decided to visit Spain in the hope that there I might find the source of whatever it was about them that had moved me. A short visit wasn't enough. I returned there and learned the language, read the literature . . .

"My intuition was correct. We have much to learn from these people with deep roots."

Mr. Frank's chance encounter in an unlikely Colorado town led to a lifelong love affair with Spanish culture, and many trips to Latin America, where he lectured extensively. In 1929 he received a doctorate of literature from the National University of San Marcos in Peru; and the University of Quito in Ecuador made him an honorary professor in 1949.

In the United States Mr. Frank compiled a reputation as a caustic critic of the American scene, fostered chiefly by two books, *Our America*, published in 1919, and *The Rediscovery of America*, issued in 1929. His discontents led to action, and Mr. Frank took part in a number of social protests in the thirties.

One of these involved taking food and clothing to striking coal miners in Harlan, Kentucky. In company with Malcolm Cowley, Edmund Wilson, and Mary Heaton Vorse, among others, Mr. Frank was arrested and ejected from Kentucky with the warning never to return.

In 1936 he joined the presidential campaign of Earl Browder, the Communist Party candidate, and the two men were arrested in Terre Haute, Indiana, because the mayor and chief of police did not want "any Communistic speeches and demonstrations" in their city. Mr. Frank and Mr. Browder were later released and told to get out of town and stay out.

Mr. Frank was not a Communist, he said, and he could point to a book, *Dawn in Russia*, published in 1932, in which he was critical of some aspects of the Soviet Union. He was also critical of the Soviet purge trials in the thirties. Nonetheless, Communists considered him a friendly liberal, at least until 1949, when he was denounced in unmeasured terms in the *Daily Worker* as a "cosmopolitan" writer and as "a stooge" of American imperialism.

Mr. Frank continued to write in his own way, however, publishing *Not Heaven*, a novel, in 1953; *Bridgehead: The Drama of Israel*, an impressionistic study of that country, in 1957; *The Rediscovery of Man* in 1958, a philosophical work; and *The Prophetic Island: A Portrait of Cuba* in 1961. In this he drew a sympathetic picture of Castroism, which he regarded as indigenous social revolt. "Cuba's was an authentic American revolution," he asserted.

In support of Castroism, Mr. Frank was chairman of the Fair Play for Cuba Committee. He was also chairman of the Committee for a Democratic Spain, whose aim was to seek withdrawal of United States support for Generalissimo Francisco Franco, the Spanish strongman.

In the late fifties Mr. Frank engaged in a losing court battle with the State Department over his request for a passport valid for Communist China. He had been invited to lecture at the University of Peking on Walt Whitman. The case went up to the Supreme Court, which decided that it could not compel the issuance of Mr. Frank's passport.

Mr. Frank was married three times. His first wife was Margaret

Naumberg, a founder of the Walden School in New York, to whom he was married in 1916. They had one child, Thomas Frank. His second marriage was to Alma Magoon in 1927. The couple had two daughters, Michal Enid and Deborah. In 1943 Mr. Frank married his secretary, Jean Klempner, and they had two sons, Jonathan and Timothy.

In his final years Mr. Frank spent most of his time at his Cape Cod home. Reviewing his works and his years of adjuring and advising his countrymen, he remarked in mellow reflection: "Every critical work that I have written has been inspired by my love of my country and by my faith in the high destiny of my country."

J ROBERT OPPENHEIMER

J Robert Oppenheimer died in Princeton, New Jersey, on February 18, 1967, at the age of sixty-five. "The father of the atomic bomb" was the most complex of men, and his obit was the product of several weeks' work, every moment of it fascinating. If my obit does not resolve all the questions about the physicist, I hope that at least it illuminates them.

STARTING AT precisely 5:30 A.M., Mountain War Time, July 16, 1945, J (for nothing) Robert Oppenheimer lived the remainder of his life in the blinding light and the crepusculine shadow of the world's first man-made atomic explosion, an event for which he was largely responsible.

That sunlike flash illuminated him as a scientific genius, the tech-nocrat of a new age for mankind. At the same time it led to his public disgrace when, in 1954, he was officially described as a security risk to his country and a man with "fundamental defects in his character." Publicly rehabilitated in 1963 by a singular government honor, this bafflingly complex person nonetheless never fully succeeded in dispelling doubts about his conduct during a crucial period of his life.

These perplexities centered on a bizarre story of attempted atomic espionage that he told army counterintelligence officers in 1943 and that he later repudiated as a fabrication. His sole explanation for what he called "a cock-and-bull story" was that he had been "an idiot." Misgivings also sprang from the manner in which he implicated a close friend in his asserted concoction.

An astonishingly brilliant nuclear physicist, with a comprehensive grasp of his discipline, Dr. Oppenheimer was also a cultivated scholar, a humanist, a linguist of eight tongues, and a solitary, brooding searcher for ultimate spiritual values. And from the moment that the test bomb exploded at Alamogordo, New Mexico, he was haunted by the implica-tions for man in the unleashing of the basic forces of the universe.

As he clung to one of the uprights in the desert control room that July morning and saw the mushroom clouds rising in the explosion, a passage from the *Bhagavad Gita*, the Hindu sacred epic, flashed through his mind. He remembered it later as: "If the radiance of a thousand suns were to burst into the sky, that would be like the splendor of the Mighty One."

And as the black, then gray atomic cloud pushed higher above Point Zero, another line—"I am become Death, the shatterer of worlds"—came to him from the same scripture.

Two years later, he was still beset by the moral consequences of the bomb, which, he told fellow physicists, had "dramatized so mercilessly the inhumanity and evil of modern war.

"In some sort of crude sense which no vulgarity, no humor, no overstatements can quite extinguish," he went on, "the physicists have known sin; and this is a knowledge which they cannot lose."

In later years, he seemed to indicate that "sin" was not to be taken personally. "I carry no weight on my conscience," he said in 1961 in reference to the atomic bombing of Hiroshima and Nagasaki. "Scientists are not delinquents," he added. "Our work has changed the conditions in which men live, but the use made of those changes is the problem of governments, not of scientists."

With the detonation of the first three atomic bombs (actually, the uranium Hiroshima bomb exploded and the plutonium-test and Nagasaki bombs imploded) and the immediate Allied victory in World War II, Dr. Oppenheimer, at the age of forty-one, reached the apogee of his career. Acclaimed as "the father of the atomic bomb," he was officially credited by the War Department "with achieving the implementation of atomic energy for military purposes." Secretary of War Henry L. Stimson led a chorus of national praise when he said of the scientist: "The development of the bomb itself has been largely due to his genius and the inspiration and leadership he has given to his colleagues."

Shortly thereafter, in 1946, Dr. Oppenheimer received a Presidential Citation and a Medal of Merit for his direction of the Los Alamos Laboratory, where the bomb had been developed.

At the same time, his prestige among physicists, especially the younger ones, and in the scientific community generally rose to spectacular heights. He was looked to as a spokesman, a senior statesman, and something of a wizard for having developed in only two years what many thought would take much longer—if indeed it could be put together at all.

In the years from 1945 to 1952, Dr. Oppenheimer was one of the foremost government advisers on key phases of United States atomic policy. He was the dominant author of the Acheson-Lilienthal Report (named for Secretary of State Dean Acheson and David Lilienthal, first chairman of the Atomic Energy Commission), which offered a plan for international control of atomic energy. He was also the virtual author of the Baruch Plan, which was based on the Acheson-Lilienthal Report, calling for United Nations supervision of nuclear power. He was consultant to Mr. Baruch and to Frederick H. Osborn, his successor, in futile United Nations negotiations over the plan, which was balked by the Soviet Union.

Furthermore, from 1947 to 1952, Dr. Oppenheimer headed the Atomic Energy Commission's General Advisory Committee of top nuclear scientists, and for the following two years he was its consultant. He also served on the atomic committee of the Research and Development Board to advise the military, the science advisory committee of the Office of Defense Mobilization, and study groups by the dozen. He had a desk in the President's Executive Offices, across the street from the White House.

This eminence ended with shocking abruptness in December 1953, when President Dwight D. Eisenhower ordered that a "blank wall be placed between Dr. Oppenheimer and any secret data" pending a security hearing. The following June he was stripped of his security clearance by the Atomic Energy Commission. It was never restored to him.

Up to 1954 Dr. Oppenheimer's big-brimmed brown porkpie hat, size 6⅞, was a frequent (and telltale) sight in Washington and the capitals of Western Europe, where he traveled to lecture or consult. (The trademark hat was also in evidence at Princeton, New Jersey, where he headed the Institute for Advanced Study from 1947 to 1966.) He was Oppy, Oppie, or Opje to hundreds of persons who were captivated by his charm, his eloquence, his sharp, subtle humor, and his easy smile or who were awed by the scope of his erudition, the incisiveness of his mind, the chill of his sarcasm, and his arrogance toward those he thought were slow or shoddy thinkers.

He was six feet tall, a bit stooped, and as thin as the wisps from his chain-smoked cigarettes or pipes. Blue-eyed, with close-cropped hair (it was dark in 1943, gray by 1954, and white a few years later) he had a mobile, expressive face that, once young and ageless and poetic, became lined and worn and haggard after his security hearings.

He was extremely fidgety when he sat, and he constantly shifted himself in his chair, bit his knuckles, scratched his head, and hooked and unhooked his legs. When he spoke on his feet, he paced and stalked, smoking incessantly and jerking a cigarette or pipe out of his mouth almost violently when he wanted to emphasize a word or phrase with a gesture of his nicotine-stained fingers.

He was an energetic man at parties, where he was usually the center of attention. He was gracious as a host and the maker of fine and potent martinis. He was full of droll stories, but he could switch in a flash from frivolity to gravity.

What bedazzled people first about Dr. Oppenheimer was his da Vinci intellect. "Robert is the only authentic genius I know," Mr. Lilienthal said of him. Echoing this appraisal, Charles Lauritsen, a former colleague at the California Institute of Technology, once remarked: "The man was unbelievable. He always gave you the right answer before you formulated the question."

Knowledge came effortlessly to Dr. Oppenheimer. As a young man he learned enough Dutch in six weeks to deliver a technical lecture while on a visit to the Netherlands. At the age of thirty he learned Sanskrit, and he used to enjoy passing notes to other savants in that language. On a train trip from San Francisco to the East Coast he read Edward Gibbon's seven-volume *The Decline and Fall of the Roman Empire*. On another such trip he read the four volumes of Karl Marx's *Das Kapital* in German. On a short summer holiday in Corsica he read in French Marcel Proust's massive *A la Recherche du temps perdu*, which he later said was one of the great experiences of his life. This almost compulsive avidity for learning was not sterile, for he invariably made some use of what he read. He was, moreover, an authority, if not an expert, in baroque and classical music, to which he liked to listen. In the words of a friend, Dr. Oppenheimer was "a culture hound."

Even as a child Dr. Oppenheimer was made much of for his formidable ability to absorb knowledge. He was born in New York on April 22, 1904, the son of Julius and Ella Freedman (or Friedman) Oppenheimer. Julius Oppenheimer was a prosperous textile importer who had immigrated from Germany, and his wife was a Baltimore artist, who died when her elder son was ten. (The younger son, Frank Friedman Oppenheimer, also became a physicist.) The family lived in comfort, with a private art collection that included three Van Goghs. Robert was encouraged to delve into rocks after he started a collection at the age of five, and he was admitted to the Mineralogical Club of New York when he was eleven.

He was a shy, delicate boy (he was once thought to have tuberculosis), concerned more with his homework and with poetry and architecture than with mixing with other youngsters. After attending the Ethical Culture School ("It is characteristic that I don't remember any of my classmates," he said), he entered Harvard College in 1922, intending to become a chemist.

He was a solitary student with an astonishing appetite for work. "I had a real chance to learn," he said later. "I loved it. I almost came alive. I took more courses than I was supposed to, lived in the [library] stacks, just raided the place intellectually." Typical of his absorption was this note that he wrote about himself: "It was so hot today the only thing I could do was lie on my bed and read Jeans's 'Dynamical Theory of Gases.' "

In addition to studying physics and other sciences, he learned Latin and Greek and was graduated summa cum laude in 1925, having completed four years' work in three.

From Harvard, Robert Oppenheimer went to the University of Cambridge, in England, where he worked in atomics under Lord Rutherford, the eminent physicist. Thence he went to the Georgia Augusta University at Göttingen, Germany, at the invitation of Max Born, also a celebrated scientist interested in the quantum theory of atomic systems. He received his doctorate there in 1927, along with a reputation for being pushy.

In 1927–28 he was a National Research Fellow at Harvard and Cal Tech, and the following year he was an International Education Board Fellow at the University of Leyden, in the Netherlands, and the Technische Hochschule in Zurich, Switzerland.

Returning to the United States in 1929, Dr. Oppenheimer joined the faculties of Cal Tech at Pasadena, California, and the University of California at Berkeley. He was attached to both schools until 1947 and rose to the rank of professor. He proved an outstanding teacher. Magnetic, lucid, always accessible, he developed hundreds of young physicists, some of whom were so devoted to him that they migrated with him back and forth from Berkeley to Pasadena and even copied his mannerisms.

Describing to his security hearings his ivory-tower life up to late 1936, he said: "I was not interested in and did not read about economics or politics. I was almost wholly divorced from the contemporary scene in this country. I never read a newspaper or a current magazine like *Time* or *Harper's*; I had no radio, no telephone; I learned of the stock-market crash in the fall of 1929 only long after the event; the first time I ever voted was in the presidential election of 1936."

However, in the 1930's Dr. Oppenheimer greatly influenced American physics as leader of a dynamic school of theoreticians in California. His influence continued in his recent years at the Institute for Advanced Study. In the words of one Nobel laureate in physics: "No one in his age group has been as familiar with all aspects of current developments in theoretical physics."

One of his earliest contributions was in 1926–27 while he was working with Dr. Born, then a professor at Göttingen. Together they helped lay the foundations of modern theory for the quantum behavior of molecules.

In 1935, he and Melba Phillips made another basic contribution to quantum theory, discovering what is known as the Oppenheimer-Phillips process. It involves the breakup of deuterons in collisions that had been thought far too weak for such an effect.

The deuteron consists of a proton and neutron bound into a single particle. The two physicists found that when a deuteron is fired into an atom, even weakly, the neutron can be stripped off the proton and penetrate the nucleus of the atom. It had been assumed that since the deuteron and nucleus are both positively charged, each would repel the other except in high-energy collisions.

Another theoretical study by Dr. Oppenheimer has figured prominently in recent efforts to explain the astronomical objects, known as quasars, that radiate light and radio waves of extraordinary intensity. One possibility is that the quasar is a cloud of material being drawn together by its own gravity.

In 1938-39, Dr. Oppenheimer with Dr. George M. Volkoff and others had analyzed such a "gravitational collapse" in terms of the general theory of relativity. Their calculations are now cited in efforts to explain the quasars.

Beginning in late 1936, Dr. Oppenheimer's life underwent a dramatic change of direction that involved him in numerous Communist, trade union, and liberal causes to which he devoted time and money and that added to his circle of acquaintances many Communists and liberals, some of whom became intimate friends. These commitments and associations, which were to be recalled with sinister overtones at his security hearings, ended around 1940, according to the scientist; or, in the version of some others, they persisted until the end of 1942, when he was about to go to Los Alamos.

One precipitating factor in Dr. Oppenheimer's awakening to the world about him was a love affair, starting in 1936, with a woman Communist now dead. (In 1940 he married the former Miss Katherine Puening, a onetime Communist whose second husband was Joseph Dallet, a Communist who died fighting for the Spanish Republican government.)

Apart from the influence exerted by his fiancée, there were other compelling elements in Dr. Oppenheimer's transformation from cloistered academician to social activist. He described them this way: "I had had a continuing smoldering fury about the treatment of Jews in Germany. I had relatives there, and was later to help in extricating them and bringing them to this country. I saw what the Depression was doing to my students. Often they could get no jobs, or jobs which were wholly inadequate. And through them, I began to understand how deeply political and economic events could affect men's lives. I began to feel the need to participate more fully in the life of the community."

Dr. Oppenheimer's activism was far-ranging, but he consistently denied that he was ever a member of the Communist Party ("I never accepted Communist dogma or theory"), and no substantial evidence was ever adduced to refute him.

Dr. Arthur H. Compton, the Nobelist, brought Dr. Oppenheimer informally into the atomic project in 1941. Within a year he had convinced Dr. Compton and military authorities that to build a bomb it was essential to concentrate qualified scientists and their equipment in a single community under a unified command.

He also impressed Lieutenant General Leslie R. Groves, in charge of the $2 billion Manhattan Engineer District, as the bomb project was code-named, who selected him for the post of director and who ordered him cleared for the job despite army counterintelligence qualms over his past associations. This action placed Dr. Oppenheimer in General Groves's debt. With the general, Dr. Oppenheimer selected the Los Alamos site for the laboratory.

"To recruit staff," he said later, "I traveled all over the country talking with people who had been working on one or another aspect of the atomic-energy enterprise, and people in radar work, for example, and underwater sound, telling them about the job, the place that we were going to, and enlisting their enthusiasm."

Dr. Oppenheimer's persuasiveness and qualities of leadership were such that he gathered a star scientific staff that numbered nearly four thousand by 1945 and lived, often amid frustrations and under quasi-military rule, in the hastily built houses of Los Alamos. Among the staff were Dr. Enrico Fermi and Niels Bohr, two physicists of immense world stature.

In the two exciting, tension-filled years that it took to construct the bomb, Dr. Oppenheimer displayed a special genius for administration, for handling the sensitive prima donna scientific staff (often he spent as much time on personal as on professional problems), and for co-ordinating their work. He drove himself at breakneck speed, and at one time his weight dropped to a precarious 115 pounds. But under the whiplash of the war he always managed to surmount whatever problem arose, and it was for this stupendous, all-around task that he was exalted as "the father of the atomic bomb."

Dr. Oppenheimer's security troubles had their fateful genesis while he was director at Los Alamos. Because a security-risk potential was imputed to him on account of past associations, he was dogged by army agents, his phone calls were monitored, his mail was opened, and his every footstep was watched. In these circumstances his overnight visit with his former fiancée—by then no longer a Communist—on a trip to San Francisco in June 1943, aroused the Counter-Intelligence Corps.

The following August, for reasons that still remain obscure, Dr. Oppenheimer volunteered to a CIC agent that the Russians had tried to get information about the Los Alamos project. George Eltenton, a Briton and a slight acquaintance of Dr. Oppenheimer, had asked a third party to get in touch with some project scientists. In three subsequent interrogations Dr. Oppenheimer embroidered his story, but he declined to name the third party who had approached him or to identify the scientists. In one interrogation, however, he gave the CIC a long list of persons he said were Communists or Communist sympathizers in the San Francisco area, and he offered to dig up information as to former Communists at Los Alamos.)

Finally, in December 1943, Dr. Oppenheimer, at General Groves's direct order, vouchsafed the third party's name as Professor Haakon Chevalier, a French teacher at Berkeley and a long-time close and devoted friend of the Oppenheimer family. At the security hearing in 1954, the scientist recanted his espionage account as a "cock-and-bull story," saying only that he was "an idiot" to have told it. Dr. Oppenheimer never gave a further explanation.

There was some basis for Dr. Oppenheimer's original story, according to him and Professor Chevalier. The professor said that Mr. Eltenton had indeed approached him in late 1942 or early 1943 with a nebulous notion about getting scientific information and had been quickly rebuffed. Professor Chevalier said that he had recounted the episode to Dr. Oppenheimer and that both had dismissed the matter. This part of the incident was corroborated by Dr. Oppenheimer in his testimony at his security hearings.

(Just how much of Dr. Oppenheimer's spy-attempt story the CIC believed is difficult to judge in the light of the fact that neither Professor Chevalier nor Mr. Eltenton was interrogated until May 1946. Neither was prosecuted. Indeed, Professor Chevalier was an interpreter on the United States staff at the Nuremberg War Crimes Trial in 1945. Twenty years later he wrote *Oppenheimer: The Story of a Friendship*, in which he charged that Dr. Oppenheimer had betrayed him out of ambition for fame and to stay in the CIC's good graces.

(A CIC operative who had questioned Dr. Oppenheimer suggested to his army superiors that an unimpeachable assistant be assigned to the scientist. The operative's memo included this sentence: "It is the opinion of this office that subject's [Dr. Oppenheimer's] personal inclinations would be to protect his own future and reputation and the high degree of honor which would be his if his present work is successful, and, consequently, it is felt that he would lend every effort to cooperation with the Government in any plan which would leave him in charge.")

With the end of World War II and Dr. Oppenheimer's return to full civilian life, he caused some disquiet in the scientific community by supporting the May-Johnson bill for military control of further atomic experiments. This was countered, however, when he later supported the McMahon bill, which created the Atomic Energy Commission, a civilian agency.

Another of the charges pressed against Dr. Oppenheimer in 1954 also had its origin at Los Alamos, and it involved the hydrogen, or fusion, bomb and his relations with Dr. Edward Teller over that super-weapon, of which the Hungarian scientist was a vociferous proponent. At Los Alamos Dr. Teller was passed over for Dr. Hans Bethe as head of the Theoretical Physics Division. Dr. Teller, meantime, worked on problems of fusion.

At the war's end, when most of the Los Alamos scientists returned to their campuses, hydrogen bomb work was generally suspended. In 1949, however, when the Soviet Union exploded its first fission bomb, the United States considered pressing forward immediately with building and testing a fusion device. The matter came to the Atomic Energy Commission's General Advisory Board, headed by Dr. Oppenheimer.

On the ground that manufacturing a hydrogen bomb was not technically feasible at the moment, the board unanimously recommended that thermonuclear research be maintained at a theoretical level only. Dr. Oppenheimer, who also thought a hydrogen bomb morally dubious, played a leading role in this proposal, and it did not endear him to Dr. Teller.

In 1950, President Harry S Truman overruled Dr. Oppenheimer's board and ordered work pushed on the fusion bomb. Dr. Teller was given his own laboratory and within a few months the hydrogen bomb was perfected with the aid of a technical (and still secret) device suggested by Dr. Teller.

It was charged at the security hearings that Dr. Oppenheimer was not sufficiently diligent himself in furthering the hydrogen bomb and that he influenced other scientists against participating in work on it. Dr. Teller testified that, apart from giving him a list of names, Dr.

Oppenheimer had not assisted him "in the slightest" in recruiting scientists for the project.

Dr. Teller, moreover, went on record as being opposed to restoring Dr. Oppenheimer's security clearance, saying: "In a great number of cases I have seen Dr. Oppenheimer act—I understood that Dr. Oppenheimer acted in a way which for me was exceedingly hard to understand. I thoroughly disagreed with him in numerous issues and his actions frankly appeared to me confused and complicated. To this extent I feel that I would like to see the vital interests of this country in hands which I understand better, and therefore trust more.

"In this very limited sense I would like to express a feeling that I would personally feel more secure if public matters would rest in other hands."

Dr. Oppenheimer, for his part, vigorously denied that he had been dilatory or neglectful in supporting the hydrogen bomb, once President Truman had acted. "I never urged anyone not to work on the hydrogen bomb project," he declared. He insisted, too, that his board had materially assisted Dr. Teller's work.

If Dr. Oppenheimer had stirred Dr. Teller's displeasure in 1949, he also aroused strong feelings in Dr. Edward U. Condon of the National Bureau of Standards for different reasons. In an appearance before an executive session of the House Un-American Activities Committee, Dr. Oppenheimer described a fellow atomic scientist as a former German Communist. When quotations from the testimony were printed in the newspapers, Dr. Condon and a number of other scientists were shocked on the ground that Dr. Oppenheimer had acted as an informer. "It appears that he [Dr. Oppenheimer] is trying to buy personal immunity from attack by turning informer," Dr. Condon wrote.

Subsequently, Dr. Oppenheimer wrote a public letter in which he attested to the atomic scientist's patriotism, but the incident perplexed a number of Dr. Oppenheimer's friends.

The security hearings for Dr. Oppenheimer were triggered late in 1953, when William L. Borden, former executive director of the Joint Congressional Committee on Atomic Energy, wrote an unsolicited letter to J. Edgar Hoover, director of the Federal Bureau of Investigation. Mr. Borden gave it as his opinion that the scientist had been "a hardened Communist" and that "more probably than not he has since been functioning as an espionage agent."

Mr. Hoover wasted little time in sending the letter and an FBI report to the White House and other agencies. It was then that President Eisenhower cut Dr. Oppenheimer off from access to secret material.

Lewis L. Strauss (pronounced Straws), then chairman of the Atomic Energy Commission, gave Dr. Oppenheimer the option of resigning his consultantship with the commission or asking for a hearing. He chose a hearing.

The action against Dr. Oppenheimer dismayed the scientific community and many other Americans. He was widely pictured as a victim of McCarthyism who was being penalized for holding honest, if unpopular, opinions. The AEC, Mr. Strauss, and the Eisenhower administration were accused of carrying out a witch-hunt in an attempt to account for Soviet atomic successes and to feed a public hysteria about Communists.

The Personnel Security Board of the AEC, consisting of Gordon Gray, an educator, chairman, Thomas A. Morgan, a businessman, and Dr. Ward V. Evans, a chemist, held hearings in Washington from April 12 to May 6, 1954. They considered a long list of specific charges, one batch dealing with Dr. Oppenheimer's past associations, another with the Haakon Chevalier incident, and another with the hydrogen bomb.

Dr. Oppenheimer testified in his own behalf, and forty great names in American science and education offered evidence of his loyalty. However, by a vote of two to one (Dr. Evans dissented) the board declined to reinstate its consultant's security clearance.

After asserting as "a clear conclusion" that Dr. Oppenheimer was "a loyal citizen," the majority report said that it had "been unable to arrive at the conclusion that it would be clearly consistent with the security interests of the United States to reinstate Dr. Oppenheimer's clearance . . ."

The report listed the following as controlling its decision:

1. We find that Dr. Oppenheimer's continuing conduct and associations have reflected a serious disregard for the requirements of the security system.

2. We have found a susceptibility to influence which could have serious implications for the security interests of the country.

3. We find his conduct in the hydrogen-bomb program sufficiently disturbing as to raise a doubt as to whether his future participation, if characterized by the same attitudes in a government program relating to the national defense, would be clearly consistent with the best interests of security.

4. We have regretfully concluded that Dr. Oppenheimer has been less than candid in several instances in his testimony before this board.

On appeal to the commission, Dr. Oppenheimer lost by a vote of 4 to 1. After declaring that Dr. Oppenheimer had "fundamental defects in his character," the majority said that "his associations with persons known to him to be Communists have extended far beyond the limits of prudence and self-restraint."

With the commission ruling, Dr. Oppenheimer returned to Princeton and the Institute he headed. There he lived in quiet obscurity until April 1962, when President John F. Kennedy invited him to a White House dinner of Nobel Prize winners.

In December 1963, as a further evidence of a rapprochement, President Lyndon B. Johnson handed Dr. Oppenheimer the highest award of the Atomic Energy Commission, the fifty-thousand-dollar tax-free Fermi Award, which is named for Enrico Fermi, the distinguished nuclear pioneer.

In his acceptance remarks Dr. Oppenheimer referred to his security hearings, saying: "I think it is just possible, Mr. President, that it has taken some charity and some courage for you to make this award today."

Dr. Oppenheimer was the author of several books: *Science and the Common Understanding* (1954), *The Open Mind* (1955), and *Some Reflections on Science and Culture* (1960).

He retired as director of the Institute, a research facility for some two hundred postdoctoral fellows in many fields, in early 1966.

In addition to the Medal of Merit and an assortment of honorary doctorates, Dr. Oppenheimer was a fellow of the National Academy of Arts and Sciences, the American Physical Society, and the Royal Society. He was also a member of the National Academy of Sciences, the American Philosophical Society, and several foreign academies.

ALICE B. TOKLAS

Alice B. Toklas died in Paris on March 7, 1967, at the age of eighty-nine. Who would Miss Toklas have been without Gertrude Stein? That is an unreasonable question; but what is recordable is what she was with Miss Stein. And that is what my obit seeks to re-create.

"WHAT WOULD Alice have been without Gertrude?" a friend of Miss Toklas and Miss Stein once asked.

For nearly forty years—from about 1907 to 1946, when Miss Stein died—Miss Toklas and the writer were inseparable companions, faces in the mirror to each other, and conductors of probably the most renowned cultural salon in the world.

At their Paris homes they gathered a dazzling array of the famous, the ambitious, the wealthy, and the curious—Ernest Hemingway, Carl Van Vechten, T. S. Eliot, Alfred North Whitehead, F. Scott Fitzgerald, Thornton Wilder, Picasso, Matisse, Gris, Braque, Virgil Thomson, Charles Chaplin, Sherwood Anderson, Glenway Wescott, Paul Robeson, Jo Davidson, Pavel Tchelitchev, Ford Madox Ford, and Richard Wright, to name some.

Miss Toklas stood so much in Miss Stein's larger reputation that it was said that "Alice sat with the geniuses' wives." In fact, however, Miss Toklas was by no means such a dimmed figure, according to Robert Lescher, Miss Toklas's editor.

She took a perceptive part in the literary and art conversations that frequently swirled all afternoon and far into the night. This is also attested by Miss Toklas's autobiography and that of Miss Stein. Nevertheless, Miss Toklas was mainly content to let Miss Stein scintillate in public, while she operated the household.

"Alice Toklas neither took life easy nor fraternized casually," Mr. Thomson wrote in *Virgil Thomson*. The composer wrote:

> She got up at six and cleaned the drawing room herself, because she did not wish things broken. (Porcelain and other

fragile objects were her delight, just as pictures were Gertrude's.) She liked being occupied anyway, and she did not need repose, ever content to serve Gertrude or be near her.

She ran the house, ordered the meals, cooked on occasion, and typed out everything that got written into the blue copybooks that Gertrude had adopted from French schoolchildren.

From 1927 or '28 she also worked petit point, matching in silk the colors and shades of designs made especially for her by Picasso.

Miss Toklas and Miss Stein were an oddly contrasted couple. Miss Stein was massive, with a large face and close-cropped gray hair. Miss Toklas was small and wispy and at one time had brown hair, which she wore bobbed and with bangs. "Nicely ugly," was the way James Beard, the gourmet and cooking authority, described her.

"Alice was one of the really great cooks of all time," Mr. Beard said. "She went all over Paris to find the right ingredients for her meals. She had endless specialties, but her chicken dishes were especially magnificent. The secret of her talent was great pains and a remarkable palate."

Miss Toklas wrote two cookery books—*The Alice B. Toklas Cook Book* and *Aromas and Flavors of Past and Present*, both published by Harper. The former contained a recipe for fudge made with marijuana or hashish, which, she said, "anyone could whip up on a rainy day." Taxed with this, Miss Toklas shrugged and remarked: "What's sauce for the goose may be sauce for the gander. But it's not necessarily sauce for the chicken, the duck, the turkey, or the guinea hen."

If Miss Stein dominated the couple's salon, Miss Toklas seemed to command Miss Stein. "Small or not, she was steel, absolutely," Mr. Lescher recalled. Several instances of Miss Toklas's influence have been recorded. One occurred in 1935, when Miss Stein was giving a shipboard interview to a group of reporters in New York.

"Miss Toklas's slight, menacing figure appeared in the doorway," The New York *Herald Tribune's* account read.

" 'Come, lovey,' said Miss Toklas in a steely-sweet voice. 'Say good-by to your guests. They are leaving.'

"Miss Stein leaped to her feet and bounded off into the corridor."

Another instance was reported by Hemingway in *A Moveable Feast*, an account of his years in Paris in the 1920's.

He had gone to the Stein-Toklas apartment, he recalled, and was waiting in the living room when he overheard a bitter quarrel between the two women.

"I heard [Miss Toklas] speaking to Miss Stein as I had never heard one person speak to another; never, anywhere, ever," Mr. Hemingway wrote. He immediately left the apartment, he said, because "it was too bad to hear." This incident was not mentioned by Miss Toklas or by Miss Stein in their published writings.

Hemingway's feelings about the two women apparently were known to Miss Toklas. Asked to give an opinion of Hemingway, she replied: "I won't give you my opinion about that. It might be unpublishable anyway."

Miss Toklas recounted her association with Miss Stein (she called her "the mother-of-us-all") in *What Is Remembered*, published in 1968. Her style, in sharp distinction to Miss Stein's convolutions, was simple, spare, and economical. It was, indeed, the same style in which Miss Stein had written her autobiography in 1933. Under the title of *The Autobiography of Alice B. Toklas*, it related Miss Stein's life as if Miss Toklas were the narrator.

Alice Toklas was born in San Francisco on April 30, 1877, the daughter of Simon and Emily Toklas. She was reared, she wrote, in "necessary luxury" and learned to play the piano well enough to think of a concert career.

Instead, she went to Paris with Harriet Levy, a girlhood friend, at the suggestion of Michael Stein, Gertrude's brother. Describing her initial meeting with Miss Stein, Miss Toklas wrote: "In the room were Mr. and Mrs. [Michael] Stein and Gertrude Stein. It was Gertrude Stein who held my complete attention, as she did for all the many years I knew her until her death, and all these empty ones since them. She was a golden brown presence, burned by the Tuscan sun and with a golden glint in her warm brown hair."

After a notable quarrel with Leo Stein, another of Gertrude's brothers, Miss Toklas and Miss Stein established their salon. Its earliest members included Picasso and Guillaume Apollinaire, the poet. Within a few years, it became one of the centers of Paris's intellectual life. With the influx of Americans after World War I, "the lost generation," the salon took on an international character and became an institution.

The thrust and parry of conversation was swift and keen, and opinions flew about the room like swarms of angry bees.

When Miss Toklas wrote her autobiography, she carried her life up through the fifties, but she dropped the final chapter in its published form. She concluded her book at Miss Stein's death.

"I sat next to her," Miss Toklas wrote, "and she said to me early in the afternoon, 'What is the answer?' I was silent. 'In that case,' she said, 'what is the question?' "

Afterward, Miss Toklas lived alone in the couple's apartment in the rue Christine, on the Left Bank, an apartment so crammed with paintings and sketches that it was a veritable museum.

Miss Stein left her property in trust, providing for the care of Miss Toklas for life. In recent years, however, a dispute over the condition of the art collection and the sale of some of it caused the art to be placed in a Paris bank vault.

Even with her income reduced, Miss Toklas insisted on preparing the finest meals and on shopping at Fauchon, Paris's smartest greengrocer. Mr. Beard recalled having fetched her a brace of grouse from there for a dinner.

Three years ago, Miss Toklas was evicted from her apartment and went to live in the rue de la Convention. She was bedridden and arthritic, and her sight and hearing were much impaired. She was supported by a fund gathered from writers and old friends and administered by Janet Flanner (Genêt), the New Yorker correspondent in Paris; Virgil Thomson; and Doda Conrad, an old friend.

DOROTHY PARKER

Dorothy Parker died in New York on June 7, 1967, at the age of seventy-three. A humorist is often thought of as a lighthearted person and superficial into the bargain. Miss Parker belied that in virtually everything she wrote and said. My obit tried to capture her sparkle, which was real, and her inner convictions, which were also real.

DOROTHY PARKER was the sardonic humorist who purveyed her wit in conversation, short stories, verse, and criticism. In print and in person, she sparkled with a word or a phrase, for she honed her humor to its most economical size. Her rapier thrust, much of it spontaneous, gained its early renown from her membership in the Algonquin Round Table, an informal luncheon club at the Algonquin Hotel in the 1920's where some of the city's most sedulous framers of bon mots gathered.

Franklin P. Adams, the somewhat informal elder statesman of the group, printed Miss Parker's remarks in his "Conning Tower" column, and fame was quickly rapping on her door.

Miss Parker was a little woman with a dollish face and basset-hound eyes, in whose mouth butter hardly ever melted. It was a case, as Alexander Woollcott once put it, of "so odd a blend of Little Nell and Lady Macbeth."

Many of Miss Parker's writings appeared in the *New Yorker*, to which she was a contributor from its second issue, February 28, 1925, until December 14, 1957. In paying tribute to her last night, William Shawn, the magazine's editor, said: "Miss Parker, along with Robert Benchley, E. B. White, James Thurber, Frank Sullivan, Ogden Nash, and Peter Arno, was one of the original group of contributors to the *New Yorker* who, under Harold Ross's guidance, set the magazine's general tone and direction in its early years."

The humorist's personal and literary style, Mr. Shawn added, "were not only highly characteristic of the twenties, but also had an influence on the character of the twenties—at least that particular nonserious, unsolemn sophisticated literary circle she was an important part of in New York City."

Her lifelong reputation as a glittering, annihilating humorist was compiled and sustained brickbat by brickbat. One of her quips could make a fool a celebrity, and vice versa. She was, however, at bottom a disillusioned romantic, all the fiercer because the world spun against her sentimental nature. She truly loved flowers, dogs, and a good cry; and it was this fundamental sadness and shyness that gave her humor its extraordinary bite and intensity.

When the mood was on her, Miss Parker's conversation was like a Fourth of July sparkler; but humor did not come easily to her pen. "I can't write five words but that I change seven," she once confessed.

The best of Miss Parker's humor was wry and dry, antic and offbeat, even that about herself. For her epitaph she suggested "Excuse my dust," and of her poetry she said, "I was following in the exquisite footsteps of Miss Edna St. Vincent Millay, unhappily in my own horrible sneakers."

She took seriously her couplet about women and glasses: "Men seldom make passes / At girls who wear glasses." Although she was quite nearsighted, she refrained from wearing her horn-rimmed spectacles in public, or when men were present. She much preferred to blink her luminous hazel-green eyes.

"Deceptively sweet" was the phrase her friends most often applied to her. And indeed she looked it, for she was elfin, with a warm smile and perfect manners and a short-stepped, ladylike walk. She had a mass of dark hair that, toward middle age, she cut off and wore in bangs.

She was the "verray, parfit gentil knyght" of the squelch, which she delivered deadpan in a clear, mellow, lamblike voice. Informed that Clare Boothe Luce was invariably kind to her inferiors, Miss Parker remarked, "And where does she find them?" Of a well-known author, "The only 'ism' she believes in is plagiarism." And of a cocky friend, "His body has gone to his head."

Of Katharine Hepburn, she remarked, "She runs the gamut of emotions from A to B."

Some of Miss Parker's other mots included these:

¶"A girl's best friend is her mutter."

¶"Brevity is the soul of lingerie—as the Petticoat said to the Chemise."

¶"It's not just 'Lady Chatterley's Husbands.' It's that, after this week's course of reading, I'm good and through with the whole matter of sex. I say it's spinach and the hell with it."

¶"As far as I'm concerned the most beautiful word in the English language is cellar-door."

¶"Most good women are hidden treasures who are only safe because nobody looks for them."

¶"Salary is no object; I want only enough to keep body and soul apart."

Miss Parker's background was not literary. She was born on August 22, 1893, in West End, New Jersey. Her father, J. Henry Rothschild, was a New Yorker of means; her mother, the former Eliza Marston, was of Scottish descent. She attended Miss Dana's School at Morristown, New Jersey, and the Sacred Heart Convent in New York.

She was, she recalled, "a plain disagreeable child with stringy hair and a yen to write poetry."

After she had by chance sent some of her verses to *Vogue* magazine, she was hired at ten dollars a week to write picture captions. At the same time, Mr. Adams, who was generally known by his initials of FPA, published some of her poetry in his column, then appearing in the *Daily Mail*.

Miss Parker worked for *Vogue* for two years, 1916 and 1917, and in the latter year was married to Edwin Pond Parker 2d. The marriage was terminated by divorce in 1928, but she retained Parker as her professional name.

After her marriage, Miss Parker became drama critic for *Vanity Fair* from 1917 to 1920, when, during an office reorganization, she resigned. It was during the following five years that she attained her celebrity for sizzling, off-the-cuff wit from her repartee at the Algonquin Round Table.

Miss Parker, Mr. Benchley, and Robert E. Sherwood were the founders of the group when they all worked at *Vanity Fair*, which had offices at 19 West 44th Street. The group got going because the Algonquin was nearby on 44th Street, and the three could not bear to suspend their office conversations.

The group rapidly expanded, and Frank Case, the hotel's proprietor, provided a round table for it. The group, usually about ten a day, lunched together for about a decade. At one time or another it included George S. Kaufman, Harold Ross, Donald Ogden Stewart, Russel Crouse, Edna Ferber, Heywood Broun, Ruth Gordon, and, of course, FPA, and the three founders.

Miss Parker was one of the luminaries, but she later took a dour view of the Round Table. "People romanticize it," she said. "This was no Mermaid Tavern. These were no giants. Think of who was writing in those days—Lardner, Fitzgerald, Faulkner, and Hemingway. Those were the real giants. The Round Table was just a lot of people telling jokes and telling each other how good they were. At first I was in awe of them because they were being published. But then I came to realize I wasn't hearing anything very stimulating.

"I remember hearing Woollcott say, reading Proust is like lying in someone else's dirty bath water. And then he'd go into ecstasy about something called *Valiant Is the Word for Carrie*, and I knew I had had enough of the Round Table.

"The one man of real stature who ever went there was Heywood Broun. He and Robert Benchley were the only people who took any cognizance of the world around them. George Kaufman was a nuisance and rather disagreeable. Harold Ross, the *New Yorker* editor, was a complete lunatic; I suppose he was a good editor, but his ignorance was profound."

As one result of her poems and stories, Miss Parker was pointed out at parties and literary gatherings, not always to her amusement.

"Are you Dorothy Parker?" a woman at one party inquired. "Yes, do you mind?" the humorist retorted.

On another occasion, assured by a drunk who accosted her that he was really a nice person and a man of talent, Miss Parker replied: "Look at him, a rhinestone in the rough."

"This reputation for homicidal humor," Miss Parker recalled in after years, "used to make me feel like a fool. At parties, fresh young gents would come up defiantly and demand I say something funny and nasty. I was prepared to do it with selected groups, but with others I'd slink away."

At one party a man followed her around all evening waiting for a bright remark. He finally apologized, saying, "You're not at all the way I thought you'd be. I'm sorry."

"That's all right," Miss Parker rejoined. "But do me a favor. When you get home, throw your mother a bone."

Miss Parker herself understood the ephemerality of conversational humor. "Wit has truth in it," she said. "Wisecracking is simply calisthenics with words."

Nonetheless, it was the sort of gymnastics at which she could be very good indeed. At a party where she was seated with Somerset Maugham, the author asked if she would write a poem for him. "I will if you like," Miss Parker said, and scribbled out:

> Higgledy Piggledy, my white hen;
> She lays eggs for gentlemen.

"Yes, I've always liked those lines," Mr. Maugham commented.

Miss Parker bestowed a cool smile and without an instant's hesitation added:

You cannot persuade her with gun or lariat
To come across for the proletariat.

Miss Parker laced her wit with heady truth as a book reviewer, first for the *New Yorker* as Constant Reader and then for *Esquire* as book review editor for many years. Her notices were written with a chatty trenchancy, as though she were talking informally to the reader; but she could (and did) impale authors who displeased her, either by synopsizing a pompous plot in all its ludicrousness or by pulverizing the book with a phrase.

She reduced A. A. Milne's sugary *The House at Pooh Corner* to water by remarking that "Tonstant Weader fwowed up" after reading one too many of the word "tummy."

Her verdict on Edith Wharton's autobiography was equally to the point: "Edie was a lady." Edward W. Bok, the prestigious editor of the *Ladies' Home Journal*, was left in tatters with Miss Parker's summary of him as "the Eddie Guest of prose."

"Inseparable my nose and thumb," she once wrote, and she delighted in wiggling her fingers at folk gods. "*In the Service of the King* has caused an upset in my long-established valuations," she wrote. "With the publication of this, her book, Aimee Semple McPherson has replaced Elsie Dinsmore as my favorite character in fiction."

Miss Parker was not entirely negative, however. She praised F. Scott Fitzgerald, the early Ernest Hemingway, some of Sinclair Lewis, James Baldwin, and Edward Albee.

Miss Parker's reputation for light poetry was based on four books of verse: *Enough Rope* (1926), *Sunset Gun* (1928), *Death and Taxes* (1931) and *Not Deep as a Well* (1936). On the surface the poems were a blend of the cynical and the sentimental—just right for the sweet-winning generation of the late 1920's and early 1930's.

If there was a touch of Miss Millay in them, there was also an overtone from Housman, as in "Pictures in the Smoke:"

Oh, gallant was the first love, and glittering and fine;
The second love was water, in a clear white cup;
The third love was his, and the fourth was mine;
And after that, I always get them all mixed up.

In Miss Parker's evocation of heartburn, there was, too, a bit of Donne and a hint of La Rochefoucauld, as in "Words of Comfort to Be Scratched on a Mirror":

Helen of Troy has a wandering glance;
Sappho's restriction was only the sky;
Ninon was ever the chatter of France;
But oh, what a good girl am I!

Miss Parker wrote her last published poem in 1944, and then gave up the craft. "Let's face it, honey," she explained, "my verse is terribly dated."

But her final poem, "War Song," was her favorite. It is quintessentially Miss Parker, and it reads:

Soldier, in a curious land
 All across a swaying sea,
Take her smile and lift her hand—
 Have no guilt of me.
Soldier, when were soldiers true?
 If she's kind and sweet and gay,
Use the wish I send to you—
 Lie not alone until day.
Only, for the nights that were,
 Soldier, and the dawns that came,
When in sleep you turn to her
 Call her by my name.

As a short-story writer, Miss Parker produced several that were more than merely excellent: *Big Blonde,* which won the O. Henry Memorial Award in 1929; *Telephone Call, Soldiers of the Republic* and *Arrangement in Black and White.*

The latter is a particularly mordant satire of a woman explaining her own and her husband's attitude toward Negroes. Its most memorable passage reads: "But I must say for Burton, he's heaps broader-minded than lots of these Southerners. He's really fond of colored people. Why, he says himself he wouldn't have white servants."

In 1933 Miss Parker was married to Alan Campbell, an actor. They were divorced in 1947 and remarried three years later. The Campbells went to Hollywood and collaborated on a number of motion-picture scenarios; between times Miss Parker wrote short stories and book notices. Mr. Campbell died in California in June 1963, and Miss Parker, already ill, moved back to New York.

Miss Parker, for all her mercury-quick mind, was a careful, even painful, craftsman. "To say that Miss Parker writes well," Ogden Nash once remarked, "is as fatuous as proclaiming that Cellini was clever with his hands."

She had her own definition of humor, and it demanded lonely, perfectionist writing to make the truly funny seem casual and uncontrived. "Humor to me, Heaven help me, takes in many things," she said. "There must be courage; there must be no awe. There must be criticism, for humor, to my mind, is encapsulated in criticism. There must be a disciplined eye and a wild mind. There must be a magnificent disregard of your reader, for if he cannot follow you, there is nothing you can do about it."

Toward the close of her life Miss Parker was convinced that humor had fallen on evil days. "There just aren't any humorists today," she said on her seventieth birthday in 1963. "I don't know why. I don't suppose there is much demand for humor. S. J. Perelman is about the only one working at it, and he's rewriting himself."

In 1953 she and Arnaud d'Usseau collaborated on *Ladies of the Corridor*, a Broadway play of middling success about the pointless lives of middle-aged women without families. She also contributed some lyrics to Leonard Bernstein's musical *Candide*.

From the late 1920's, when Miss Parker was fined five dollars for "sauntering" in a Boston demonstration against the execution of Nicola Sacco and Bartolomeo Vanzetti, she was active in liberal causes. In the Spanish Civil War and afterward, she was national chairman of the Joint Anti-Fascist Refugee Committee and active in its behalf. This had repercussions in 1951 when she was cited, by the House Un-American Activities Committee, with three hundred other writers, professors, actors, and artists, for affiliation with what the committee designated as "Communist-front" organizations. One committee witness identified her as a member of the Communist Party, an accusation she persistently denied.

In her final illness Miss Parker was melancholy about her life's accomplishments. She wanted to write again, especially short stories, but she lacked the strength.

The summing up came from Edmund Wilson, the critic, who wrote: "She is not Emily Brontë or Jane Austen, but she has been at some pains to write well, and she has put into what she has written a voice, a state of mind, an era, a few moments of human experience that nobody else has conveyed."

ALBERT LUTHULI

Albert Luthuli was killed by a train near his home in Groutville, South Africa, on July 21, 1967. He was believed to be sixty-nine years old. A Zulu and the winner of the Nobel Peace Prize for 1960, he epitomized one aspect of the new Africa, the black man's yearning for independence and self-determination. His obit gave me a chance to say something about South Africa as well as to describe an obviously great man.

ALBERT JOHN LUTHULI, a Zulu only two generations removed from primitivism, was the acknowledged leader of millions of oppressed black men in South Africa. He was a moderate who advocated nonviolence and passive resistance.

Although he favored cooperation with whites to achieve equal citizenship for the blacks, he was spurned and reviled by the white-supremacist leaders of South Africa, whose policy of apartheid seeks to keep blacks and whites strictly segregated.

So fearful of Mr. Luthuli was the South African government that since 1959 it had banished him to his twenty-five-acre sugar farm near the Zulu village of Groutville. As an additional restriction, the government forbade newspapers to quote his words. And it positively discouraged visits to him. The ban on visits was grudgingly relaxed in June 1966, when Senator and Mrs. Robert F. Kennedy were in South Africa. Shepherded by government officials and police, the Kennedys were flown to the ramshackle reservation for an hour's chat with the winner of the 1960 Nobel Prize for Peace. As had scores of others before him, the Senator described Mr. Luthuli as "one of the most impressive men I have met."

Gray-haired, stockily built, and immensely dignified, Mr. Luthuli uttered his political views in calm and measured phrases. Summarizing these, he once said: "We are not content to accept apartheid, which denies us equality in an integrated society and at the same time denies us independence 'in our own areas.' We demand the right of all free peoples, the right to self-determination and equality, the right to decide our future for ourselves. We want to end white supremacy and oppression, which are leading our country to chaos and our peoples to endless suffering and misery."

But even in the years of his banishment, which many regarded as a living death, Mr. Luthuli declined to express hatred for the whites. "I am no racist," he said on one occasion. "South Africa is large enough to accommodate all people if they have large enough hearts."

Mr. Luthuli's leadership of the black four-to-one majority in South Africa was exercised through the African National Congress, of which he was president. Although the movement was outlawed in 1960, it flourished underground.

Its program was chiefly economic. It (and Mr. Luthuli) favored peaceful work stoppages or "stay-at-homes," because of their immediate effect on the economy, which is dependent on cheap African labor. The Congress also urged boycotts of certain goods and services as further means of exerting economic pressure on the government.

In contrast to his political intransigence, Mr. Luthuli's manner was courteous. He smiled readily and his frank eyes, set in a round face, twinkled. Some Africans thought him too deferential toward whites, but his politeness seemed natural in a man with pride for his racial heritage.

He was born in Rhodesia of South African parents. "I cannot be precise about the date of my birth, but I calculate that I was born in the year 1898, and certainly before 1900," he wrote in his autobiography, Let My People Go. His father died when he was an infant, and his mother returned with him to South Africa. He was raised in Groutville, where his uncle was a Zulu chief.

In the village he attended the Congregationalist mission school and then went on to Adam's Mission Station College, a church-run secondary school near Durban. The Congregationalist training gave Mr. Luthuli lifelong religious convictions, a respect for Western civilization, and a sturdy belief in the inherent equality of all men.

Becoming fluent in English, he qualified, in 1921, as an instructor at the Adam's institution and seemed destined to lead the life of a successful "mission boy." After fifteen years as a teacher, however, Mr. Luthuli was elected chief of the five-thousand-member Abasemakholweni tribe, one of the few Zulu tribes to choose their leaders democratically.

He was urged to reject the honor because a chief was widely regarded as little more than a government stooge, but, proud of his traditions, he accepted and served for seventeen years. Shortly after his election he ventured into politics by joining the African National Congress, then a somnolent body of professional men.

At that period in his life Mr. Luthuli began to lose his faith in the promises of white men, a skepticism that increased after World War II, when white pledges of rights for Africans were hastily forgotten.

When African politics began to bubble in 1951, Mr. Luthuli was elected president of the Natal division of the Congress and helped organize its defiance campaign. To crush it, the government, in 1952, rounded up and jailed eight thousand Africans and Indians. Chief Luthuli was told to give up his paid chieftainship or his unpaid Congress post. He chose to stay in the Congress, and soon he was named its general president. "I only pray to the Almighty to strengthen my resolve," he said of his choice, "for the sake of the good name of our beloved country, the Union of South Africa, to make it a true democracy and a true union, in form and spirit, of all the communities in the land."

When Mr. Luthuli, by now a national figure, declined to bow to the government, his tribal elders, in a gesture of support, refused to elect a new chief. At the same time, the government prohibited him from visiting the major towns and cities in South Africa.

Not content with this ban, the government, in 1953, restricted Mr. Luthuli to his home in Groutville for two years. Nonetheless, his messages, composed slowly in longhand, were circulated, and in 1956 he was one of 156 African freedom leaders arrested on charges of high treason. After a year's detention, he was freed of the charge and renewed his public activities.

Despite harassments, Mr. Luthuli managed to keep his sense of wry humor. "The white detectives who follow me around," he said at the time, "seem to think I am criticizing them personally. There is one very nice Afrikaner detective who appreciates the Zulu language. I always said to myself, 'When I am arrested, I would like him to arrest me.'"

Exasperated by having failed to dampen the Africans' enthusiasm for Mr. Luthuli, the government in 1959 banished him for five years to Groutville under the Suppression of Communism Act and the Riotous Assemblies Act. Mr. Luthuli was not a Communist. "Extreme nationalism is a greater danger than Communism, and a more real one," he asserted.

In March 1960, the government permitted Mr. Luthuli to testify at a treason trial in Pretoria. Simultaneously the Africans started a mass protest against the "pass" system, which requires all black men to carry a special identification card. In a peaceful demonstration against the "pass" at Sharpeville, seventy-two Africans were killed by whites.

Mr. Luthuli burned his own pass in protest and called a national day of mourning for the massacre victims. The government declared a state of emergency and hustled Mr. Luthuli out of sight and back to Groutville.

It was there in October 1961 that he was notified that he had received the Nobel Peace Prize for 1960 "because in his fight against racial discrimination he had always worked for nonviolent methods."

Mr. Luthuli had been nominated for the award by the late Reverend Dr. Andrew Vance McCracken of Bronxville, New York, editor of *Advance* magazine, a Congregational Church publication. The two men had met in 1948, when Mr. Luthuli had lectured in the United States for the American Mission Board.

After an initial outburst of anger for the world honor bestowed on Mr. Luthuli, the South African regime gave him a ten-day passport to travel to Oslo to accept the prize. In an eloquent speech there he termed the award a paradox: "How great is the paradox and how much greater the honor that an award in support of peace and the brotherhood of man should come to one who is a citizen of a country where the brotherhood of man is an illegal doctrine," he said.

Mr. Luthuli also voiced serene optimism in the eventual success of his struggle. "In a strife-torn world, tottering on the brink of complete destruction by man-made nuclear weapons, a free and independent Africa is in the making, in answer to the injunction and challenge of history: 'Arise and shine, for thy light is come,' " he said.

Two years after winning the Nobel award, Mr. Luthuli was named rector of Glasgow University, but the South African government would not let him leave the tin-and-concrete house to which he was confined after his trip to Scotland.

Although his health was failing in recent years, Mr. Luthuli's devotion to the cause of freedom for the 10 million black Africans in South Africa was undimmed.

His wife, Nokukanya, shared his banishment. The couple, who were married in 1927, had two sons and three daughters.

ILYA EHRENBURG

Ilya Grigorievich Ehrenburg was seventy-six years old when he died in Moscow on September 1, 1967. Known only remotely in the United States for his novel The Thaw, *he was nonetheless an important European and Russian writer with a considerable gift for passionate description. His death was reported on page one of* The Times, *and my article was written on deadline.*

Two STALIN PRIZES for Literature, one International Stalin Peace Prize, one Lenin Peace Prize, two Orders of Lenin, one Order of the Red Banner of Labor, one Order of the Red Star. Such were the principal tangible honors accumulated by Ilya Grigorievich Ehrenburg in his long, agile, and stormy life as a writer.

Few Soviet writers were so bemedaled, few so criticized. Indeed, some of his severest critics were the Soviet authorities who cascaded emoluments on him. Their criticisms, however, were quite different from those directed at him from abroad. In the West he was sometimes thought of as a clever survivor, a sort of Abbé Emanuel-Joseph Sieyès of the Russian Revolution, who had put expediency above personal integrity.

In the Soviet Union, Mr. Ehrenburg was something of an odd man out. A man of cosmopolitan tastes and literary background, an expatriate for many years, a latecomer to Communism, he was one of Josef Stalin's favorite writers and among those least liked by Nikita S. Khrushchev. Sympathetic, at the close of his life, to the aspirations of young writers seeking a more flexible freedom of expression, he omitted to attend last spring's congress of the Union of Soviet Writers.

Mr. Ehrenburg was publicly rebuked for his absence by Mikhail Sholokhov, the novelist. Remarking on the incident last July in an interview with Harrison E. Salisbury, an assistant managing editor of *The New York Times*, the white-haired, dark-eyed writer said: "When Sholokhov attacked me, many in the congress envied me. Many readers wrote, asking me how he dared to attack me. He has written nothing for many years. One thing can be said for him, however: he always says something at a congress to wake up the members."

Mr. Ehrenburg could well afford the sarcasm, for more than 10 million copies of his works in thirty languages had been published in the Soviet Union. His novels, mainly of Russian life, were marked by interesting plots, dynamic narration, and original style. His vitriolic war reportage was read by millions. And his autobiography, recounting his life with remarkable candor, was a Soviet best seller over the last five years.

At his death Mr. Ehrenburg was working on the concluding volumes of his memoirs. He had completed six, bringing his life up to 1954. These have been published in English as *Men, Years, and Life*.

In the memoirs he dealt with the question of his own survival, how it was that so many of his friends and colleagues and fellow Jews had fallen victims to Stalin's purges and why he had escaped.

"Many of my contemporaries have found themselves under the wheels of time," he wrote. "I have survived, not because I was stronger or more far-seeing but because there are times when the fate of a man is not like a game of chess dependent on skill, but like a lottery."

In his talk with Mr. Salisbury, Mr. Ehrenburg expanded on this. He denied that he had been spared because of a special association with Stalin. Indeed, he said, he had had only one telephone call from Stalin in his life and that was in April 1941.

At that time, according to the writer, he was trying in vain to publish his *Fall of Paris*, a pro-French, anti-German chronicle of the collapse of France in 1940. The Moscow-Berlin Pact was then in force and Mr. Ehrenburg said he feared for himself because his views were so out of line with prevailing policy. One day, he recounted, he received a call from Stalin, who said he had been reading the manuscript and liked it. Mr. Ehrenburg explained that he couldn't seem to find a publisher.

"Let's work together, you and me, and see if we can't push it through," Mr. Ehrenburg quoted Stalin as having said.

The following day there was a publishers' clamor for the novel which went on to win Mr. Ehrenburg his first Stalin Prize. The story of French social decay, reflecting the author's lifelong love affair with Paris, is regarded as among his best.

To further illustrate his lack of official protection, Mr. Ehrenburg told Mr. Salisbury that in the postwar purge years of 1948–49 he expected daily to be arrested. Finally, he said, he wrote to Stalin, saying that he couldn't stand the suspense and that if there were charges against him he would like them brought. The next day, Mr. Ehrenburg related, Georgi Malenkov phoned and said: "Comrade Stalin received your letter and can't understand it, for there are no charges against you."

Shortly thereafter, the writer said, he was besieged with offers to write articles.

In the view of qualified Westerners, Mr. Ehrenburg owed his survival chiefly to his talents as a writer and to his fiery patriotism, a combination exhibited at its finest in World War II. As a war correspondent for the army newspaper *Red Star*, he attained tremendous popularity.

Many a Red Army commander later reported that without the savage hatred for the Germans inspired by Mr. Ehrenburg's flaming articles, their soldiers would have been unable to withstand the onslaughts of the Wehrmacht. Day after day, in the paper that went to all Soviet fighting forces, the writer preached the doctrine that the only good German was a dead one. He published accounts of atrocities and war crimes that fanned popular anger against the Hitlerites.

For these services, he received his first Order of Lenin. It was personally conferred by Stalin in 1944.

Having held a lucky lottery ticket, Mr. Ehrenburg appeared to feel, judging from his memoirs, an obligation to re-create the mainstream of Russian culture, which had been diverted in the Stalin years. In addition to set pieces praising artists and writers who had been purged, he sought to speak to the younger generation of "rebel" writers, acquainting them with the heritage of European culture and with modernist trends in Soviet life. Earlier, in 1954, he himself had tried to pave the way for freer artistic expression with his novel *The Thaw*.

The book, which deals with life in a provincial town, was mediocre as literature but frank in its discussion of the shortcomings of Soviet life under Stalin. It also epitomized Mr. Ehrenburg's nonconformity, a trait that characterized his life.

Ilya Ehrenburg was born in Kiev, the Ukraine, January 27, 1891. His parents were middle-class Jews, a generation removed from the Czarist ghettos. The family moved to the outskirts of Moscow when Ilya was five, and his father was for a time manager of a brewery. The boy's early years were brightened by Maxim Gorky, the noted writer, who lived in the Ehrenburg home and often read stories to him.

At school Ilya was exposed to revolutionary ideas and was expelled in 1907 for leading a student strike. It was the end of his formal education. He was twice arrested and, after five months in jail in 1908, he was exiled from Moscow. He shortly departed Russia and settled in Paris, where he was initially influenced by Roman Catholic writers and began to write poetry.

In World War I, he worked first as a freight handler and then as a war correspondent with the French forces for Russian papers. He returned to his homeland in 1917; but, unable fully to accept the Bolshevik Revolution, he was back in Western Europe in 1921.

Barred from Paris as a suspected Communist agent, Mr. Ehrenburg lived in Belgium and Germany, where he completed his first novel, *Extraordinary Adventures of Julio Jurenito and His Disciples*. Its nihilistic and cynical hero was patterned on Diego Rivera, the Mexican muralist and a friend of the author. The book satirized the capitalist West, but many of its barbs also fell on revolutionary Russia. Nevertheless, Lenin was reportedly charmed by Mr. Ehrenburg's deft touches.

Paris relented in 1924 and the writer installed himself on the Left Bank, principally at the cafe La Coupole, on Montparnasse. There he talked and formed friendships with virtually every modern writer and artist—Paul Eluard, Louis Aragon, André Malraux, Picasso, Matisse, and Chagall, among others. He also got to know Einstein and Joliot-Curie, the scientists, and Pablo Neruda, the Chilean poet.

Mr. Ehrenburg's novels in this period were tinged with skepticism and satire. *The Self-Seeker*, which appeared in 1925, dealt harshly with the speculators that emerged in the Soviet Union under Lenin's New Economic Policy. *A Street in Moscow*, published two years later, was a vivid picture of the seamy side of life in a Moscow slum.

Neither novel earned him much praise in the Soviet Union, although orthodox Communist critics did not dismiss him entirely. One reason was that he also wrote an acceptable biographical novel about Gracchus Babeuf, a radical hero of the French Revolution, as well as a series of sardonic exposés of such aspects of capitalism as automobile manufacturing and motion-picture producing.

In the early thirties there was a marked shift in Mr. Ehrenburg's outlook. The emergence of Fascism, he said later, convinced him that "one ought to take one's place in the fighting ranks." He abandoned his satire and began to write novels that fitted the official Soviet doctrine of socialist realism. One called *Out of Chaos* centered on workers building a steel mill under the Five-Year Plan.

It appeared that Mr. Ehrenburg had joined the Soviet establishment, for in 1932 he became a regular correspondent for *Izvestia*, the government newspaper; and in the following eight years he traveled the face of Europe, reporting the Saar Plebiscite, the Austrian Anschluss, and the Spanish Civil War. He took part in the combat and his dispatches from the Loyalist trenches are among the most graphic and poignant of all his writings.

Mr. Ehrenburg was a striking-looking correspondent. Of medium height and slightly stoop-shouldered, he had a mane of tousled wiry hair that he flung back as he spoke. A cigarette usually drooped from one corner of his mouth, and the ashes inevitably deposited themselves on his vest front, from which he would sweep them with a careless gesture. He was a brilliant conversationalist, by turns charming and acerbic, with an extraordinary range of literary and historical information.

He had a magpie mind for telling incident and an acid way of writing. Both aptitudes he put to use in World War II in his savage articles about the Germans. These were so vitriolic, in fact, that Mr. Ehrenburg was denounced by name by Hitler and Josef Goebbels, his Propaganda Minister.

Even after the war was over, Mr. Ehrenburg kept on pen-lashing the Germans until *Pravda*, the Communist Party paper, rebuked him for failing to distinguish between the Nazis and the German people.

Although Mr. Ehrenburg was uncomfortable in postwar Russia, he conceded later that he refrained from speaking out against Stalin. A novel he wrote in 1947 called *The Storm* earned him a second Stalin Prize. It was an indifferent work, although it was intended to be a sequel to *The Fall of Paris*.

For several years after a visit to the United States in 1946 he turned out journalistic polemics against this country as the aggressor in the Cold War. To many in the West he seemed, in Malcolm Muggeridge's phrase, "a dictatorial regime's tame intellectual: Stalin's Malraux or Schlesinger."

At the same time Mr. Ehrenburg became a founder and one of the most active members of the Soviet international peace movement. He was among the first Soviet spokesmen to assail Voice of America programs beamed at the Soviet Union. He coined the word "atomshik" to describe Americans who, he said, were engaged in "atomic blackmail."

For his work in the World Peace Council he received a Soviet peace prize in 1952. At his death he was deputy chairman of the Soviet Committee for the Defense of Peace, for which he also won a prize.

With Stalin's death in 1953 Mr. Ehrenburg published *The Thaw*, which has been described as a political bombshell, and a sequel, *The Spring*. Although the Soviet Writers Congress criticized him for his frankness, his attempt to liberate Soviet writers from the rigid censorship of Stalinism seemed to prevail, for other writers and artists soon followed his lead in producing unstereotyped works.

"Novels," he said at the time, "are not mined like coal. They do not wear out like shoes. Russia needs great works, but it is impossible to plan them or order them."

Mr. Ehrenburg's outspokenness finally irked Premier Khrushchev, who dressed him down in 1963 for "corrupting the morals of our youth." It was a serious moment for Mr. Ehrenburg, but he managed to escape virtually unscathed. Eventually, the Premier relented in his criticism.

In his talk with Mr. Salisbury, Mr. Ehrenburg said that he had visited the Premier. "I told him some things he didn't like," the writer recalled. "He held his temper. He got red in the face, but he held himself in."

Later, discussing the differences between Mr. Khrushchev and Stalin, Mr. Ehrenburg said: "Stalin talked in terms of great humanitarianism, used good language, and never appeared angry, but he killed many people. Khrushchev used violent language, scolded everyone, but didn't kill anyone. He banged on the table with his shoe, but no one was frightened. He never did anything bad."

Mr. Ehrenburg's own summation of his life came in his memoirs, and they revealed a man not fully at ease with himself. This is what he wrote:

"Western journalists have accused me and still accuse me of tendentiousness, of political bias, of subjecting truth to narrow ideology, and even to directives from higher up. Some Soviet journalists, on the other hand, have contended and still contend that I suffer from excessive subjectivity, but equally from objectivity, that I am unable to separate the new awareness of reality from the rubbish of obsolete emotions.

"All my life I have tried, for my own satisfaction, to link justice with beauty and the new social order with art. The two Ehrenburgs in me seldom lived at peace with each other; often the one would subjugate and trample the other; there was no duplicity here but the uneasy fate of a man who made a great many mistakes and yet passionately abhorred the idea of treachery.

"It is not so much my book as my life that has been and will be criticized. But I cannot begin my life anew. I have admitted my many mistakes and instances of thoughtlessness too often to assume the role of an aged mentor. I myself, for that matter, would gladly listen to the wise men capable of answering the questions that still harass me."

ANDRE MAUROIS

André Maurois died in Paris on October 9, 1967, at the age of eighty-two. Talking to him in Paris earlier that year, I was impressed by his literary professionalism: he was a man of letters who worked at his trade and produced some splendid books. I was also impressed by his candor and by his French sense of logic and order. I must say that I admired Maurois, and I think the obituary shows it.

MASTER OF a pellucid and colorful prose style, prolific and versatile, André Maurois was among the most widely known French writers of his day. He was a jack of almost all genres—biography, history, fiction, essays, and criticism of manners. Biography, however, was his true genius and the basis for his enduring reputation. His affinity was for such nineteenth-century literary and political titans as Victor Hugo, George Sand, Lord Byron, and Disraeli. His craftsmanship advanced with his years: his masterwork, *Prometheus: The Life of Balzac*, was produced at the age of eighty.

Although Mr. Maurois was indubitably French in his sensibility, the appeal of his writing was international. He was read and admired in Britain and the United States, where his biographies were best sellers, as well as on the Continent. He regarded biography as an art, and to it he applied a sophisticated and vivacious mind and the keen perceptions of a man who had begun his literary career as a novelist.

"Except in those rare cases in which [the biographer] is writing the history of a man whose life happens to have constructed itself, he is obliged to take over a shapeless mass, made up of unequal fragments and prolonged in every direction by isolated groups of events which lead nowhere," he once remarked of his craft, adding: "There are deserts in every life, and the desert must be depicted if we are to give a fair and complete idea of the country. It is [also] true that these long periods of empty monotony sometimes throw up the color of the livelier periods into greater relief.

"Balzac was not afraid of deserts in his novels. But the biographer will never have the luck to find a life perfectly grouped around a single passion. Thus the biographer has greater difficulty than the novelist in composition. But he has one compensation: To be compelled to take over the form of a work ready-made is almost always a source of power to the artist. It is painful, it makes his task more difficult; but at the same time it is from this struggle between the mind and the matter that resists it that a masterpiece is born."

Another of Mr. Maurois's precepts was never consciously to think about morals. "Every biographer should write on the first page of his manuscript: 'Thou shalt not judge,'" he said. "Moral judgment may be hinted at; but as soon as it is formulated, the reader is recalled to the sphere of ethics and the sphere of esthetics is lost to him."

To a marked degree Mr. Maurois chose his biographical subjects because they reflected problems or predicaments associated with his life. "The need to express oneself in writing springs from a maladjustment to life, or from an inner conflict, which the adolescent (or the grown man) cannot resolve in action," he said.

Elaborating this dictum with a New York Times reporter who visited him in the spring of 1967 in his sumptuously furnished Paris apartment, Mr. Maurois explained: "My first biography—Ariel: The Life of Shelley —I did because it was an expression of one of my conflicts. Shelley had come from a family from which he wanted to escape, and so did I. The problem of Shelley was also my problem."

The writer was alluding to a family that had not had much sympathy with his literary aspirations.

"My personality was also expressed in Disraeli," he went on in his precise tenor. "He was Jewish. I was Jewish myself. He was for me an example of how to get on with a Christian society."

Turning slightly away from his desk in his cushioned swivel chair, Mr. Maurois paused to ponder his other selections. "Proust, Chateaubriand, and Balzac I did because I admired them as writers," he said after a moment. "The choices were guided by my inner feelings, whether I can get on with this man or this woman. I couldn't accept the idea of spending three years of my life with someone I didn't like."

Mr. Maurois's habit was to absorb himself in his subject. "It is arduous, hard work to do research," he commented; and he entrusted the task to no one but himself and his wife. This perfectionism carried over to his writing. He worked with a fountain pen on unlined white paper and made frequent revisions. "Words flow easily," he said, "but not when first written."

Because Mr. Maurois was able to produce so consistently and on such a diversity of subjects (some of his books and essays were serious criticism, some were fripperies about love and marriage), some critics passed him off as superficial. Harold J. Laski, the British Socialist leader, for example, once remarked that Mr. Maurois "ministers to those who want the elements of culture without the need to stir the muddy waters of scholarship."

Other critics thought of him as a literary factory; and, in a way, he was. "I get up at seven and am at my desk at eight and work all day long," he confided to his American visitor. "I write every day except for Sunday, either here or at my country home in the Perigord region. The job of a writer is to write."

In Perigord, his house was atop a high hill. "From my window," he said, "I look out on nothing but tree- and heather-covered slopes, with cows grazing in the meadows and farm carts laden with hay, while far away is the village with its church steeple. There I escape from the agitation of Paris."

In Paris, Mr. Maurois's study was a large, square book-lined room on the Boulevard Maurice-Barrès overlooking the Bois de Boulogne. He dressed each day as if he were going out to a business office. Typically, he wore a blue serge suit with a vest and a neatly knotted four-in-hand tie. His sole concession to informality was a pair of expensive brown leather slippers.

One of the least bohemian of writers, he relished the deluxe things of life—a pleasant dinner, truffles, noble wines, good table talk, an evening at the cinema or the theater, a walk every day. Mr. Maurois's pen earned him a great deal of money, which he was not ashamed to spend on his own comforts.

Mr. Maurois was born into well-to-do circumstances. His name was actually Emile Herzog, which he changed legally in 1947. His father, Ernest, was an Alsatian who had moved his textile factory to Normandy in the Franco-Prussian war of 1871. Emile was born in Elbeuf, near Rouen, on July 26, 1885.

The boy was a brilliant student. He took many prizes at the Elbeuf secondary school, at the Lycée Corneille in Rouen and at the University of Caen, where he studied philosophy under Emile Chartier, better known by his pseudonym of Alain.

"I wanted to write, but I did not know if I should be able to do it," Mr. Maurois recalled. "My father wished me to enter his factory. The man who had the greatest influence on my life [Alain] advised me to do what my father wanted. 'If you wish to write,' he told me, 'nothing will be more useful to you than to have lived first, to have employed yourself in a trade and to have known responsibility.'

"The greatest influences of my youth were, first, that of Alain, who was himself a remarkable writer, and next, among books, those of Anatole France, the great French classics, and also the works of Kipling, whose philosophy of action pleased me."

Mr. Maurois remained at the family factory until World War I broke out. Since he knew English, he was attached first as an interpreter, then as a liaison officer to the British Army in France. As he had been doing for years, he wrote for his own pleasure, describing what came under his eye, and his notes were read by a fellow French officer, who took it upon himself to have them published. "These notes formed my first book, Les Silences de Colonel Bramble [The Silence of Colonel Bramble]," Mr. Maurois recalled. "This book, partly because of the circumstances—it was published in 1918 in the midst of the war—had a great popular and critical success, so that I found myself, from one day to the next, transformed from a factory official and an officer into an author. After that I was naturally only too happy to continue a career that had been since my childhood the object of my desires."

The name Maurois, that of a French village, was signed to the first book mostly because the author liked its somber sound. He continued to use it with his other books.

Now a man of letters, Mr. Maurois began in earnest to pursue his profession. Although he wrote his biography of Shelley in 1924, it was as a novelist that he first achieved renown. In addition to The Silence of Colonel Bramble, he wrote in the twenties Bernard Quesnay and Climats, both of which had enormous sales in Europe.

"My novels are better known in France and Europe than my biographies," Mr. Maurois said in his eighty-second year. "Climats sold two million copies in France, but it was not a success in the United States, where only forty thousand were sold. As to why Climats and my other novels were not well received in the United States, the ideas of love and marriage are not the same in France as in America. The hero of Climats was a sentimental man. Americans don't like to talk about emotion; they prefer physical love, what goes on behind the bedroom door. For the French it is what precedes the bedroom door that counts. 'Every beginning is lovely' is a saying that fits the case perfectly."

In between novels and biographies Mr. Maurois wrote short stories that, he said, "may turn out to be the best things I have written." These, too, had to do with emotional and romantic situations in the bourgeois world. It was a limitation that Mr. Maurois recognized. "In my novels and short stories I wrote about a rather limited world," he said in retrospect. "The difference between me and Balzac is that Balzac knew all classes of French society, gangsters and bankers. My type of

life made me know bourgeois society much better. I don't know the
underworld and can't write about it."
    Following the life of Shelley, Mr. Maurois dealt with Benjamin Dis-
raeli, the nineteenth-century British Prime Minister, in 1927. Still in
an English mood, he did Byron in 1930. In that decade he wrote some
of his major biographies: those of Marshal Louis Hubert Lyautey, a
close friend and the pacifier of French Morocco; of Voltaire, King Edward VII, Charles Dickens, and François de Chauteaubriand, the poet
and statesman who was also a notable lover.
    Honors fell upon Mr. Maurois in the thirties, as each new book
added to his luster. He was made a Knight of the Order of the British
Empire, a Commander of the Legion of Honor, and, as a climax, he
was elected to the French Academy in 1938. "I like the French Academy," he said in 1967. "It's a nice place and I enjoy meeting my friends
there once a week on Thursday. They are the companions of my life."
These included François Mauriac and Jules Romains, both novelists of
his age.
    In World War II, Mr. Maurois became a captain in the French
Army, attached to British General Headquarters. After the fall of France
in 1940, he and his wife came to the United States, living in New
York and Kansas City, where he taught at the University of Kansas
City. He described his temporary exile in two autobiographical volumes,
I Remember, I Remember and From My Journal. Published after the war
was his History of the United States. Reviewers found it "pleasantly styled" and sympathetic, but neither profound nor particularly
illuminating.
    In 1943, Mr. Maurois went to North Africa as a volunteer in the
French forces and returned to his Paris apartment and his Perigord
farm after the Germans had been thrown out of France. One of his
first books was Eisenhower, the Liberator, and it was quickly followed
by Franklin: The Life of an Optimist and Washington: The Life of a
Patriot. None of these was among his more memorable biographies.
    Mr. Maurois hit his stride again, however, in the fifties and early
sixties with Proust: Portrait of a Genius, Lelia: The Life of George
Sand, Olympio: The Life of Victor Hugo, The Titans: A Three-
Generation Biography of the Dumas, and his biography of Balzac.
    Of this Orville Prescott wrote in The New York Times: "His book
is enriched by much enlightening criticism of all Balzac's books sep-
arately and with a brilliant exposition of La Comédie Humaine as a
whole. Mr. Maurois recognizes minor flaws in Balzac's novels and certain clumsinesses in Balzac's style; but his fervent enthusiasm is eloquent
and persuasive."

Francis Steegmuller, another critic, hailed Mr. Maurois's book as "the most engrossing chronicle conceivable of a literary genius."

Mr. Maurois's graceful style survived translation into English, as this passage from his life of Balzac indicates: "He [Balzac] read a great many books on these matters [medicine]. The medical profession at the time was divided into three schools: the vitalists, who believed that a man possessed a 'life force,' which was another name for the soul; the mechanistic-chemical school, which scorned all metaphysical concepts and saw only organs, actions, and reactions; and the 'eclectic' school, which advocated the empirical approach. There was Dr. Virey, a vitalist, whose theories broadly corresponded with Honoré's beliefs— that longevity was to be attained by husbanding the vital forces; that these were squandered no less by intellectual labor than by dissipation, and that chastity led to the accumulation of a reserve of energy which, concentrated in thought, produced physical results. To these principles Balzac added the one with which he had always been obsessed, namely that man is able, by the use of his will, to control his own vital force and project it beyond himself. Hence the magnetic healing which he practiced, like his mother, by the laying-on of hands."

Critics also thought highly of The Titans. His purpose, Mr. Maurois said, was "to study, through three generations, the successive manifestations of a temperament so fantastic as to have become legendary." It began with Alexandre Dumas, the mulatto son of a Frenchman of gentle birth and a black slave girl of Santo Domingo, who rose from private to general in the wars of the French Revolution. The second in line, writer of some of the most popular plays and novels in European history, was a man who, according to Mr. Maurois, "loved women en bloc." The third, of course, wrote hugely popular plays, chiefly problem melodramas.

In addition to his biographies, Mr. Maurois kept up a steady stream of serious comment in literary reviews, including The New York Times Book Review, and in newspapers and magazines. In a less weighty mood, he wrote often in women's magazines as a sort of counselor on love and marriage. He was a favorite with editors because his witty articles, on virtually any subject, emerged with a swiftness that never missed a deadline.

In his later years more honors were showered on him. He received the Grand Cross of the Legion of Honor; he was made a Grand Officer of the British Empire; he got the Prix des Ambassadeurs for his writings in general; and he became an honorary doctor of such universities as Oxford, Edinburgh, and Princeton.

Unlike some of his colleagues, Mr. Maurois refused to subordinate literature to the fierce political debates of the times. Although he took exception to Jean-Paul Sartre's militant leftist politics, Mr. Sartre was his choice for the Nobel Prize for Literature in 1964, and he supported his subsequent refusal of it.

Mr. Maurois was twice married. His first wife, whom he wed in 1912, was Jeanne-Marie Wanda de Szymkiewicz. The couple had three children, Michelle, Gerald, and Oliver. After the death of his first wife, Mr. Maurois married Simone de Caillavet in 1926. They had a daughter, Françoise, who died in 1930.

Even in old age Mr. Maurois, a slight man with a sharp face and a long nose, did not give the appearance of venerability. His face was virtually unlined, his mind was keen, and his blue-gray eyes were quick. He felt sad, though, that his life was behind him.

"I don't like being old; it's unpleasant," he said. "I hope there are not too many more years for me."

JOHN NANCE GARNER

John Nance Garner died in Uvalde, Texas, on November 7, 1967, at the age of ninety-eight, a quarter of a century after he had ended his duties as Vice-President. His influence in national politics had also ended in 1941. He (and his era) were worth being re-created, however, for he was so much the politician of our pre-World War II innocence. He was not nearly so malevolent as John L. Lewis said, but there was no question of the fact that he was poker-playing and whiskey-drinking. And very good at political dealing, too.

THE TEXAN who was the thirty-second Vice-President of the United States was never fully happy in the eight years he spent in that office from 1933 to 1941.

More accustomed to the congressional committee room and the small gatherings of influential legislators, he frequently said that he had been just "a spare tire of the government" in the first two terms of President Franklin D. Roosevelt's New Deal.

"Worst damn-fool mistake I ever made was letting myself be elected Vice-President of the United States," he remarked after he had left office. "Should have stuck with my old chores as Speaker of the House. I gave up the second most important job in the government for one that didn't amount to a hill of beans."

Although Mr. Garner disparaged his job, he was nonetheless one of the most influential men on Capitol Hill in the first years of the New Deal. Having been in the House of Representatives since 1903 and a member of its powerful Ways and Means Committee for many years, he was practiced, as few other legislators were, in the intricate and offstage business of getting bills through Congress.

As presiding officer of the Senate and as Mr. Roosevelt's designated "Mr. Common Sense," Mr. Garner put his political knowledge to work in obtaining passage of New Deal legislation. He was more conservative than his President, and he did not wholeheartedly approve of much of the legislation he promoted, yet personal friendship (Mr. Roosevelt and he played poker together) and party loyalty persuaded him to help gather the necessary votes and to direct legislative strategy. Mr. Garner did most of his wheeling and dealing in a private office in the rear of the Senate chamber, to which he quietly invited key legislators to join him in what he called "striking a blow for liberty." The Vice-President's excellent bonded bourbon and his persuasive, often sarcastic, tongue succeeded in persuading his guests to vote his way.

However, after the election of 1936, Mr. Garner found himself increasingly out of step with Mr. Roosevelt. Their political differences reached a breaking point over the President's proposal to enlarge the Supreme Court to obtain judicial approval of New Deal statutes. The Vice-President was against the plan, and when he knew how the votes were tending he told the President.

"How do you find the court situation, Jack?" Mr. Roosevelt asked.

"Do you want it with the bark on or off, Cap'n?" Mr. Garner countered.

"The rough way," Mr. Roosevelt replied.

"All right, you are beat," Mr. Garner said. "You haven't got the votes."

Mr. Roosevelt then agreed to drop his proposal and commissioned Mr. Garner to patch up as best he could the party feuds that the court plan had engendered. Although the two men remained friendly, Mr. Garner was dropped from the circle of White House intimates and from the list of those who lunched with the President at his desk.

The Vice-President was persuaded by his conservative friends to harbor ambitions for the White House, but these were effectively frustrated by his lack of touch with organized labor, especially its militant leaders in the Committee for Industrial Organization, later the Congress of Industrial Organizations.

The mark of labor's disenchantment was stamped on Mr. Garner by John L. Lewis, head of the CIO, in a memorable display of his phrase-coining talents. The occasion was a hearing on July 28, 1939, before the House Labor Committee, which was considering liberalizing changes in the Wage-Hours Act, which Mr. Garner opposed. Referring to this, Mr. Lewis labeled the Vice-President a "poker-playing, whisky-drinking, labor-baiting, evil old man."

The description hurt Mr. Garner politically, and so did his opposition to a third term for President Roosevelt. They added to the sourness with which he left Washington in 1941 for his home in Uvalde. He vowed never again to come east of the Potomac, and he never did.

In his Washington years, Mr. Garner was a man of striking appearance. He was somewhat under average height, but his ruddy complexion, white hair, and slanting blue eyes under shaggy eyebrows made him difficult to forget. He was not given to speeches (he boasted that he had not made a single formal speech as Vice-President) but he was an industrious and powerful member of the House. The nickname Cactus Jack, given to him because he came from an infertile area of Texas, remained with him all his life.

Although he became a millionaire from business interests in his home state, he lived simply in Washington. For many years his wife, the former Ettie Rheiner, whom he married in 1895, performed all his secretarial duties and prepared their lunch on a range in his congressional office. Because he spent so penuriously, Mr. Garner had a wide reputation as a tightwad, which he did nothing to dispel.

Apart from baseball, pecan growing, and farming (he raised fowl), Mr. Garner's chief avocation was poker. He was so adept at the game that his winnings in some sessions of Congress exceeded his pay of ten thousand dollars a year.

A product of the rugged frontier, John Nance Garner was born on November 22, 1868, in a mud-chinked cabin near Detroit, Texas. His father, John Nance Garner III, had been a Confederate cavalry trooper who had migrated to Texas from Tennessee.

The boy's education was so sketchy that he had trouble keeping up with his classmates when he went to Vanderbilt University. Returning home, he read law with a lawyer in Clarksville, was admitted to the bar at the age of twenty-two, moved to Uvalde, near the Mexican border, and joined a law firm that eventually became Clark, Fuller & Garner.

When he acquired a newspaper, the Uvalde Leader, as part of a legal fee, he made his name known and was elected county judge of Uvalde County, a post corresponding to county executive in other states.

From county judge, Mr. Garner moved to the Texas legislature, which he entered in 1898. In his two terms he fought railroad interests in behalf of his Populist-minded small-farmer constituents, who sent him to Congress in the election of 1902.

"When I entered Congress," Mr. Garner once reminisced, "the autocratic leaders of the [Democratic] party thought I was just another cow thief from Texas. They 'rolled' me on committees, giving me minor assignments. I kicked until they put me on the Foreign Affairs Committee. Being the newest Democrat, I sat beside Nicholas Longworth, the junior Republican. That was how we struck up our friendship.

"It was darned peculiar that a silver-spoon aristocrat like him and one of the common people should hit it off, but we tried to outsmart each other for thirty years."

Over the years Mr. Garner formed friendships with men who exerted great influence in national affairs—Joseph T. Robinson of Arkansas, Carter Glass of Virginia, James F. Byrnes of South Carolina, Sam Rayburn of Texas, George W. Norris of Nebraska, Andrew W. Volstead of Minnesota, and William Randolph Hearst, the publisher.

Increasingly, the Texan was admitted to the inner circles of the House leadership, those who frequented a Capitol hideaway and were known collectively as "the Board of Education."

Mr. Garner, a party stalwart except in international affairs, moved into the national spotlight in 1928, when he was elected House minority leader. As such, he was active in the election of 1930, in which the Republican majority in the House was cut almost to the vanishing point. In those days a new Congress did not organize until thirteen months after an election, and by the time the House met in December 1931, the Republican majority had disappeared, owing to deaths, including that of Speaker Longworth.

Mr. Garner was elected Speaker by three votes, a margin that obliged him to exercise his skill as a politician to obtain the legislative results sought by his party.

In the jousting for the Democratic nomination for President in 1932, Mr. Garner was Texas's favorite son. He was also, because of his conservative and isolationist views, the choice of Mr. Hearst, a major force in the party, who had, most improbably, won the California delegation for Mr. Garner. On the first convention ballot in Chicago, Mr. Roosevelt had 666 votes of the 770 needed for nomination. Alfred E. Smith, the former New York Governor and the candidate in 1928, was second, and Mr. Garner was a poor third.

By the third ballot, Mr. Roosevelt had gained only 16 votes, and James A. Farley, his campaign manager, was fearful that on the next ballot delegates would slip away to Mr. Smith or to Newton D. Baker, an internationalist who had been President Woodrow Wilson's Secretary of War.

Thus it came down to Mr. Hearst and Mr. Garner's 86 votes, 44 of them from California. At first Mr. Hearst refused to listen to Mr. Farley's entreaties until he received assurances, in phone calls to San Simeon, his California castle, that Mr. Roosevelt would eschew internationalist policies.

Then Mr. Hearst made his decision. Although he did not particularly care for Mr. Roosevelt, he cared far less for Mr. Smith and not at all for Mr. Baker. Through an intermediary, the publisher got in touch with Mr. Garner in Washington.

According to *Citizen Hearst*, W. A. Swanberg's authoritative biography, "Garner knew that he owed Hearst the strength that he had. He thought it over and agreed [to deliver his California votes to Mr. Roosevelt]."

Although there have been denials, it has been widely accepted that the *quid pro quo* was the vice-presidential nomination for Mr. Garner. In any event, Mr. Roosevelt was nominated on the fourth ballot and Mr. Garner was chosen as his running mate without significant opposition. In the election Mr. Garner's homespun manner and conservative fiscal views added strength to Mr. Roosevelt's appeal among those who regarded the New Yorker with skepticism.

As Vice-President Mr. Garner adhered to the then current tradition —to be seen very little and not to be heard at all. Instead, he confined himself to the task he liked (and knew) best—maneuvering legislation through Congress.

He liked to joke about himself in this respect. One day a circus clown met him in the Senate Office Building and said by way of introduction: "I am head clown in the circus."

"And I am Vice-President of the United States," Mr. Garner replied solemnly. "You'd better stick around here awhile—you might pick up some new ideas."

When Mr. Garner, at the age of seventy-two, retired to his house in Uvalde, set among live oaks and pecan trees, he said that he wanted to live in quiet until he was ninety-three. If he attained that age, he explained, he could say that he had spent half his life in public office and half as a private citizen.

He passed much of his time looking after his ranch holdings, real estate, and banking interests.

He rejected offers for his memoirs, and, it was said, he burned his letters and other material bearing on his service in Washington.

When his wife died in 1948, he moved out of the main house into a smaller frame building nearby. He was generally known among his neighbors as Judge Garner, the title he had held in his first office. He read a bit, mostly history, and celebrated his birthdays with a special cake and a modest party. Several years ago he gave up whiskey on his physician's suggestion and cut down smoking the strong Mexican cigars to which he had been addicted for scores of years.

Starting in 1961, he made gifts that eventually totaled $1 million to Southwest Texas Junior College, an institution on the outskirts of

Uvalde. Pressed as to the reasons for his philanthropy, he said: "I don't want these kids around here to have to suck on the hind teat when it comes to getting a good education. I can't explain my time schedule on what I've given to the college except to say that when you get in your nineties you can't afford to be a *mañana* man."

Although Mr. Garner only dressed in what he called his "store clothes" for such occasions as his birthday, he was the object of some attention and curiosity on the part of visitors to Uvalde.

"People come by here to see me," he once explained. "They want to see what a former Vice-President looks like. They expect to see some big imposing man, and it's me. I'm just a little old Democrat."

FANNIE HURST

Fannie Hurst died in New York on February 23, 1968, at the age of seventy-eight. It is perhaps trite to suggest that a writer's popularity does not have a necessary connection with stylistic elegance. Miss Hurst proved that truism just as she demonstrated that warmth is a quality highly esteemed by millions of readers.

FANNIE HURST, the American short-story writer and novelist whose romances included *Back Street*, *Great Laughter*, and *Anitra's Dance*, was active at her typewriter until her final illness. Only a few weeks ago she turned in two finished manuscripts to her literary agent, Perry Knowlton, president of Curtis Brown, Ltd. One was untitled and the other she called *Lonely Is Only a Word*. Miss Hurst's last published novel, *Fool, Be Still*, appeared in 1964. There were about thirty others.

A gifted salonnière who enjoyed the company of celebrities, Miss Hurst was equally at ease with the unsophisticated, for whose emotional crises she displayed great tenderness and understanding. It was largely from the experiences of these friends that she fashioned the heart-throbbing love stories that were read under every hairdryer in America.

The greatest Fannie Hurst love story, however, was the true-life romance of the writer and her husband, Jacques S. Danielson. She brought about her marriage with the pianist against her family's opposition, maintained it in secrecy from 1915 to 1920, nurtured it with rare tact until her husband's death in 1952, and thereafter continued to feel so close to his spirit that she addressed a weekly letter to him for the rest of her own life.

Such delicacy of feeling as she showed in marriage was not a quality attributed to her by literary critics. She was frequently called "the sob sister" of American letters. A generation of literature students made fun of her use of clichés and awkward words even while millions of readers, especially women, enjoyed everything she wrote.

Kenneth McCormick, vice-president and editor in chief of Doubleday & Company, her editor from 1958 on, said of her recently: "She is basically a fairly corny artist. We all know people who write beautifully and can't tell a story worth a damn. She is a really wonderful storyteller."

The storytelling gift, the popularity with women readers, and the wisdom shown in her marriage all came from a common element. Warmhearted herself, she had a sensitivity about the emotions of other people. This manifested itself in civic and charitable activities of many kinds and most of all in the love story of the Danielsons.

A variance in age and background stood between them when they first met. Mr. Danielson, a handsome man of the world in his midthirties, was the assistant to the noted concert pianist Rafael Jossefy. His father had been court sculptor for the Czar of Russia but, growing fearful because of the pogroms there, had brought his son to the United States when the boy was sixteen. The pianist never forgot that in his youth he had seen fellow Jews spat upon in Russia.

Miss Hurst was in her early twenties. Born in Hamilton, Ohio, on October 18, 1889, she had grown up in St. Louis as an only child after the death of a sister at the age of four. Her father, Samuel Hurst, who came from Mississippi, owned a shoe factory. Her mother, who was Rose Koppel, came from an Ohio farm family.

The parents were Jewish, but Mr. Hurst felt that the family had to be extra careful not to go in for any display that would set them apart from other people. Mrs. Hurst had a low opinion of Russian Jews. Young Fannie suffered embarrassment that her Jewish background seemed to set her off from schoolmates.

She was bedeviled, too, by the feeling that she was too fat. Fighting against chubbiness, she played basketball and engaged in other athletics in high school and at Washington University in St. Louis, but she remained sensitive on this subject. It worried her when she came to know her beloved Jack, as she called him, at a Michigan spa and later in New York.

He was profoundly educated in music, she knew nothing of it. She worked incessantly at writing, he regarded her stories with casual interest. He worried about the difference in their ages and the prospect, which developed while they were getting to know each other, that she would earn more money than he, but she swept these considerations aside and proposed marriage.

When he at length gave in, she went to St. Louis and was subjected to an all-night denunciation of the proposed marriage during which her uncles and aunts were dragged in to support her parents. Out of a sense of duty to her parents, she telegraphed her Jack that a postponement was necessary.

He reacted by avoiding her for eight weeks until she went to his apartment and induced him to go to Lakewood, New Jersey, for a secret marriage. She telephoned the news to her parents. Cold at first, they came to accept the situation and suggested that the secrecy be ended, but Miss Hurst sensed that the marriage had more chance of working if her husband and she were to lead separate lives while also having a life together.

For five years they kept their secret, living in separate apartments, following their own careers, having their own circles of friends, and stealing off together as if they were illicit lovers. Miss Hurst, when she suggested this conduct to her husband, used a phrase that might have come from one of her romances: "We'll keep the dew on the rose."

The secrecy ended in 1920 when Paul Degan, an Associated Press reporter, discovered records of the marriage in Lakewood. He telephoned and Miss Hurst confessed the truth. She told of the separate apartments. He asked, "You mean you never meet for breakfast?"

Her phrase for the marriage came to mind. "Oh, two or three times a week," she said. "Our way of keeping the dew on the rose." The phrase enchanted people around the world, and she did not hear the end of it for many years.

Once the news of the marriage got out, she encountered more and more occasions calling for tact in dealing with her husband. He was a gifted musician who hated public appearances and made his career mostly in teaching. She became known as a vastly successful writer. She had to shield him from being treated as "Mr. Hurst."

She avoided any pressure on him to accompany her on occasions when she would overshadow him. Mrs. Franklin D. Roosevelt asked her to join the inner circle of friends who sat with the then Governor of New York on the night in 1932 that he was elected President. Mr. Danielson declined and his wife, understanding the workings of his mind, went alone to spend election night at Hyde Park.

In 1958, six years after her husband's death, the novelist told of her concern for his feelings in her autobiography, *Anatomy of Me: A Wanderer in Search of Herself*, published by Doubleday. One of her observations was: "Every career woman with a private-life mate is faced with this problem in one form or another: the dignity of her male."

One of the things that she did was to turn all her business affairs over to her husband. She tried to learn from him about music and gave up only when he recognized her lack of aptitude for the subject and tapered off the instruction. She got back from him, in return for her love and her sensitivity about his feelings, love and gay companionship. He died saying, "Don't leave me . . . don't leave me."

Every Monday morning in the years after his death—Monday being the day he had died—she wrote a chatty note addressed to him. Frequently, she used a simple Fannie Hurst phrase: "We had it nice."

Miss Hurst made a financial success at writing in her twenties in the years just before her marriage in 1915. However, success came only after much effort. She told friends that her rejection slips could stretch all the way from New York, where she was writing when prosperity came to her, to St. Louis, where she began to try to sell stories to magazines at the age of fourteen.

Writing at home with her well-meaning but not exactly helpful mother around was not easy. Mrs. Hurst would stand in the doorway of her daughter's room and comment, "You just sit. You don't write. If I had such a terrible time over something I did not have to do, I would quit." But Miss Hurst persevered, attacking an old standard typewriter with ferocity when the words came to her.

Before she turned into a professional writer, she had to harden herself against the feelings of her parents and establish herself in New York. She discovered that her sympathies were stirred by the great mass of the people of New York and that the people were individuals.

She worked briefly and ineptly as a waitress at Child's and as a salesgirl in Macy's, went regularly to Night Court, spent days at Ellis Island with the immigrants, and roamed the Lower East Side. Characters out of the life she saw appeared in her stories.

Day after day, she pounded the old typewriter for six hours, mailed out her stories, and just as regularly got them back. Finally, there were comments in the margin of returned stories, phrases like "Good try," and then sales began. When one of her stories appeared in the *Saturday Evening Post,* demand for her work began and magazines bought stories of hers that they had previously rejected.

Prices for her work shot up. The *Saturday Evening Post* paid her $1200 for a story, *Metropolitan,* $1400, and *Cosmopolitan,* under Ray Long, editor, began to give her $5000 a story and later raised that.

Newspapers around the country came to refer to Miss Hurst as the highest-paid short-story writer in America. She herself considered this a legend when such authors as Willa Cather and Edna Ferber were writing, not to forget Somerset Maugham, whose stories were appearing in American magazines. She certainly did command prices near the top, with *Cosmopolitan* paying her $70,000 for the serial rights to the novel

Back Street and *Liberty* giving her $50,000 for a novelette in a prize contest.

The description of highest-paid short-story writer gave her an uneasy feeling. She never considered that she had a literary ranking with such writers as Sinclair Lewis and Theodore Dreiser, and she was so impressed by Miss Cather that she was tongue-tied with her even when invited to her home in Greenwich Village. Striving for literary recognition, she tried writing novels.

When Miss Hurst started a novel called *Lummox*, which appeared in 1923, her mother weighed in by mail with her usual comments: "What are you writing that takes so long? Isn't there more money in short stories than in such slow novels?" Miss Hurst plodded on with this story about an orphan servant girl, and it became her own favorite of all her work.

The story began: "Nobody quite knew just what Baltic blood flowed in sullen and alien rivers through Bertha's veins—or cared, might be added. Bertha, least of all. She was five feet nine and a half, of flat-breasted bigness, and her cheek-bones were pitched like Norn's. Little tents. There must have been a good smattering of Scandinavian, and even a wide streak of western Teutonic. Slav, too. Because unaccountably she found herself knowing the Polish national anthem. Recognized it with her heart as it rattled out of a hurdy-gurdy."

That was pure Fannie Hurst—a story about an unprepossessing heroine made important by the intense interest of the author. Miss Hurst's stories were not all of one type, however, ranging by her own listing through "realistic, romantic, tragic, buoyant, or grim."

The plot of her popular novel *Back Street* (1930), for example, instead of being about a poor girl's life, was about the secret love of an apparently happily married man; the unmarried woman in the case followed the couple wherever they traveled, and privately saw her lover and in the end (when he died) sat in discreet sorrow in the back of the church.

Literary critics often jumped with both feet on her writing, as when K. S. Kosin wrote that at her worst her work was "a glorified *True Confessions* story." Sterling North commented that her writing "flows like the Mississippi—wide, deep, and rather muddy." But the note struck by critics was often that of Wilbur Watson in *The New York Times*: "The pulse of life is always there."

Some of her stories were made into films that proved popular, even though critics did not join in the praise. Her novel *Imitation of Life*, which was about mother love, home versus business, and racial complications, was made into a film in 1934 with Claudette Colbert and again in 1959 with Lana Turner. *The New York Times* film critic described it the first time as "the most shameless tear-jerker of the fall" and twenty-five years later Bosley Crowther, in turn, called it "the most shameless tear-jerker in a couple of years."

It is impossible to determine how much money Miss Hurst made, in the opinion of Mr. McCormick and of others in the book world. When her husband died, he left her $423,580, some of which probably had been her own earnings. She once discovered that a reporter for a press association had written an advance obituary about her in which he stated that she had made more money at writing than any other woman.

"I like that," she told him. "That is true."

Because of her constant worry about being fat, Miss Hurst was always dieting. Linked with that fear was her habit of getting up at 5:30 A.M. and walking around the perimeter of much of Central Park before breakfast. She had natural good looks, with dark hair usually drawn back in a bun, and most people took her anxiety about her weight in a light way as contrasted with her seriousness.

Marvin McIntyre, one of President Roosevelt's secretaries, used to tell a story in the 1930's about Miss Hurst. She had been on a reducing cure just before being invited to be a guest at the White House, and she arranged with Mr. McIntyre to be slipped into the President's office so that she might astound him with the change in her appearance.

President Roosevelt looked up curiously as she suddenly appeared, motioned to her to make a slow turn around in front of him and then commented, "The Hurst may have changed, but it's the same old fanny." Miss Hurst was always mortified at this slang word and she spoke bitterly about her mother for the choice she made of a name for her daughter, between Beulah and Fannie. Miss Hurst observed, "No one ever sat on her beulah."

Miss Hurst's interest in the poor and forlorn of New·York, which probably was actuated in part by a search for material in her early days, developed through the years into a wide concern for social and charitable activities. It was characteristic that she got to know the Roosevelts by writing a message of approval to Mrs. Roosevelt for suggesting that domestic workers should organize.

Some of the organizations that Miss Hurst aided were the New York Urban League, United Neighborhood Houses, the Heckscher Foundation, the Russell Sage Foundation, the American Cancer Society, the Federation of Jewish Philanthropies, Hadassah, and the Albert Einstein College of Medicine of Yeshiva University. Miss Hurst gave this last institution $360,000 for cardiovascular research in memory of her husband.

Miss Hurst also found time to crusade for antivivisection legislation, civil rights, workmen's compensation, and slum clearance. She conducted a five-day-a-week television program and on several occasions told stories to children at the Hans Christian Andersen statue in Central Park. Her trademark was the calla lily, which she associated with peace and beauty and which was always a part of any costume she wore.

HELEN KELLER

Helen Keller died in Westport, Connecticut, on June 1, 1968, at the age of eighty-seven. "You are one of that select company of men and women whose achievements have become legendary in their own time," John F. Kennedy once told Miss Keller. That remark sums up her life, in which she made hundreds of impossibilities come true. Miss Keller was beyond praise but not beyond human foibles; and the task I set myself was to make her real, which indeed she was.

FOR THE FIRST eighteen months of her life Helen Keller was a normal infant who cooed and cried, learned to recognize the voices of her father and mother, took joy in looking at their faces and at objects about her home. "Then," as she recalled later, "came the illness which closed my eyes and ears and plunged me into the unconsciousness of a newborn baby."

The illness, perhaps scarlet fever, vanished as quickly as it struck, but it erased not only the child's vision and hearing but also, as a result, her powers of articulate speech. Her life thereafter, as a girl and then as a woman, became a triumph over crushing adversity and shattering affliction. In time, Miss Keller learned to circumvent her blindness, deafness and muteness; she could "see" and "hear" with exceptional acuity; she even learned to talk passably. Her remarkable mind unfolded, and she was in and of the world, a full and happy participant in life.

What set Miss Keller apart was that no similarly afflicted person before had done more than acquire the simplest skills. But she was graduated from Radcliffe; she became an artful and subtle writer; she led a vigorous life; she developed into a crusading humanitarian who espoused Socialism; and she energized movements that revolutionized help for the blind and the deaf.

Her tremendous accomplishments and the force of assertive personality that underlay them were released through the devotion and skill of Annie Sullivan Macy, her teacher through whom in large degree she expressed herself. Mrs. Macy was succeeded, at her death in 1936, by Polly Thompson, who died in 1960. Since then Miss Keller has had several specially trained communicators.

Miss Keller's life was so long and so crowded with improbable feats—from riding horseback to learning Greek—and she was so serene yet so determined in her advocacy of beneficent causes that she became a great legend. She always seemed to be standing before the world as an example of unquenchable will.

Many who observed her—and to some she was a curiosity and a publicity-seeker—found it difficult to believe that a person so handicapped could acquire the profound knowledge and the sensitive perception and writing talent that she exhibited when she was mature. Yet no substantial proof was ever adduced that Miss Keller was anything less than she appeared—a person whose character impelled her to perform the seemingly impossible. With the years, the skepticism, once quite overt, dwindled as her stature as a heroic woman increased.

Miss Keller always insisted that there was nothing mysterious or miraculous about her achievements. All that she was and did, she said, could be explained directly and without reference to a "sixth sense." Her dark and silent world was held in her hand and shaped with her mind. Concededly, her sense of smell was exceedingly keen, and she could orient herself by the aroma from many objects. On the other hand, her sense of touch was less finely developed than in many other blind people.

Tall, handsome, gracious, poised, Miss Keller had a sparkling humor and a warm handclasp that won her friends easily. She exuded vitality and optimism. "My life has been happy because I have had wonderful friends and plenty of interesting work to do," she once remarked, adding: "I seldom think about my limitations, and they never make me sad. Perhaps there is just a touch of yearning at times, but it is vague, like a breeze among flowers. The wind passes, and the flowers are content."

This equanimity was scarcely foreshadowed in her early years. She was born Helen Adams Keller on June 27, 1880, on a farm near Tuscumbia, Alabama. Her father was Arthur Keller, an intermittently prosperous country gentleman who had served in the Confederate Army. Her mother was the former Kate Adams. After Helen's illness, her infancy and early childhood were a succession of days of frustration, manifested by outbursts of anger and fractious behavior. "A wild, unruly child" who kicked, scratched, and screamed was how she afterward described herself.

Her distracted parents were without hope until Mrs. Keller came across a passage in Charles Dickens' *American Notes* describing the training of the blind Laura Bridgman, who had been taught to be a sewing teacher by Dr. Samuel Gridley Howe of the Perkins Institution in Boston. Dr. Howe, husband of the author of *The Battle Hymn of the Republic,* was a pioneer teacher of the blind and the mute.

Shortly thereafter the Kellers heard of a Baltimore eye physician who was interested in the blind, and they took their daughter to him. He said that Helen could be educated and put her parents in touch with Dr. Alexander Graham Bell, the inventor of the telephone and an authority on teaching speech to the deaf. After examining the child, Dr. Bell advised the Kellers to ask Dr. Howe's son-in-law, Michael Anagnos, director of the Perkins Institution, about obtaining a teacher for Helen.

The teacher Mr. Anagnos selected was twenty-year-old Anne Mansfield Sullivan. Partly blind, Miss Sullivan had learned at Perkins how to communicate with the deaf and blind through a hand alphabet signaled by touch into the patient's palm.

"The most important day I remember in all my life is the one on which my teacher came to me," Miss Keller wrote later. "It was the third of March 1887, three months before I was seven years old.

"I stood on the porch, dumb, expectant. I guessed vaguely from my mother's signs and from the hurrying to and fro in the house that something unusual was about to happen, so I went to the door and waited on the steps."

Helen, her brown hair tumbled, her pinafore soiled, her black shoes tied with white string, jerked Miss Sullivan's bag away from her, rummaged in it for candy, and, finding none, flew into a rage.

Of her savage pupil, Miss Sullivan wrote: "She has a fine head, and it is set on her shoulders just right. Her face is hard to describe. It is intelligent, but it lacks mobility, or soul, or something. Her mouth is large and finely shaped. You can see at a glance that she is blind. One eye is larger than the other and protrudes noticeably. She rarely smiles."

It was days before Miss Sullivan, whom Miss Keller throughout her life called "Teacher," could calm the rages and fears of the child and begin to spell words into her hand. The problem was of associating words and objects or actions: What was a doll, what was water? Miss Sullivan's solution was a stroke of genius. Recounting it, Miss Keller wrote: "We walked down the path to the well-house, attracted by the fragrance of the honeysuckle with which it was covered. Someone was drawing water and my teacher placed my hand under the spout.

"As the cool stream gushed over one hand she spelled into the other the word 'water,' first slowly, then rapidly. I stood still, my whole attention fixed upon the motions of her fingers. Suddenly I felt a misty consciousness as of something forgotten—a thrill of returning thought; and somehow the mystery of language was revealed to me.

"I knew then that 'w-a-t-e-r' meant the wonderful cool something that was flowing over my hand. That living word awakened my soul, gave it light, hope, joy, set it free! There were barriers still, it is true, but barriers that in time could be swept away."

Miss Sullivan had been told at Perkins that if she wished to teach Helen she must not spoil her. As a result, she was soon locked in physical combat with her pupil. This struggle was to thrill theater and film audiences many years later when it was portrayed in *The Miracle Worker* by Anne Bancroft as Annie Sullivan and Patty Duke as Helen.

The play was by William Gibson, who based it on *Anne Sullivan Macy: The Story Behind Helen Keller* by Nella Braddy, a friend of Miss Keller. Opening in New York in October 1959, it ran for 702 performances.

Typical of the battles between child and teacher was a dinner-table struggle in which Helen, uttering eerie screams, tried to jerk Miss Sullivan's chair from under her.

"She pinched me and I slapped her face every time she did," Miss Sullivan wrote. "I gave her a spoon which she threw on the floor. I forced her out of the chair and made her pick it up. Then we had another tussle over folding her napkin. It was another hour before I succeeded in getting her napkin folded. Then I let her out into the warm sunshine and went to my room and threw myself on the bed, exhausted."

Once Helen became more socialized and once she began to learn, her hunger for knowledge was insatiable. In a few hours one April day she added thirty words to her vocabulary. Abstractions—the meaning of the word "love," for example—proved difficult, but her teacher's patience and ingenuity prevailed.

Helen's next opening into the world was learning to read. "As soon as I could spell a few words my teacher gave me slips of cardboard on which were printed words in raised letters," she recalled. "I quickly learned that each printed word stood for an object, an act, or a quality.

"I had a frame in which I could arrange the words in little sentences; but before I ever put sentences in the frame I used to make them in objects. I found the slips of paper which represented, for example, 'doll,' 'is,' 'on,' 'bed' and placed each name on its object; then I put my doll on the bed with the words *is, on, bed* arranged beside the doll, thus making a sentence of the words, and at the same time carrying out the idea of the sentence with the things themselves."

Helen read her first connected story in May 1887, and from that time "devoured everything in the shape of a printed page that has come with the reach of my hungry finger tips."

After three months with her pupil, Miss Sullivan wrote to Mr. Anagnos: "Something tells me that I am going to succeed beyond all my dreams."

Helen's progress was so rapid that in May 1888 she made her first trip to the Perkins Institution in Boston, where she learned to read Braille and to mix with other afflicted children. For several years she spent the winters in the North and the summers with her family. It was in the spring of 1890 that Helen was taught to speak by Sarah Fuller of the Horace Mann School.

"Miss Fuller's method was this," Miss Keller recalled. "She passed my hand lightly over her face, and let me feel the position of her tongue and lips when she made a sound. I was eager to imitate every motion and in an hour had learned six elements of speech: M, P, A, S, T, I. I shall never forget the surprise and delight I felt when I uttered my first connected sentence: 'It is warm.'"

Even so, it took a long time for the child to put her rushing thoughts into words. Most often Miss Sullivan or Miss Thompson was obliged to translate the sounds, for it took a trained ear to distinguish them accurately. When Miss Keller spoke very slowly and employed monosyllabic words, she was fairly readily understandable.

At the same time the child learned to lip-read by placing her fingers on the lips and throat of those who talked with her. But one had to talk slowly with her, articulating each word carefully. Nonetheless, her crude speech and her lip-reading facility further opened her mind and enlarged her experience.

Each of the young girl's advances brought pressure on her from her elders for new wonders and this inevitably fed public skepticism. This was intensified when, in 1892, a story appeared under her name that was easily identified as similar in thought and language to an already published fable. Although she denied the charge of plagiarism, the episode hurt Miss Keller for many years.

In that period, she was also exploited through such incidents as publicized trips to Niagara Falls and visits to the World's Fair of 1893 in the company of Dr. Bell.

When she was fourteen, in 1894, Miss Keller undertook formal schooling, first at the Wright-Humason School for the Deaf in New York and then at the Cambridge (Massachusetts) School for Young Ladies. With Miss Sullivan at her side and spelling into her hand, Miss Keller prepared herself for admission to Radcliffe, which she entered in the fall of 1900. It was indeed an amazing feat, for the examinations she took were those given to unhandicapped applicants, but no more astonishing than her graduation cum laude in 1904, with honors in German and English. Miss Sullivan was with her when she received her diploma, which she obtained by sheer stubbornness and determination. "I slip back many times," she wrote of her college years. "I fall, I stand still. I run against the edge of hidden obstacles. I lose my temper and find it again, and keep it better. I trudge on, I gain a little. I feel encouraged. I get more eager and climb higher and begin to see widening horizons."

While still in Radcliffe, Miss Keller wrote, on her Hammond typewriter, her first autobiography. *The Story of My Life* was published serially in the *Ladies' Home Journal* and, in 1902, as a book. It consisted largely of themes written for the English composition course conducted by Professor Charles Townsend Copeland, Harvard's celebrated "Copey." Most reviewers found the book well written, but some critics, including that of *The Nation*, scoffed. "All of her knowledge is hearsay knowledge," *The Nation* said, "her very sensations are for the most part vicarious and she writes of things beyond her power of perception with the assurance of one who had verified every word."

Miss Keller's defenders replied that she had ways of knowing things not reckoned by others. When she wrote of the New York subway that it "opened its jaws like a great beast," it was pointed out that she had stroked a lion's mouth and knew whereof she spoke. At a circus zoo she had also shaken hands with a bear, patted a leopard, and let a snake curl itself around her.

"I have always felt I was using the five senses within me, that is why my life has been so full and complete," Miss Keller said at the time. She added that it was quite natural for her to use the words "look," "see," and "hear" as if she were seeing and hearing in the full physical sense.

After college Miss Keller continued to write, publishing *The World I Live In* in 1908, *The Song of the Stone Wall* in 1910, and *Out of the Dark* in 1913. Her writings, mostly inspirational articles, also appeared in national magazines of the time. And with Miss Sullivan at her side she took to the lecture platform.

After her formal talks—these were interpreted sentence by sentence by Miss Sullivan—Miss Keller answered questions, such as "Do you close your eyes when you go to sleep?" Her stock response was, "I never stayed awake to see."

Meantime, Miss Keller was developing a largeness of spirit on social issues, partly as a result of walks through industrial slums, partly because of her special interest in the high incidence of blindness among the poor and partly because of her conversations with John Macy, Miss Sullivan's husband, a social critic. She was further impelled toward Socialism in 1908 when she read H. G. Wells's *New Worlds for Old*.

These influences, in turn, led her to read Marx and Engels in German Braille, and in 1909 she joined the Socialist Party in Massachusetts. For many years she was an active member, writing incisive articles in defense of Socialism, lecturing for the party, supporting trade unions and strikes, and opposing American entry into World War I. She was among those Socialists who welcomed the Bolshevik Revolution in Russia in 1917.

Although Miss Keller's Socialist activities diminished after 1921, when she decided that her chief life work was to raise funds for the American Foundation for the Blind, she was always responsive to Socialist and Communist appeals for help in causes involving oppression or exploitation of labor. As late as 1957 she sent a warm greeting to Elizabeth Gurley Flynn, the Communist leader, then in jail on charges of violating the Smith Act.

When literary tastes changed after World War I, Miss Keller's income from her writings dwindled, and, to make money, she ventured into vaudeville. She, with Miss Sullivan, was astonishingly successful; no Radcliffe graduate ever did better in variety than she. Harry and Herman Weber, the variety entrepreneurs, presented her in a twenty-minute act that toured the country between 1920 and 1924. (Although some of her friends were scandalized, Miss Keller enjoyed herself enormously and argued that her appearances helped the cause of the blind.)

In the Keller-Sullivan act, the rising curtain showed a drawing room with a garden seen through French windows. Miss Sullivan came on stage to the strains of Mendelssohn's *Spring Song* and told a little about Miss Keller's life. Then the star parted a curtain, entered, and spoke for a few minutes. The *Times* review of her debut at the Palace said: "Helen Keller has conquered again, and the Monday afternoon audience at the Palace, one of the most critical and cynical in the world, was hers."

On the vaudeville tour, Miss Keller, who had already met scores of famous people, formed friendships with such celebrities as Sophie Tucker, Charlie Chaplin, Enrico Caruso, Jascha Heifetz, and Harpo Marx.

In the twenties, Miss Keller, Miss Thompson (who had joined the household in 1914), Miss Sullivan, and her husband moved from Wrentham, Massachusetts, to Forest Hills, Long Island. She used this home as a base for her extensive fund-raising tours for the American Foundation for the Blind, of which she was counselor until her death. In this effort she talked in churches, synagogues, and town halls. She not only collected money, but she also sought to alleviate the living and working conditions of the blind. In those years the blind were frequently ill educated and maintained in asylums; her endeavors were a major factor in changing these conditions.

A tireless traveler, Miss Keller toured the world with Miss Sullivan and Miss Thompson in the years before World War II. Everywhere she went she lectured in behalf of the blind and the deaf; and, inevitably, she met everyone of consequence. She also found time for writing: *My Religion* in 1927; *Midstream—My Later Life* in 1930; *Peace at Eventide* in 1932; *Helen Keller's Journal* in 1938, and *Teacher* in 1955.

The *Journal*, one of her most luminous books, discloses the acuity and range of Miss Keller's mind in the thirties. In her comments on political, social, and literary matters, she condemned Hitlerism, cheered the sitdown strikes of John L. Lewis's Committee for Industrial Organization, and criticized Margaret Mitchell's *Gone with the Wind* as overlooking the brutalities of Southern slavery.

Although she did not refer to it conspicuously, Miss Keller was religious, but not a churchgoer. While quite young she was converted to the mystic New Church doctrines of Emanuel Swedenborg. The object of his doctrine was to make Christianity a living reality on earth through divine love, a theology that fitted Miss Keller's sense of social mission.

Although Miss Keller's serenity was buttressed by her religious faith, she was subjected, in adulthood, to criticisms and crises that sometimes unsettled her. Other people, she discovered, were attempting to run her life, and she was helpless to counter them. The most frustrating of these episodes occurred in 1916 during an illness of Miss Sullivan. For a while the household was broken up. Miss Thompson was ministering to Miss Sullivan in Puerto Rico, and Miss Keller was left in the house with Peter Fagan, a twenty-nine-year-old newspaperman, who was her temporary secretary, and her mother. Miss Keller, then thirty-six, fell in love with Mr. Fagan, and they took out a marriage license, intending a secret wedding. But a reporter found out about the license, and his witless article on the romance horrified the stern Mrs. Keller, who ordered Mr. Fagan out of the house and broke up the love affair.

"The love which had come, unseen and unexpected, departed with tempest on his wings," she wrote in sadness, adding that the love remained with her as "a little island of joy surrounded by dark waters."

For years her spinsterhood was a chief disappointment. "If I could see," she said bitterly, "I would marry first of all."

With Miss Sullivan's death in 1936, Miss Keller and Miss Thompson moved from New York to Westport, Connecticut, Miss Keller's home for the rest of her life. At Westport she made friends with its artists (Jo Davidson executed a sculpture of her) and its writers (Van Wyck Brooks wrote a biographical sketch).

With Mr. and Mrs. Davidson, Miss Keller and Miss Thompson toured France and Italy in 1950, where Miss Keller saw great sculptures with her fingers under Mr. Davidson's tutelage. "What a privilege it has been," Mrs. Davidson remarked to a friend, "to live with Helen and Polly. Every day Helen delights us more and more—her noble simplicity, her ability to drink in the feel of things, and that spring of joyousness that bubbles up to the surface at the slightest pressure."

In her middle and late years Miss Keller's income was derived from her book royalties and a stipend from the Foundation for the Blind. After Miss Thompson's death in 1960, a trustee conducted most of her affairs.

For her work in behalf of the blind and the deaf, in which she was actively engaged up to 1962, Miss Keller was honored by universities and institutions throughout the world—the universities of Harvard, Glasgow, Berlin, and Delhi among them. She was received in the White House by every President from Grover Cleveland to John F. Kennedy.

Despite the celebrity that accrued to her and the air of awesomeness with which she was surrounded in her later years, Miss Keller retained an unaffected personality and a certainty that her optimistic attitude toward life was justified.

"I believe that all through these dark and silent years God has been using my life for a purpose I do not know," she said recently, adding: "But one day I shall understand and then I will be satisfied."

RICHARD MANEY

Dick Maney died of pneumonia on July 1, 1968, in the Norwalk (Connecticut) Hospital at the age of seventy-seven. The theatrical press agent usually operates in anonymity; but Mr. Maney's personality and accomplishments were such that he achieved the status of a Broadway character. I knew Dick from a distance, having watched him frequently in his furious pursuit of victory in the match game at the Artists and Writers Restaurant, better known as Bleeck's, a saloon on West 40th Street whose habitués were mostly newspapermen. A large, gray-haired man whose suits were carelessly rumpled, he stood for long hours at the bar with his chosen companions. He was not a quiet man, especially late in the evening when the liquor was beginning to tell; but he was amusing himself and those with whom he played, and it was all innocent fun. By the time Dick left Broadway in 1966, the fun had gone out of press agentry and he knew it.

IN A FIELD devoted to fashioning halos for personalities, Richard Sylvester Maney was so adept a press agent that he acquired a special Broadway nimbus. In the course of beating the drums for three hundred shows he became accustomed to hearing himself flattered as Broadway's Boswell or as the Homer of the Great White Way.

He took these compliments as his due, for Mr. Maney was a man without illusion about his clients, most of whom he considered his inferiors. "There are a good many press agents in New York who operate on a sort of man-to-man basis," Wolcott Gibbs wrote in the *New Yorker* in 1941, adding that Mr. Maney "is the only one who persistently treats them with the genial condescension of an Irish cop addressing a Fifth Avenue doorman."

A few performers were admitted to Mr. Maney's circle of equality —Noel Coward, Maurice Evans, and Tallulah Bankhead—but membership was likely to be precarious.

Yet in his own gruff and gravelly way Mr. Maney had a fondness for his feckless clients, and he bestowed his talents on them with genuine affection. "Press agentry," he once remarked, "is no business for people with nerves. But it can be a gay life for one with detachment, with sympathy for the deranged, and with an understanding of why the theater's children behave the way they do.

"Despite the pettiness, the egomania, and the persecution complex of stage folk, they are more amusing, more generous, and more stimulating than any other professional group."

As a press representative, Mr. Maney was employed mostly by producers. He held them, particularly, in low esteem. "Producing is the Mardi Gras of the professions," he said on several occasions. "Anyone with a mask and enthusiasm can bounce into it."

He went even further in 1930 in an article for the New York *Herald Tribune*. He not only assailed the theater for "its notorious affair with mediocrity" but he also urged critics "to bat the ears off" cheap and vulgar plays. "The statutes covering indecent exposure have been breached long enough," Mr. Maney said.

Commenting on Mr. Maney's propensity to inflict stigmas on his employers, Russel Crouse, the playwright and producer who was once a press agent, wrote in 1945: "The hands that feed Maney include those of practically every producer of standing on Broadway and they are practically porous with Maney's teeth marks. He has corrected Gilbert Miller's English, questioned Orson Welles's veracity, blithely deflated Jed Harris, and publicly derided Billy Rose—all the while being paid by them."

Nonetheless, producers vied for his services. "There must be a reason for this," Mr. Crouse remarked. "Foremost, I should think, is Maney's vicious, vituperative, almost sadistic honesty. There isn't any question of Maney's talking behind your back unless you turn it."

Mr. Maney was candid about his work. "The press agent's role is to foment publicity, i.e., free publicity, and fan it once it starts to glow," he once observed. He was uncertain, however, of the effect of his exertions, remarking: "Regardless of my industry and ingenuity, more than once I've been haunted by the suspicion that I'm yodeling in an echo chamber."

One instance of this took place in 1941 when Mr. Maney was handling *The Corn Is Green*, starring Ethel Barrymore. Toward the close of the drama's run Miss Barrymore marked her fortieth anniversary as a star, and Mr. Maney arranged a cascade of publicity for the event that included an hour-long nationwide radio testimonial.

"And what was the effect on the b.o. of *The Corn Is Green?*" Mr. Maney asked, majestically, recollecting the incident a few years ago.

He licked his lips. His voice sank to a one-block whisper. "It tapered off."

Mr. Maney's apotheosis was *My Fair Lady*, the musical that opened on Broadway in January 1956, and ran for four years. "It automatically reversed my professional position," Mr. Maney said. "The editors whom I commonly besieged, now besieged me [for interviews with the stars]."

This was not strictly accurate, for Mr. Maney's fame was early established on Broadway. In fact, the press agent in the 1932 play *20th Century*, by Ben Hecht and Charles MacArthur, was modeled after him. Moreover, actresses and actors had long insisted on Mr. Maney in their contracts.

There were two explanations for this. First, he was highly regarded by drama reporters and editors for his accuracy and honesty. They paid him the compliment of accepting him as one of themselves. Once, when publicizing a show that was cluttered with props and sets, he described it in a handout as "the triumph of lumber over art."

Secondly, he was a readable writer with a pleasantly rococo style. Newspapers and magazines paid him to spread across their pages, in his witty fashion, yarns about his shows and the people in them—or even about himself.

Mr. Maney brought a high standard of literacy to press agentry. He knew by heart large chunks of Chaucer's *Canterbury Tales* and he was fluent in Shakespearean English. He was, in addition, always ready with the appropriate adjective or metaphor.

An actor who displeased him was dispatched as "a malevolent Etruscan," and a producer was skewered as "a penthouse Cagliostro," after the noted impostor.

Virtually all Mr. Maney's life after adolescence was spent in the theater. He was born on June 11, 1891, in Chinook, Montana, the son of John and Elizabeth Bohen Maney. His father was a bullwhacker and teacher. The family moved to Seattle, where Richard attended high school and the University of Washington, from which he was graduated in 1912.

He got his first theater job in 1913 as one of four advance press agents for the cross-country tour of *Anna Held and Her All-Star Jubilee*. He was not too successful, and for five or six years he toiled as associate editor and editor of the *American Angler*, a fishermen's monthly. He signed on as a press agent for *Frivolities of 1920*, and remained a part of the Broadway scene for forty-six years.

He recounted most of those years in *Fanfare*, an autobiography published in 1957. In it he extolled few theater people; but he made an exception for Miss Bankhead, clearly one of his favorite friends.

Mr. Maney helped materially to build Miss Bankhead's career. He saw to it that she was quoted, sparklingly, in Broadway columns, and he was her ghostwriter for many years. The two, it was said, liked to drink together and to argue for hours about sports and politics.

Besides *The Corn Is Green* and *My Fair Lady*, his major shows included *The Front Page, 20th Century, Sailor, Beware!, The Little Foxes, The Male Animal, Arsenic and Old Lace, The Skin of Our Teeth, Private Lives, Come Back, Little Sheba, Dial 'M' for Murder*, and *Camelot*.

Mr. Maney's first office was at the now-vanished Empire Theater. He moved to the 48th Street Theater, now the Playhouse, where to producers, actors and writers he was, he once said, "a fusion of midwife, clairvoyant, public address system, and hypnotist." There he also turned out his bravura prose.

And from there he sallied to the saloons and bars, where he delighted in spending his evenings. At various times he was banned from the Stork Club and "21," among others.

At one fashionable saloon he was barred after describing the owner as an inflated busboy; at another he called a patron, to her face, "my painted Jezebel."

The bar that enjoyed Mr. Maney's steadfast patronage was Bleeck's, on West 40th Street near the back door of the *Herald Tribune*. He liked it for its newspaper atmosphere, for its copious drinks, and for the match game, which was frequently in progress. In this game, the contestant attempts to guess the total number of matches in his closed fist and that of his opponent. Mr. Maney was a wildly enthusiastic but not highly skilled participant.

His retirement from Broadway in 1966 lacked his usual fanfare. The news came out only after a friend had phoned his office to get a pass to Mr. Maney's then-current show, *Annie Get Your Gun*. Mr. Maney returned the call from his home in Westport and told the pass-seeker he had stepped down. He was asked to dictate his retirement notice, and this is what he said:

"Richard Maney, reformed altar boy, who entered this vale of tears in Chinook, Montana, in 1891 to the obbligato of coyote yelps, after fifty years of inflating and/or deflating the theater's famous and infamous, slapped the cover over his Underwood for the last time today.

" 'Press agentry is an exciting profession,' says Mr. Maney, 'for one who can tolerate the pranks and prattle of children.'

"What is Mr. Maney going to do? Retire to my Connecticut estate and contemplate my navel."

NORMAN THOMAS

Norman Thomas died in a Long Island nursing home on December 19, 1968, at the age of eighty-four. He "kept the faith," President Lyndon B. Johnson said in his tribute to a man who was often the voice of conscience for his countrymen. I had heard Mr. Thomas speak a number of times, and I had interviewed him in his final years, the last time a month before he died. What I found remarkable then and earlier was his passion for what he deemed the correct course for Americans. The nation, as Hubert Humphrey said, was the better for him.

In 1964, when Norman Thomas was eighty years old, bent and hobbled by arthritis, hard of hearing, and so blind he could not read without the aid of a magnifying glass, several thousand friends gave him a birthday reception at the Astor Hotel. When it was over a young reporter asked the gaunt, dignified, white-haired guest, "What will you do now, sir?"

The reply was unhesitating. "The same thing I've always done."

For Mr. Thomas "the same thing" was to serve as the Isaiah of his times, the zealous and eloquent moralistic prophet who for a half century warned his countrymen of "the evils of capitalism" while pointing out to them the pathways of social, economic, and political justice.

Once scorned as a visionary, he lived to be venerated as an institution, a patrician rebel, an idealist who refused to despair, a moral man who declined to permit age to mellow him.

Times changed, but Norman Thomas appeared steadfast. He spoke to the mind; he appealed to ethical sensibilities; he thundered at malefactors; he counseled with doubters; he goaded the lethargic and chided the faint of heart; he rallied the committed.

If his moralism was stern, his manner was gentle and his words were good-humored. But the message—and Mr. Thomas always had a message—was the need for reformation of American society.

The general toleration, even acceptance and respectability, that Mr.

Thomas achieved in his long career had a number of explanations. Passionate critic though he was, he lived within the accepted social order and conformed to most of its standards of propriety: he used perfect English, had excellent table manners, lived in or near fashionable Gramercy Park, had a family life that was a model of decorum, and possessed a captivating personality. Esteem for him was personal to the point where he conferred a certain cachet on dissent.

A further explanation for Mr. Thomas's position was that, although he was the voice of the mute and the tribune of the disenfranchised, his brand of Socialism was mild. It shunned class conflict, the dictatorship of the proletariat, and the violence of revolution. It was to Marxism what Muzak is to Mozart. In Leon Trotsky's celebrated gibe, "Norman Thomas called himself a Socialist as a result of misunderstanding."

Mr. Thomas, who was anti-Communist and anti-Soviet to a marked degree, wrote extensively on what he regarded as the shortcomings of Marxism. One of his favorite arguments was expressed in question form: "Can a generation which has had to go far beyond Newtonian physics or atomic chemistry or Darwinian biology be expected to find Marx, who was also the child of his time, infallible?"

In his own philosophy, Mr. Thomas seemed ultimately to lean to democracy, albeit a radical one by some standards. "For the believer in the dignity of the individual," he once declared, "there is only one standard by which to judge a given society and that is the degree to which it approaches the ideal of a fellowship of free men. Unless one can believe in the practicability of some sort of anarchy, or find evidence there exists a superior and recognizable governing caste to which men should by nature cheerfully submit, there is no approach to a good society save by democracy. The alternative is tyranny."

There was irony in the fact that Mr. Thomas lived to see many of his specific prescriptions for social ills filled by other parties. Running for President in 1932, in one of six such races, Mr. Thomas's platform called for such Depression remedies as public works, low-cost housing, slum clearance, the five-day week, public employment agencies, unemployment insurance, old age pensions, health insurance for the aged, the abolition of child labor, and minimum wage laws.

Each of these then-radical proposals is now an accepted part of the fabric of American life. Mr. Thomas once acknowledged this state of affairs. "It was often said by his enemies that [Franklin D.] Roosevelt was carrying out the Socialist Party platform," he said in a bitter moment. "Well, in a way it was true—he carried it out on a stretcher."

Mr. Thomas later explained what he had in mind. "You know, despite the fact that the New Deal took over many of the ideas we

Socialists campaigned for, I have been profoundly disappointed," he said. "Some of our major concepts have not been accepted, but time has not changed my advocacy of them. I still heartily yearn for the nationalization of the steel industry, for example. In fact, I'm for public ownership of all natural resources. They belong to all the people and should not be for the private enrichment of the few."

Mr. Thomas summed up his alternative to capitalism as "the cooperative commonwealth." Its main features were public ownership and democratic control of the basic means of production as well as long-range economic planning.

Because he campaigned for both his long-term and his short-term reforms so assiduously and yet with so little likelihood of winning office, critics accused him of lack of realism. To these he said, "Vote your hopes and not your fears" or "Don't vote for what you won't want and get it."

Mr. Thomas was also criticized for being too professorial. According to a sketch of him in 1932, he "looks like a cultivated aristocrat, with his high-domed head, his thin gray hair, his narrow nose, firm lips and thoughtful blue-gray eyes.

"He belongs to the Woodrow Wilson type, depending more upon logic than upon emotions, and his manner is faintly academic." That appraisal appeared in the old New York Sun, an impeccably Republican newspaper.

In the opinion of the late F. O. Matthiessen, the social historian, Mr. Thomas "never served to do much more than educate some middle-class intellectuals." Echoing that assessment, a fellow Socialist told Mr. Thomas: "Most of your time is devoted to the LID [League for Industrial Democracy, an educational organization] instead of to the workers in the factories, mines, and mills. I suppose Karl Marx must have said: 'Students, lawyers, doctors, ministers of the world, unite!' instead of 'Workers of the world, unite!'"

Mr. Thomas tended to be wry with his critics, one of whom was President Roosevelt. Twitting the Socialist leader at a White House tête-à-tête in 1935, Mr. Roosevelt said, "Norman, I'm a damned sight better politician than you." "Certainly, Mr. President," Mr. Thomas shot back, "you're on that side of the desk and I'm on this."

It was not for want of trying that Mr. Thomas was always on the visitor's side of the desk. He campaigned for the presidency at four-year intervals from 1928 through 1948; he ran for Governor of New York, for Mayor twice, for state Senator, for Alderman, and for Congress. He also lectured two or three times a week (for a fee whenever possible) and wrote innumerable articles. His subjects were world peace, anti-

Communism, civil liberties, Negro rights, and all manner of specific causes that he believed had a place under the umbrella of social justice. Mr. Thomas had a truly awesome capacity for work. "Some of my friends and members of my family wanted me to go slow during the recent presidential campaign," he said at the age of eighty. "How could I? Oh, I wasn't all the way with LBJ—only most of the way—but I was all the way against Barry Goldwater, a dangerous man, the prophet of war. So I made speeches from Massachusetts to Hawaii."

Almost two years later he was still going about the country, living out of a battered duffel bag, lecturing to campus groups, talking at sit-ins, voicing moral indignation over United States military involvement in Vietnam and Southeast Asia. Young people ordinarily skeptical of anybody over thirty flocked to hear Mr. Thomas, to watch his years fall away as he denounced the Vietnam conflict as "an immoral war ethically and a stupid war politically." "We are ruining a country and ourselves in the process," he said; but he declined to incriminate President Lyndon B. Johnson, whom he described as "a sincere man" who had been "caught in the meshes of an inherited system."

Arguing against militarism and war in the 1960's, Mr. Thomas even softened somewhat his anti-Communism. "If you cannot learn to live with Communists," he told his audiences, "then you might begin to think about dying with them."

His fears were of thermonuclear war. "Kennedy said that if we had nuclear war we'd kill 300 million people in the first hour," he would declare in a typical thrust. Then there would be a rhetorical pause and this clincher: "McNamara, who is a good businessman and likes to save, says it would be only 200 million!"

Those who saw and heard Mr. Thomas in his declining years could still gather some impression of the man in his prime, for he was tall, he had presence and self-command. Murray B. Seidler, a friend and biographer, once described him this way: "He can communicate warmth and friendliness to widely varying types of people. The handshaking art of politics . . . comes easily to him because he likes people and is interested in the problems of individuals as well as those of mankind en masse. Although he is probably more keenly sensitive to the problems of society than to problems confronting individuals, it is not difficult to address him as Norman; most of his political associates have done so."

Mr. Thomas was probably one of the finest platform orators of his day. Having learned the art before electronics altered the nature of speaking to large masses of people, he strongly resembled, in his style, such virtuoso spellbinders as William Jennings Bryan, Eugene Victor Debs, Woodrow Wilson, Billy Sunday, and Franklin Roosevelt.

Mr. Thomas possessed a booming, virile, organ-roll voice that he could modulate from a roar to a whisper. And part of the magic of his eloquence resided in his gestures—the pointing finger, the outflung arm, the shaking of the head.

H. L. Mencken heard Mr. Thomas in the campaign of 1948. "It was extempore throughout, and swell stuff indeed," he wrote. "It ran on for more than an hour, but it seemed far shorter than an ordinary political speech of twenty minutes.

"It was full of adept and memorable phrases, some of them apparently almost new. It shined with wit and humor. The speaker poked gentle but devastating fun at all the clowns in the political circus, by no means forgetting himself. There was not a trace of rancor in his speech, and not a trace of Messianic bombast.

"His voice is loud, clear, and a trifle metallic. He never starts a sentence that doesn't stop, and he never accents the wrong syllable in a word or the wrong word in a sentence."

In his battles Mr. Thomas frequently had the support of many men of intellectual substance—John Dewey, John Haynes Holmes, Rabbi Stephen S. Wise, Reinhold Niebuhr, to mention but a few—but he lacked in quantity. Congratulated on the lofty caliber of his campaigns, his reply was, "I appreciate the flowers; only I wish the funeral weren't so complete."

And on another occasion he said, "While I'd rather be right than be President, at any time I'm ready to be both." But his presidential vote was always slender. In 1928, in his first White House bid, he was credited with 267,420 votes. In 1932 the votes counted for him soared to 884,781—his record. Four years later the tally slipped to 187,342. In 1940 it was 116,796; and in 1944 a total of 80,518 votes were recorded for him. In his final race, in 1948, his supporters numbered 140,260.

When the results were in that year, showing President Harry S Truman returned to office over Governor Thomas E. Dewey of New York, a prominent New York Democrat remarked: "The best man lost."

"You mean Dewey?" a listener asked.

"No, Thomas."

The feeling that Mr. Thomas was "the best man" was widely shared, and many who were not Socialists voted for him because of disenchantment with what he called "the Tweedledum and Tweedledee" choice offered by the two major parties. On the other hand, there were many who believed such a protest vote wasted because Mr. Thomas's chances at the polls were obviously so slim.

Mr. Thomas himself was very aware of this situation. In 1932, with the Depression searing the nation, many supporters predicted a vote of perhaps two million; but he knew better. Sitting with his associates on election eve, he said: "I want to tell all of you that I'm not going to get a big vote tomorrow. It's going to be a lot smaller than anybody thinks. For instance, at my wonderful meeting in Milwaukee last Saturday, hundreds came to shake my hand. One young man came up to me with tears in his eyes and said, 'I believe in everything you say and I agree entirely with your principles, but my wife and I can't vote for you. The country can't stand another four years of Hoover.'

"You can multiply that couple by thousands, if not millions. I can't help but sympathize with the feelings of that young man, but our vote will be small."

In the race of 1932, as in every other, Mr. Thomas campaigned earnestly. He toured the country by auto and train (sleeping in an upper berth to save money) and he spoke to whatever crowds could be drummed up. Apart from the needle trades workers in New York, however, Mr. Thomas did not get the labor vote, a painful anomaly for a professed Socialist. But the truth was that Mr. Thomas was not a trade-union figure, although a number of his close associates—David Dubinsky, Walter Reuther, Victor Reuther, and Emil Rieve—were union officials.

Unlike Eugene Debs, his predecessor as a party leader, Mr. Thomas did not have a working-class or trade-union background. His natural idiom and style, moreover, were those of the sack suit, not the overalls. His intellectualism and his moralism were part of his heritage and of his own early life. Both his grandfathers had been Presbyterian ministers, as was his father; and he himself remained a clergyman until 1931.

He was born November 20, 1884, in Marion, Ohio, where his father, Welling Evan Thomas, had a pastorate. His mother was the former Miss Emma Mattoon, whose surname was her son's middle name. Norman, the eldest of six children, attended the local schools and earned pocket money by delivering Warren G. Harding's *Marion Star*. In 1901 the Thomas family moved to a new pastorate in Lewisburg, Pennsylvania, where Norman entered Bucknell. After a year he transferred to Princeton when an uncle offered to pay four hundred dollars of his yearly expenses. He was graduated in 1905 as class valedictorian.

Still basically conservative in his outlook, Mr. Thomas was jolted by the urban blight he saw in his first job—that of a social worker at the Spring Street Presbyterian Church and Settlement House in New York. After a world trip he continued his social service as a pastoral assistant at Christ Church. Then, while serving as an associate at the Brick Presbyterian Church, he attended Union Theological Seminary, from which he received his divinity degree in 1911.

At the seminary he was influenced by the writings of Dr. Walter Rauschenbusch, who taught a theology that accented the Protestant churches' social responsibility. This helped to prepare Mr. Thomas for pastoral work among Italian immigrants in East Harlem, where he lived and worked for the next several years.

Meantime, in 1910, he had married Frances Violet Stewart, who came from an aristocratic banking family and who shared his social service work. Their union was extremely happy. Until her death in 1947, Violet Thomas, as she was known, devoted her life to her husband and to the rearing of their children. The Thomases were the parents of six: Norman, Jr. (who died in childhood), William, Polly, Frances, Becky, and Evan.

The family lived on a basic income of about ten thousand dollars a year that was provided to Mrs. Thomas through a legacy. This was supplemented by sums she earned by breeding cocker spaniels at the family summer home in Cold Spring Harbor, Long Island, and by Mr. Thomas's fees from lectures and writing.

For many years Mr. Thomas had his office in his New York home. This permitted him to take a greater part in family life than his otherwise crowded schedule might have allowed.

A number of developments helped to bring Mr. Thomas to Socialism. In his introduction to A Socialist's Faith, published in 1951, he wrote: "I had come to Socialism, or more accurately to the Socialist Party, slowly and reluctantly. From my college days until World War I my position could have been described, in the vocabulary of the times, as 'progressive.'

"Life and work in a wretchedly poor district in New York City drove me steadily toward Socialism, and the coming of the war completed the process. In it there was a large element of ethical compulsion."

His initial overt step was taken toward the end of 1916, when he joined the Fellowship of Reconciliation, a Christian pacifist group. Shortly afterward he became a member also of the American Union Against Militarism, in which social workers and intellectuals were active. "War and Christianity are incompatible," he said at the time, and this was the theme of scores of speeches. In his activities he met Socialists, read their books and articles, and was impressed by the party's opposition to American entry into the war. And, in 1917, when Morris Hillquit ran for Mayor of New York on a Socialist antiwar platform, Mr. Thomas supported him.

A year later, in October 1918, he joined the Socialist Party with this statement: "I am sending you an application for membership in the Socialist Party. I am doing this because I think these are the days when radicals ought to stand up and be counted. I believe in the necessity of establishing a cooperative commonwealth and the abolition of our present unjust economic institutions and class distinctions based thereon."

Meanwhile, Mr. Thomas had resigned his church post to work full time for the Fellowship of Reconciliation and to edit *The World Tomorrow*, its monthly magazine. He was also active, with Roger Baldwin, in the National Civil Liberties Bureau, which became the American Civil Liberties Union in 1920. Mr. Thomas was a leading figure in that organization for the rest of his life, and a tireless advocate of individual rights. To this end he helped to organize or joined hundreds of committees over the years that sought justice for persons of all political views. Some were futile, some were frivolous, but many were effective.

Although Mr. Thomas was primarily an evangelist, he never hesitated to join a picket line in a good cause no matter what the personal risk. He was active, for example, in the famous textile workers strike in Passaic, New Jersey, in 1919 and again in 1926. In the latter strike he was arrested and jailed until bail could be raised, but a grand jury declined to indict him.

In 1922 he became co-director, with Harry W. Laidler, of the League for Industrial Democracy, a post he held until 1937. The LID, the educational arm of the Socialist Party, sponsored thousands of Mr. Thomas's speeches. Through them he preached Socialism across the country, becoming in the process the recognized leader of the party, the successor to Eugene Debs after his death in 1926.

In this capacity Mr. Thomas was the presence and spokesman for the party rather than an organizer or administrator. Nonetheless, he undoubtedly drew into it thousands of native-born Americans and helped it to outgrow its ethnic and European origins.

Mr. Thomas made his first bid for public office in 1924 as the Socialist candidate for Governor of New York. Running against Governor Alfred E. Smith, a popular liberal who was also a friend of labor, he polled 99,854 votes.

A year later he was campaigning for Mayor of New York against James J. Walker, the Democrat, and Frank Waterman, Republican. The Socialist platform called for city-owned housing and public ownership of the transit system. Mr. Thomas trailed the field, of course, with only 39,083 votes. He ran again in 1929 with the endorsement of the Citizens Union and amassed 175,000 votes. A major issue was corruption, but Mayor Walker won easily.

In the early 1930's Mr. Thomas turned his tremendous energies to causes growing out of the Depression. He spoke in behalf of the unemployed; he helped set up the Workers Defense League; he was an active sponsor of the Southern Tenant Farmers Union, a sharecropper organization; and he marched in countless picket lines and signed countless petitions.

Mr. Thomas was a critic of the New Deal, although he conceded in after years that "we would have had very bad times" if Mr. Roosevelt had not been elected in 1932. "In retrospect, I wouldn't change many of the criticisms I then made," he said. "Yet the net result was certainly the salvation of America, and it produced peacefully, after some fashion not calculated by Roosevelt, the welfare state and almost a revolution."

Chiefly, the Socialist leader regarded the New Deal as a device to bail out capitalism; he considered President Roosevelt too facile; and he liked to note that full employment was not achieved until the nation entered World War II.

Many Socialists, especially labor-union officials, disagreed with their leader's assessment. The result was a party split, in which such unionists as David Dubinsky and Sidney Hillman broke away to support the New Deal on the ground that labor could bargain with Mr. Roosevelt to its advantage.

At the same time Mr. Thomas was beset by the Communists. Prior to 1936 he was denounced as "a social Fascist" for reputedly being too soft on the New Deal. Then, during a united front period, he was wooed in the name of workers' unity against Fascism. Next, he was assailed as anti-Soviet; but in the final period of his life, when he was opposing the Vietnam War, he was viewed more leniently.

Mr. Thomas was stoutly anti-Communist. "The differences between us preclude organic unity," he said in 1936 of the Communist Party. "We do not accept control from Moscow, the old Communist accent on inevitable violence and party dictatorship, or the new accent on the possible good war against Fascism and the new Communist political opportunism."

And after a disillusioning visit to the Soviet Union in the late thirties, he said: "More and more it becomes necessary for Socialists to insist to the whole world that the thing which is happening in Russia is not Socialism and it is not the thing which we hope to bring about in America or in any other land."

Mr. Thomas was involved in several free-speech incidents, perhaps none more dramatic than that in Jersey City in 1938 against Mayor Frank Hague. Mr. Hague, who once boasted, "I am the law," declined to sanction a Socialist May Day rally in his city. Mr. Thomas showed up anyhow to the cheers of a crowd in Journal Square. The police roughed him up, shoved him in a car, and "deported" him to New York with a warning never to return. He was back later that evening and was again ejected.

Mr. Thomas went to nearby Newark a few weeks later to thunder at "Hagueism" from that quarter. He also initiated court action and instigated a Federal Bureau of Investigation inquiry into Mr. Hague's affairs.

The result of these actions, and complementary ones by the Committee for Industrial Organization, was a federal court ruling against Jersey City. Mr. Thomas immediately returned to Journal Square and made a speech to a big throng.

With the gathering of war clouds in Europe in 1938–39, Mr. Thomas acted to stem the trend to United States involvement. With his most passionate feelings aroused, he helped to set up the Keep America Out of War Congress. "We who insist that Americans must keep out of war," he said, "do not do it because we condone Fascism, but because American participation in war will bring new horrors and sure Fascism to America without curing Fascism abroad." To the dismay of many of his friends Mr. Thomas, in 1940–41, also spoke to audiences of the America First Committee, an isolationist group.

When the United States entered the war Mr. Thomas felt a personal setback. "Pearl Harbor meant for me the defeat of the dearest single ambition of my life: that I might have been of some service in keeping my country out of a second world war," he said.

During the war he led his party in a program of what he termed "critical support" of American actions. He was afraid that whichever side triumphed democracy would suffer, but he ultimately decided that the "lowest circle of hell" would be a Fascist victory. On the home front he protested the internment of Japanese-Americans in 1942 and, in the presidential campaign of 1944, he argued against the Roosevelt policy of unconditional surrender, calling instead for a statement of democratic peace terms.

Mr. Thomas denounced in the strongest terms the atomic bombing of Hiroshima and Nagasaki in 1945. "Proof of the power of atomic energy did not require the slaughter of hundreds of thousands of human guinea pigs," he said. "We shall pay for this in a horrified hatred of millions of people which goes deeper and farther than we think."

To the end of his life he spoke out boldly and earnestly for proposals to restrict or outlaw thermonuclear war. He also pleaded for world disarmament "down to the police level" and called for an end to conscription. He set up the Post War Council and wrote its bimonthly newsletter. The organization, he said, "concerns itself with matters of foreign policy and, especially, with a crusade for universal disarmament under effective international control, coupled with a war on the world's poverty, in which lie the seeds of true world government."

In his final campaign, in 1948, he hit hard at the threat of war, which he saw "in the aggression of the Soviet empire" as "encouraged by the blunders of American policy." He favored the Marshall Plan for European recovery while dissenting from the military emphasis in the Truman Doctrine of aid to Greece and Turkey. He was, at the same time, scornful of Henry A. Wallace and the Progressive Party on the ground that they gave "blanket endorsement to the foreign policy of the aggressive Soviet dictatorship."

Two years after that race he counseled his party to drop its election activity in favor of an educational approach, but the party overruled him and ran national candidates in 1952 and 1956. In that year they received 2,044 votes. There was no ticket in 1960 or 1964. Mr. Thomas resigned his party posts in 1955, but remained as a member.

Although he stopped running for office, Mr. Thomas did not relinquish his basic role as a social philosopher, nor did his zest diminish. "I enjoy sitting on the sidelines and Monday-morning quarterbacking other people's performances," he said. However, he was so busy bouncing around the country that he rarely sat. He was among the leading opponents of McCarthyism and of the government's loyalty-security program to screen alleged subversives. And in speeches and articles he maintained a drumfire of comment on current events, especially topics having to do with foreign affairs, Negro rights, the John Birch Society, and individual freedoms.

Mr. Thomas was a prolific writer. He was the author of twenty books, scores of pamphlets, and almost numberless newspaper and magazine articles. He also served as editor or associate editor of a variety of Socialist publications.

Toward the end of his life, he was asked what he thought he had achieved. His reply was this: "I suppose it is an achievement to live to my age and feel that one has kept the faith, or tried to. It is an achievement to be able to sleep at night with reasonable satisfaction.

"It is an achievement to have had a part, even if it was a minor one, in some of the things that have been accomplished in the field of civil liberty, in the field of better race relations, and the rest of it.

"It is something of an achievement, I think, to keep the idea of Socialism before a rather indifferent or even hostile American public. That's the kind of achievement I have to my credit, if any. As the world counts achievement, I have not got much."

Reminded on another occasion that he was known as America's greatest dissenter, he said that he had never dissented for its own sake. "The secret of a good life," he declared, "is to have the right loyalties and to hold them in the right scale of values. The value of dissent and dissenters is to make us reappraise those values with supreme concern for truth.

"Rebellion per se is not a virtue. If it were, we would have some heroes on very low levels."

JOHN STEINBECK

John Steinbeck died in New York on December 20, 1968, at the age of sixty-six. The Nobel Prize novelist struck me then as a tragic figure. He wrote one great book and spent the rest of his life in its shadow. He never seemed able to come to terms with the experiences that shaped The Grapes of Wrath, *to synthesize what the Joads were all about, and to go on from there. My feeling is implied in the obit.*

OF JOHN STEINBECK's twenty-four works of fiction, one novel, *The Grapes of Wrath*, was the anchor of his fame. A compassionate, realistic, and deeply emotional account of a farm family's forced migration from the Depression dustbowl of Oklahoma to the exploitive migrant labor camps of California, the book, published in 1939, brought its thirty-seven-year-old author overnight praise and denunciation.

The acclaim was for the novel's lucid and powerful narrative of the Joads and their fellow Okies and migrants, whose human frailties made more poignant their desperate struggle to survive. Their survival was not a triumph of heroic individualism but the result of a painfully learned lesson in the importance of cooperation to achieve a common purpose. This was a story—and a theme—that was especially congenial to Depression-era readers, many of whom had jettisoned the concept of rugged individualism.

The criticism was for Mr. Steinbeck's apparent attack on capitalism and his suggestion that it could produce the poverty and the dislocation that all but swept the Okies under. Many of these critics were certain that the writer was a Communist (he was not), and his book was banned as subversive by a number of libraries. Actually, *The Grapes of Wrath* contains a specific defense of private property and private enterprise, although this was overshadowed by the book's denunciation of big business as irresponsible.

Whatever the author's ideology, however, his novel touched off a national explosion of protest and indignation over the plight of the dispossessed. "No novel of our day has been written out of a more genuine humanity, and none, I think, is better calculated to arouse the humanity of others," was how Louis Kronenberger expressed it in *The Nation*. The book was read and debated less as a novel than as a sociological document, so much so that it was compared, in its impact on the public, to Harriet Beecher Stowe's *Uncle Tom's Cabin*.

Although the comparison turned out to be facile—Mr. Steinbeck was not nearly so radical as Mrs. Stowe—*The Grapes of Wrath* became a classic because its drama of humanity dealt with real people in real situations. It won a Pulitzer Prize in 1940 and was made into a memorable movie of social protest that starred Henry Fonda and Jane Darwell. The book has sold over 3 million copies in various American editions, and has long been required reading in scores of colleges and universities.

The Grapes of Wrath made its California author an unwilling celebrity, a condition he resisted all his life. "I am not neurotic about personal publicity," he said. "I just think it's foolish. The fact that I have housemaid's knees or fear of yellow gloves has little to do with the books I write."

He shunned award ceremonies, dodged interviews, and declined as often as he could to pose for photographs. "They ain't going to lionize me," he told a friend in 1940.

Zealously guarding his privacy, Mr. Steinbeck took little part in the public literary life of his time. He rarely served on committees, signed appeals, attended parties, lectured at colleges, or commented on the work of other writers. He lived simply, inconspicuously and off the beaten track—in a ranch house in California, in a cottage at Sag Harbor, Long Island, in a nondescript brownstone on New York's Upper East Side.

Because Mr. Steinbeck isolated himself so much, he was considered reserved and difficult to get to know really well. "John always seemed occupied with his inner thoughts," an acquaintance of many years said recently. "He had a way of putting you off if you tried to probe him and a way of making you feel as if you were being observed under his microscope."

In another view, Mr. Steinbeck was accounted a delightful companion in a small circle of intimates that included Nathaniel Benchley, Elia Kazan, Arthur Miller, Edward Albee, Abe Burrows, John Huston, and Thomas Guinzburg, his publisher. "John was a very soft man, once you got to know him," Mr. Guinzburg said. "He was wonderfully kind. He was pleased by small things, just like a big kid."

Mr. Steinbeck felt very much at home with people of no pretension—the Okies among whom he lived and worked for a while, workers in a fish-canning factory, ranch hands, apple pickers, and paisanos. He delighted to talk with them, drink with them, and worry over their day-to-day problems. And for their speech he developed a marvelously accurate ear and for their ways a keen eye.

A husky six-footer with brown hair that turned to gray with age, the writer was ill at ease in conventional attire. He preferred sweaters, baggy trousers, and battered shoes to sack suits, and for years he did not own a dinner jacket.

Early in his adulthood he grew a mustache and, later, a beard. Over the years this underwent a number of changes in style, but it seemed to be fixed in his last years as a short Vandyke, which gave his face a Mephistophelean cast.

At Sag Harbor, he wrote in a small building apart from his cottage, to which he retired for a few hours every day. He wrote in pencil on yellow lined paper, and his manuscripts were transcribed by a typist at Viking Press, his publisher. His novels, according to Mr. Guinzburg, required only light editing.

Mr. Steinbeck liked to putter and to do things with his hands. In time he acquired considerable skill in woodworking, and, in proof of his talent, delivered the manuscript of *East of Eden* in a handcrafted box of complicated design.

The simple, even casual life was part of John Ernst Steinbeck, Jr.'s, California heritage. He was born on February 27, 1902, in the town of Salinas of German, Irish, and New England extraction. He was the only son of a miller who was once treasurer of Monterey County. His mother was Olive Hamilton Steinbeck, a teacher in the Salinas Valley schools. As a youth John played basketball and excelled at track, but he spent much of his spare time in the out-of-doors and in reading. His fare was Malory's *Morte d'Arthur*, Milton's *Paradise Lost*, the Bible, Hardy's *The Return of the Native*.

From this reading sprang a lifelong absorption in allegory, a form around which most of his fiction is built. His reading also turned him toward mythopoetic expression, which is also intricately woven into the fabric of his novels.

After his high school years, young Steinbeck entered Stanford University, which he treated as an academic adventure. He tasted the curriculum, taking courses in literature, science, and writing; and he wrote poems and comic satire for college publications.

Restless and seemingly undirected, he worked as a ranch hand and toiled on a road-building gang and in a sugar-beet factory. He left Stanford in 1925 without a degree but with a passion to write and went to

New York to establish himself. He worked briefly as a reporter for the New York *American* (facts eluded his grasp and he was dismissed) and as a hod carrier in the construction of Madison Square Garden.

When a publisher rejected Mr. Steinbeck's manuscript, a collection of stories, he returned to California, where he took a job as a lodge caretaker at Lake Tahoe in the Sierras. There in loneliness he created his first novel, "Cup of Gold," a historical extravaganza about Sir Henry Morgan, a seventeenth-century Caribbean pirate.

Containing strong hints of its source in the Arthurian quest for the Holy Grail, the novel is an allegory designed to convey the notion that swashbuckling heroes are out of place in the modern world, that civilization destroys innocence.

The book, appearing in 1929, sold about fifteen hundred copies and excited no critical interest. Undiscouraged, Mr. Steinbeck married Carol Henning and moved to Pacific Grove on a monthly allowance of twenty-five dollars from his family. He tried to sell short stories, fashioned a new novel, and formed a fast friendship with Edward Ricketts, a marine biologist.

Mr. Steinbeck told the story of his profound intellectual and emotional debt to this man in *About Ed Ricketts*, a memoir issued in 1948 after his death. Mr. Ricketts gave coherence to the writer's philosophical attitudes, providing him with the arguments for a biological view of man that infuses his novels.

This view—that man must adapt to his environment if he is to survive—was presented in *The Grapes of Wrath* and in *Cannery Row*, where it is suggested that men should accept themselves as they are and stop persecuting others for being different from them.

Mr. Ricketts, in addition to being the writer's mentor, was his closest drinking and talking companion. Slightly disguised, the biologist appeared in three of his friend's novels—*In Dubious Battle, Cannery Row*, and *Sweet Thursday*.

Mr. Steinbeck's second novel, *The Pastures of Heaven*, came out in 1932, followed a year later by *To a God Unknown*. The former was a satire of mediocrity, the latter an allegory about the breakdown of a family. Although neither was a popular success, each stirred the interest of a Chicago bookseller, who, in turn, insisted that Pascal Covici, the publisher, read them. He was impressed sufficiently to publish *Tortilla Flat*, Mr. Steinbeck's next book and the one that earned his first critical huzzas.

Tortilla Flat was at once a pointed satire of middle-class values and a tragic story of a man who fails while trying to achieve greatness. The people of the novel were a group of paisanos, a band of idlers who shunned the amenities of civilization and pursued their own eccentric moralities.

Warm, sentimental, offbeat, the novel quickly became a best seller and was purchased by Hollywood—but not filmed for ten years (and then badly). With the money from the book, Mr. Steinbeck had his first taste of affluence and the heady experience of being in demand as a writer.

He followed his success with *In Dubious Battle*, the story of an apple pickers' strike that attacked both insensitive employers and militant strike leaders. Although the author's sympathies were clearly with the strikers—"the working stiffs"—he pictured them as exploited by both the capitalists and the Communists.

On the strength of the book, Mr. Steinbeck was hired by the San Francisco *News* to write about California's migrant labor camps, and from this searing experience came the idea for *The Grapes of Wrath*. Meantime, however, he wrote *Of Mice and Men*, a tragic fable of the strong and the weak, published in 1937. The book introduced Mr. Steinbeck to Broadway, where *Of Mice and Men* was converted into a play with George S. Kaufman's help. Although the play barely missed winning the Pulitzer Prize, it did take the New York Drama Critics Circle Award and went on to become a movie.

The night the play opened, its author was in a migrant camp, having traveled to California from Oklahoma with some of its inhabitants. All the pathos of these uprooted people was translated into *The Grapes of Wrath*, which made its author a national figure in spite of himself. To escape, he and Mr. Ricketts journeyed to the Gulf of California. Their adventure is described in *Sea of Cortez*, a semitravel book.

Shortly afterward, Mr. Steinbeck went to Mexico to make *The Forgotten Village*, a notable documentary film about the introduction of modern medicine to a backward village.

Restless, he took to traveling, which over the years became virtually a way of life for him. These trips caused his wife to divorce him in 1942. She received a $220,000 settlement.

The following year, with Paul de Kruif, the medical writer, serving as best man, he married Gwyndolen Conger, who became the mother of his two children, Thom and John. This marriage lasted until 1948. His third marriage, which was said to be happier, came in 1950, when he wed Elaine Scott, divorced wife of Zachary Scott, the movie actor.

With his second marriage, Mr. Steinbeck moved to New York, a change of milieu that, in the opinion of many critics, adversely affected the quality of his fiction.

After the high point of *The Grapes of Wrath*, his next novel, *The Moon Is Down*, an abstract account of the German occupation of a Scandinavian country, was coolly received. More enthusiasm greeted his film script for *Lifeboat*, an allegory about a world adrift, which starred Tallulah Bankhead. The movie was a hit on its release in 1944.

Mr. Steinbeck's first postwar novel, *Cannery Row*, returned to the scene of his earlier triumphs. A story of the denizens of Monterey's Cannery Row, it described the destructive force of respectability. Two years later, in 1947, he published *The Wayward Bus*, a semiphilosophical examination of a group of stranded bus riders. It failed to attract much attention, as did *A Russian Journal*, an account of a trip to the Soviet Union with Robert Capa, the photographer. The novelist turned again to the movies, working on the script for Marlon Brando's *Viva Zapata!* in 1950. The same year his play *Burning Bright* failed on Broadway after thirteen performances.

Mr. Steinbeck's literary (or at least popular) stock rose markedly in 1952 with *East of Eden*, a lusty family chronicle that developed into an intricate gloss on the Cain-and-Abel theme. Although critics tended to disparage it as rambling, the book sold well, and Elia Kazan transmuted part of it into a movie in which James Dean made his screen debut.

Nonetheless, *Sweet Thursday* was only indifferently received in 1954, as was *Pipe Dream*, the musical comedy version of the book. In those years Mr. Steinbeck wrote for magazines, including *Holiday* and the *Saturday Review*, and did an introduction to the collected campaign speeches of Adlai E. Stevenson. Warren French, a sympathetic critic, called most of the writer's output during the 1950's "superficial journalism."

Mr. Steinbeck made a comeback of sorts in 1961 with *The Winter of Our Discontent*, an inversion of the Gospel story in modern dress that portrayed the decline of moral standards in the United States. But to many it seemed more of a sermon than a novel, and it did not do very well for all its articulateness.

Although Mr. Steinbeck had been mentioned years earlier as a possible Nobelist, the awarding of the prize to him in 1962 was a surprise. The citation, calling attention to his "sympathetic humor and social perception," implied that it was his sociological fiction that had captivated the judges. At the same time, it was said that the jury had also liked *The Winter of Our Discontent* because of its "instinct for what is genuinely American, be it good or bad."

Even so, some American critics, including Arthur Mizener, believed the judges had erred. "It is difficult," he wrote at the time in *The New York Times*, "to find a flattering explanation of awarding this most distinguished of literary prizes to a writer whose real but limited talent is, in his best books, watered down by twentieth-rate philosophizing and, in his worst books, is overwhelmed by it."

Mr. Steinbeck was one of six Americans who won the Nobel Prize for literature since the prizes were instituted in 1901. The others were Ernest Hemingway, William Faulkner, Pearl Buck, Eugene O'Neill, and Sinclair Lewis.

With the prize Mr. Steinbeck appeared to have lost his fictive voice altogether. "The prize did terrible things to John's ability to create fiction," Mr. Guinzburg said. "He felt vastly frustrated and he wouldn't fool around with an entertainment, or something light, to break the tension."

The year of the Nobel Prize Mr. Steinbeck published *Travels with Charley*, a whimsical chronicle of a trip across the United States with his poodle. The book affirmed his attachment to America as well as his fondness for, and rapport with, simple people. "I began to feel that Americans exist, that they really do have generalized characteristics regardless of their states, their social and financial status, their education, their religious, and their political conviction," he wrote, adding cryptically: "But the more I inspected this American image, the less sure I became of what it is."

In the middle sixties, Mr. Steinbeck talked from time to time of writing a "big" novel, but seemed unable to put it together. His most recent book, *America and Americans*, was a collection of thoughts on the United States that accompanied 105 photographs of the national scene.

In the Vietnam War he dismayed and puzzled his friends in the intellectual community, most of whom opposed the war. Mr. Steinbeck, who took a trip to South Vietnam, aired his hawkish views in columns he wrote for *Newsday*, the Long Island newspaper. These were titled *Letters to Alicia*, the reference being to Alicia Patterson, the paper's founder, who had died several years before the columns appeared.

He was also censured in a poem by Yevgeny Yevtushenko, the Soviet writer, as "betraying" his principles. Mr. Steinbeck, who maintained that the Vietnam conflict was "a Chinese-inspired war" that the United States must win, replied to the Soviet poet. He challenged Soviet authorities to print his tart letter, which accused them of perpetuating the war. The challenge was accepted, and the letter appeared on the front page of a Moscow newspaper.

In recent years, Mr. Steinbeck secluded himself in his Sag Harbor home. He declined to see interviewers, although he was available, as always, to his close friends. In the early summer of 1967 he was in the hospital for the removal of a tumor that was diagnosed as benign. Later in the year he underwent a successful operation for a ruptured lumbar disk.

BORIS KARLOFF

Boris Karloff died in Midhurst, England, on February 2, 1969, at the age of eighty-one. The actor chilled millions in film and stage horror roles; and, thanks to television, his movies of the thirties and forties are a legacy of sorts that modern viewers can and do enjoy. It may astonish some of these to learn what he was like off camera.

WITHOUT uttering a single intelligible word, a gentle, amiable, obscure British-born actor achieved virtually instant motion-picture stardom, creating at the same time a genre from which he never truly escaped. The actor was Boris Karloff; the role was the Monster in *Frankenstein,* a Universal film of 1931; and the genre was that of the horror movie.

"*Frankenstein* transformed not only my life but also the film industry," he said later in his well-tailored voice. "It grossed something like $12 million on a $250,000 investment and started a cycle of so-called boy-meets-ghoul horror films."

Mr. Karloff appeared in many of these, including several extensions of his original triumph—*Bride of Frankenstein, Son of Frankenstein, House of Frankenstein,* and *Frankenstein 1970,* the last issued in 1958.

On the strength of his sensitive film portrayals—that Mr. Karloff was an elegant actor was sometimes overlooked—he went on to a triumph on Broadway as Jonathan Brewster, the zesty murderer, in Joseph Kesselring's *Arsenic and Old Lace* and as Mr. Darling and Captain Hook in James M. Barrie's *Peter Pan.*

But it was as a movie horror man that Mr. Karloff attained lasting celebrity. He looted graves in *The Body Snatchers,* wielded the ax as the leering executioner in *Tower of London,* frightened people to death in *The Walking Dead,* cheated death in *The Man They Could Not Hang,* invoked the curse of the pharaohs in *The Mummy,* was the sadistic prison warder in *Bedlam,* and corrupted Jackie Cooper as a narcotics peddler in *Young Donovan's Kid.*

Chance opened Mr. Karloff's path to stardom. He was forty-two years old and unrenowned ("I quit writing home—for I had nothing to write about") when he got his break one lunchtime in the Universal commissary.

Recalling the incident thirty years afterward, Mr. Karloff said: "Someone tapped me on the shoulder and said, 'Mr. Whale would like to see you at his table.' Jimmy Whale was the most important director on the lot. 'We're getting ready to shoot the Mary Shelley classic, *Frankenstein*, and I'd like you to test—for the part of the Monster,' Whale said.

"It was a bit shattering, but I felt that any part was better than no part at all. The studio's head make-up man, Jack Pierce, spent evenings experimenting with me. Slowly, under his skillful touch, the Monster's double-domed forehead, sloping brow, flattened Neanderthal eyelids, and surgical scars materialized. A week later I was ready for the test. I readily passed as a monster."

As the Monster, the soulless creation of Frankenstein from parts of human cadavers, Mr. Karloff wore make-up that took four hours to apply and that was excruciating to work in. Even so, he was initially so subordinate to the stars of the film, Colin Clive and Mae Clarke, that he was not invited to the premiere on December 6, 1931.

Nor when the film opened at the Mayfair in New York was Mr. Karloff especially remarked upon. For example, Mordaunt Hall's comment in *The New York Times* was spare. "Boris Karloff undertakes the Frankenstein creature," he wrote, "and his make-up can be said to suit anybody's demands."

The movie's producers believed at the time that their melodrama might be overly horrifying for young eyes, but it turned out that teenagers and even children found *Frankenstein* absorbing and Mr. Karloff fascinating. He became a folk hero in the tradition of Lon Chaney, the repellent Quasimodo in *The Hunchback of Notre Dame*. And he was responsible in part for the rise of two other horror actors—Bela Lugosi and Peter Lorre, with whom Mr. Karloff played in 1941 in an indifferent picture called *You'll Find Out*.

The Monster followed Mr. Karloff wherever he went. "On a motoring holiday in France, I lost my way," the actor once recalled. "In the dreadful remains of my schoolboy French, I inquired in a tiny village butchershop. The proprietor looked me in the face and exclaimed, 'Frankenstein's Monster!' That sort of thing has lasted for thirty years."

Not only did Monster fans send Mr. Karloff voodoo dolls, but he was also made the butt of a good deal of Hollywood gallows humor. For years Groucho Marx's standard greeting was, "How much do you charge to haunt a house?"

On a more serious professional level, J. B. Priestley almost rejected him for the part of the kindly Professor Linden in the 1947 production of *The Linden Tree*. "Good God, not Karloff!" Mr. Priestley told Maurice Evans, the producer. "Put his name up on the marquee and people will think my play is about an ax murder." Only Mr. Karloff's solemn assurance that he possessed inner tender sentiments persuaded the playwright to withdraw his objections.

Although the Monster type-cast the actor (it also made him wealthy) he insisted that he liked the role. "Favorite role?" he said in reply to an interviewer. "Frankenstein's Monster, I guess. He had no speech and hardly any intelligence, yet you had to convey a tragic part."

Mr. Karloff became an actor for want of a vocation as a diplomat. He was born William Henry Pratt in London November 23, 1887, the youngest of eight sons of Edward Pratt, a member of the British Indian Civil Service, and Eliza Sara Millard Pratt. His parents died when he was a child, and he was reared in serene circumstances by a stepsister and his elder brothers, who wanted him to enter the diplomatic service.

He began to veer from that objective when he was nine and acted the Demon King in a school play, Cinderella. He attended King's College, London, but so unnotably the family exported him to Canada in 1909. There he worked briefly as a farmhand and as a ditchdigger in Vancouver, British Columbia.

"Then one day in an old copy of *Billboard*," he recounted, "I came across the advertisement of a theatrical agent in nearby Seattle. His name was Kelly. I went to him and shamelessly told him I'd been in all the plays I'd ever seen. Two months later, while chopping trees, I received a brief note, 'Join Jean Russell Stock Company in Kamloops, B.C.—Kelly.' I left my ax sticking in a tree."

On the journey to Kamloops, the actor invented his stage name, taking the "Karloff" from a maternal relative and the "Boris" from thin air. He made his debut in Ferenc Molnar's *The Devil*, and from 1910 to 1916 he learned the acting profession in a series of stock companies that played western Canada and the United States.

"In some towns we stayed a week; in others we settled down for a run," he said. "It was in Minot, North Dakota, that we stayed fifty-three weeks and I played 106 parts. I was a quick study and the quickest study got the longest parts."

In 1917, Mr. Karloff found himself in Los Angeles and without funds, a state to which he had become inured as a stock player. He got a job piling sacks of flour in a storeroom. "Then I wandered into the movies, via a five-dollar-a-day extra role as a swarthy Mexican soldier in a Doug Fairbanks Sr. film, *His Majesty, the American*," Mr. Karloff recalled.

Between extra roles the actor drove a truck until his fortunes improved and he received some bit parts, mostly those of sweet and kindly characters. But what brought him to Mr. Whale's notice was his portrayal of Galloway, the convict-killer, in *The Criminal Code*.

Frankenstein was Hollywood's first monster film of any significance, and it was produced with some trepidation lest it might not pass the Hays office, the censorship agency of the time. Two endings were filmed, one faithful to the Gothic novel, in which Frankenstein died; another contrived, in which he lived. The second ending was ultimately used in order to elicit sympathy for the young scientist.

In both endings, however, the Monster was consumed in a crackling windmill fire that the villagers set. That awful mistake became quickly evident as Depression audiences flocked to see the film and demanded more of the Monster.

Hollywood's best brains proved equal to the contretemps, for drum-beaters for the sequel, *Bride of Frankenstein*, explained that the Monster had not actually been burned to death, but instead had fallen through the flaming floor into the cool waters of the millpond below.

"The watery opening scene was filmed with me wearing a rubber suit under my costume to ward off the chill," Mr. Karloff recalled. "But air got into the suit. When I was launched into the pond, my legs flew up in the air and I floated there like some sort of an obscene water lily while I, and everyone else, hooted with laughter. They finally fished me out with a boat hook and deflated me."

After ten years of Hollywood fun and games, Mr. Karloff was pleased to be able to make his New York stage debut at the Fulton Theater on January 10, 1941, in *Arsenic and Old Lace*. The Russel Crouse–Howard Lindsay production ran for 1,444 performances.

Appearing with Josephine Hull and Jean Adair, the two sweet and kindly Brewster sisters of Brooklyn who poison lonely old men, Mr. Karloff was their equally homicidal brother, whose victims' remains were scattered around the world. "As the evil one, Mr. Karloff moves quietly through the plot and poison without resorting to trickeries," Brooks Atkinson of *The Times* wrote in his notice of the comedy.

Mr. Karloff became almost as much attached to his stage role as to his film one, for he played Jonathan Brewster on the road for years, venturing as far afield as Alaska. As late as 1961 he was in a television revival of the play with Dorothy Stickney.

Following *Arsenic and Old Lace*, Mr. Karloff was a hit with Jean Arthur in *Peter Pan*. As Captain Hook he was a favorite with children in the audience.

"After the show," he said, "I'd corral as many [children] as my dressing room would hold and ask, 'Would you like to try on my hook?' Even little blond angels would reply, 'Yes, sir.'"

Mr. Karloff's professional life was enormously busy. He was in more than a hundred films and a dozen legitimate plays. In addition to the Frankenstein movies, he played such roles as James Lee Wong, the Chinese detective, and Dr. Fu Manchu in *The Mask of Fu Manchu*. His final film was *Targets*, released here last year, when he was eighty. In it he was the aged monarch of Hollywood shockers.

In private life, the actor was an affable, urbane six-footer with a wry sense of humor. In late life his hair was gray, as were his bushy eyebrows and his colonial mustache. He bore himself with impeccable dignity, and enjoyed watching cricket, rugby football, and field hockey, sports in which he had indulged as a younger man.

Mr. Karloff's first wife was Dorothy Stine, from whom he was divorced in 1946 after seventeen years of marriage. His second wife was Evelyn Hope Helmore, to whom he was married in 1946.

In his later years the actor lived in Cadogan Square, a fashionable area of London. At seventy-seven he carried on the traditions of trouper by acting in the film *The House at the End of the World*. It was a horror film, although he objected to the adjective.

"I never liked the word horror," he explained. "It should have been terror. They needed a word [in 1931] to describe what we were filming, but they just picked the wrong one.

"Horror means something revolting, but I don't think there's been anything revolting in the parts I've played.

"I believe in fear and excitement, in shock that emerges from the story, in terror—not horror."

JOHN L. LEWIS

John L. Lewis died in Washington on June 11, 1969, at the age of eighty-nine. A man of folkloric proportions, he was a giant of the American labor movement, especially in the 1930's, when his name helped to draw millions of workers into trade unions. His strengths and weaknesses are an essential part of our recent past, and his story, I believe, is well worth knowing something about.

For forty years, and especially during the turbulent 1930's, 1940's, and early 1950's, John Llewelyn Lewis, a pugnacious man of righteous wrath and rococo rhetoric, was a dominant figure in the American labor movement. He aspired to national political and economic power, but they both eluded his grasp except for fleeting moments. He nudged greatness as a labor leader only to end in isolation from the mainstream of trade unionism.

But in his headline years Mr. Lewis, with his black leonine mane, his snaggly reddish eyebrows and his outthrust-jaw stubbornness, was an idol without peer to millions of workers and the symbol of blackest malevolence to millions in the middle and upper classes.

Gruff and unsmiling in public, his broad-brimmed fedora tilted over his eyes, he reveled in the dramatic tensions he helped to create, and he sparkled whether he was in center stage or whether he was the deep stentorian voice from the wings. As the thunderer for labor he was unexcelled.

Starting in 1935, when coal was the country's kingpin fuel and he was president of the United Mine Workers of America, Mr. Lewis shattered the complacent craft-union American Federation of Labor by setting up the Committee for Industrial Organization to organize workers into single unions for each big industry. He went on to lead convulsive sitdown strikes, to humble the auto industry and Big Steel, to endorse and then to break bitterly with President Franklin D. Roosevelt, to defy the government in coal-mine disputes during World War II, to battle with President Harry S Truman in two coal strikes (in which Mr. Lewis was twice held in contempt of federal court and fined), to ease the way for mechanization of bituminous mining, and to pioneer in the establishment of a pension and welfare fund for his miners.

Once denounced for balking the authority of the government, he later received the Medal of Freedom, the highest civil honor the President can bestow. It was given him in 1964 as one of "the creators" in American life.

In the course of tumultuous labor politics, Mr. Lewis's wealthy and influential union left the American Federation of Labor and then rejoined it after leaving the Congress of Industrial Organizations, the successor to the Committee for Industrial Organization. Finally, Mr. Lewis took his union out of the AFL in the late 1940's, and went it alone. Although he wrote history for all labor, and with seldom a dull line, the mine union, which he ruled with fierce pride, held his steadiest focus.

Addressing the miners, he summed up his efforts in their behalf: "I have never faltered or failed to present the cause or plead the case of the mine workers of this country. I have pleaded your case not in the quavering tones of a mendicant asking alms, but in the thundering voice of the captain of a mighty host, demanding the rights to which free men are entitled."

Soot-smirched miners heeded Mr. Lewis without question. If he called for a shutdown, the pits were deserted. If he wanted the mines run on a three-day week, as he did during contract talks in 1949–50, that was the way they were operated. For their unswerving loyalty the miners received periodic wage increases, vacation pay, pensions at age sixty, pay for underground travel time, improved mine safety, and many other benefits. There was, however, little democracy within the union: Mr. Lewis did not like to have his judgments questioned or challenged.

In the larger context of American life, Mr. Lewis, by force of personality, was able to bend public officials to his will. Perhaps the most notable instance of this occurred during the sit-down strike in 1937 at General Motors plants in Flint, Michigan. The strikers had ignored an injunction to leave the factories, and Governor Frank Murphy was about to declare a state of insurrection and order the National Guard to evict the workers. The Governor took a copy of his order to Mr. Lewis in his Detroit hotel in an eleventh-hour effort to get him to end the strike.

After Mr. Lewis had refused, Mr. Murphy asked him what he would do if the Guard were called out. Following a suitable pause Mr. Lewis replied: "You want my answer, sir? I give it to you. Tomorrow morning,

I shall personally enter General Motors plant Chevrolet No. 4. I shall order the men to disregard your order. I shall then walk up to the largest window in the plant, open it, divest myself of my outer raiment, remove my shirt and bare my bosom. Then when you order your troops to fire, mine will be the first breast those bullets will strike.

"And as my body falls from that window to the ground, you listen to the voice of your grandfather [he had been hanged in Ireland by the British for rebellion] as he whispers in your ear, 'Frank, are you sure you are doing the right thing?' "

Color draining from his face and his body quivering, the Governor left the room. The order was not issued. The next day General Motors capitulated.

Mr. Lewis was also the master of the oblique approach, which he demonstrated in dealings with Myron Taylor, chairman of the United States Steel Corporation, in 1937. He charmed the industrialist by chatting with him in his Fifth Avenue mansion about Gothic tapestries and statuary. He flattered Mrs. Taylor. He also convinced Mr. Taylor, in a series of conversations, that Big Steel would be wise to recognize the Steel Workers Organizing Committee of the CIO. Mr. Taylor, in turn, persuaded other steelmen to deal with Mr. Lewis. The result was a stunning victory for the CIO.

A superb orator with a bass-baritone that could shake an auditorium without electrical amplification or that could be muted to a whisper audible in the last rows, Mr. Lewis swayed thousands of emotion-hungry audiences. Describing him in his prime, one observer said: "He can use his voice like a policeman's billy or like a monk at orisons. He can talk an assemblage into a state of eruption. He can translate a group of people into a pageant of misery and back again."

With mine operators in wage negotiations Mr. Lewis was equally effective. C. L. Sulzberger, in his Sit Down with John L. Lewis, related this episode from contract talks in the early thirties:

"Lewis began to walk up and down. Back and forth he went, deftly, stolidly, with a peculiar, light-footed stride, throwing his chest forward. He stuck a cigar in his mouth, folded his nubby hands behind him.

" 'Gentlemen,' he said, speaking in a slow, tricky way. 'Gentlemen, I speak to you for my people. I speak to you for the miners' families in the broad Ohio Valley, the Pennsylvania mountains and the black West Virginia hills.

" 'There, the shanties lean over as if intoxicated by the smoke fumes of the mine dumps. But the more pretentious ones boast a porch, with the banisters broken here and there, presenting the aspect of a snaggly tooth child. Some of the windows are wide open to flies, which can feast near by on garbage and answer the family dinner call in double quick time.

" 'But there is no dinner call. The little children are gathered around a bare table without anything to eat. Their mothers are saying "We want bread."

" 'They are not asking for more than a little. They are not asking for a $100,000 yacht like yours, Mr. ———,' suddenly pointing his threatening cigar, 'or for a Rolls-Royce limousine like yours, Mr. ———,' transfixing him with his bettle-browed gaze. 'A slim crust of bread . . .' "

The operators, according to Mr. Sulzberger's book, squirmed, and one of them muttered, "Tell him to stop. Tell him we'll settle."

On other contract occasions he could be more blunt. In 1949 talks, A. H. Raskin of *The New York Times* reported, Mr. Lewis intransigently told the chief negotiator for the operators:

"You need men and I have all the men and they are in the palm of my hand; and now I ask, 'What am I bid?' "

Many thought Mr. Lewis merely theatrical. In a sense he was, for his histrionics were in the grand manner; but when he was speaking from a position of strength there was nothing hollow about his acting. On the other hand, when he lacked public sympathy as in his court battles in the late forties—he tended to bombast.

Those who crossed Mr. Lewis discovered there was sting to his tongue. When, in 1939, John Nance Garner, then the Vice-President, took exception to some of the labor leader's views, Mr. Lewis called him "a labor-baiting, poker-playing, whiskey-drinking, evil old man."

Of William Green, the president of the AFL, he once said: "I have done a lot of exploring of Bill's mind and I give you my word there is nothing there."

He characterized Walter Reuther, head of the United Automobile Workers Union, as "an earnest Marxist chronically inebriated, I think, by the exuberance of his own verbosity."

George Meany, president of the AFL-CIO, was dismissed as "an honest plumber trying to abolish sin in the labor movement."

Mr. Lewis's showmanship sometimes tended to obscure his matchless fund of knowledge about coal production and marketing. In appearances before congressional committees he was the professor lecturing sophomores on fuel economics.

He was also exceedingly well read in the classics of English literature, in the Bible, in Napoleonic lore, in American history, and in labor-industry problems. His speeches and even his conversations were laced with literary allusions.

Mr. Lewis was often pictured as a radical, especially by those who opposed his type of trade unionism. Basically, however, Mr. Lewis's economic and political views tended to be conservative. A Republican in the twenties, he was twice considered for appointment as Secretary of Labor. He supported Roosevelt in 1936 and was on close personal terms with him until the outbreak of World War II in Europe in 1939, when, fearing American involvement, he switched to Wendell L. Willkie, the Republican leader. He later fell out with President Truman, and, although he never again became an ardent Republican, neither was he a stanch Democrat. He backed Democrats perfunctorily in 1956, 1960, and 1964.

Although much of the public may have equated Mr. Lewis with bellicosity, he was actually an amiable and courtly person, possessed of a nimble wit and a pleasant laugh. In private he was also gracious and conciliatory; he conversed congenially and temperately on a wide range of subjects; and he was hospitable, even to those with whom he disagreed.

"I am not disappointed about anything," he remarked toward the close of his active union leadership, when it was suggested that he had failed to exercise enduring labor and political influence. "When you see those editorials about me being a bitter, disappointed old man, just remember that I do my laughing in private."

Mr. Lewis, whose salary rose over the years to fifty thousand dollars a year plus expenses, was not a flashy liver. He had a modest, book-lined house on a quiet street in Alexandria, Virginia, and shunned most Washington parties.

Fastidious about the trim of his hair and his sartorial appearance, he had a fondness for well-tailored suits and excellent shirts and ties. He liked to travel in high-powered motor cars and he liked to lunch at the Sheraton-Carlton in Washington. But he passed up choice viands for meals of steak or roast beef and potatoes, topped off with banana cream pie, which accounted for his weight of 230 pounds in his earlier years. He occasionally sipped a glass of sherry or a weak highball for sociability's sake. He smoked Havana cigars, or sometimes chewed them unlighted.

John Lewis was born to the coal mines and to unionism. His father was Thomas Lewis, a miner who had emigrated from Wales to Lucas, Iowa. His mother, Louisa Watkins, was also Welsh and the daughter of a miner. John, their first child—there were in all six sons and two daughters—was born February 12, 1880, in Lucas.

For his role in a Knights of Labor strike Thomas Lewis was black-listed for several years; talk of militant trade unionism and of the miners' hazardous and besooted lot filled John's childhood.

The youngster left school after the seventh grade and was toiling in the mines at fifteen. In his leisure time he organized and managed both a debating and a baseball team. And he read, at first planlessly and then guided by Myrta Bell, the daughter of a Lucas physician, who became his wife in 1907.

But before that, when John was twenty-one, he left Lucas and wandered the West as a casual laborer for five years. He mined copper in Montana, silver in Utah, coal in Colorado, gold in Arizona. He also was one of the rescue squad in a Wyoming coal mine disaster in which 236 men were killed.

Returning to Lucas and a mine job, he was elected a delegate to the national convention of the United Mine Workers, which traced its history to 1849. It was his first step to union leadership. The next was to move to Panama, Illinois, with his five brothers, and in a year he was president of the local mine union.

Shortly he became Illinois lobbyist for the union and, in 1911, he was named general field agent for the AFL by Samuel Gompers, then its president. This gave him a chance to travel widely and to get to know the ins and outs of labor politics, of which Mr. Gompers was a master. One result was that Mr. Lewis built a large personal following in the mine union, for which he became chief statistician in 1917 and later that year vice-president. Two years later he was acting president, and president in 1920. He did not relinquish the office for forty years.

In World War I he sat on the National Defense Council, where he successfully opposed proposals for government operation of the mines. His first major confrontation with the government occurred in 1919 in a strike of four hundred thousand miners. It was denounced by President Woodrow Wilson, and Mr. Lewis sent his men back to the pits after the government obtained an injunction.

All through the twenties, Mr. Lewis worked to consolidate his power in the union and to enlarge its membership. He fought the operators on the one hand and the Communists on the other. He earned a reputation as a Red-baiter and for his imagination for "Moscow plots." He purged his union opponents from time to time on, it was said, flimsy charges.

His attitude toward the Communists softened in the thirties, when party members were among the most active organizers of the CIO. Chided, he retorted: "Industry should not complain if we allow Communists in our organization. Industry employs them."

The genesis of the CIO was in the plague years of the Depression, when unemployment mounted to 15 million workers. Union working and wage standards were toppled, and the AFL lost thousands of members, and with them its effectiveness. The mine union itself dropped to a hundred thousand members.

At the same time it became clearly evident that organization of workers by skilled crafts, which was the basis of the AFL, was unrealistic in most major industries, where unskilled or semiskilled workers constituted the bulk of employees. This situation led to the CIO's efforts to organize the unorganized.

That was made possible in part by Section 7A of the National Industrial Recovery Act, adopted in 1933 as part of President Roosevelt's attempt to reverse the Depression. Section 7A, often called Labor's Magna Carta, gave workers the right to organize and bargain collectively through representatives of their choice. It was Mr. Lewis who was chiefly instrumental in getting the section into the NIRA.

With its adoption he sent scores of organizers into the coal fields with the cry, "The President wants you to join the union," and in two years membership rose to four hundred thousand.

The CIO came into being after the AFL convention of 1935 in which tensions between industrial and craft unions erupted in a fist fight between William Hutcheson of the Carpenters Union and Mr. Lewis. Immediately the convention adjourned Mr. Lewis met to form the CIO with, among others, Charles P. Howard of the Typographical Union; David Dubinsky of the International Ladies Garment Workers Union; Max Zaritsky of the Hat, Cap and Millinery Workers; Thomas McMahon of the Textile Workers; and Sidney Hillman of the Amalgamated Clothing Workers.

Subsequently these and other unions backing the CIO were expelled from the AFL, but it was an empty gesture, for, virtually from the outset, workers responded to the CIO campaigns in the basic industries. First autos capitulated, then Big Steel, then others until 4 million workers were enrolled in CIO unions. But the steady procession of successes was interrupted in late 1937 by Little Steel, the smaller fabricators, and especially by Tom Girdler of Republic Steel.

The Little Steel strike, an old-fashioned walkout, was marked by violence. In Chicago on Memorial Day the police shot and killed ten strikers and sympathizers, and there was sporadic shooting elsewhere. In the course of the strike, which was lost, President Roosevelt was asked what he thought of the dispute. "A plague on both your houses," he replied, a remark that enraged Mr. Lewis, whose union had contributed $500,000—$120,000 as an outright gift—to the President's 1936 campaign. His retort was: "It ill behooves one who has supped at labor's table and who has been sheltered in labor's house to curse with equal fervor and fine impartiality both labor and its adversaries when they become locked in deadly embrace."

Mr. Lewis followed this excoriation with others equally acerbic in the campaign of 1940, in which he sought to rally organized labor against Mr. Roosevelt's third-term bid. "Sustain me now, or repudiate me," he said in accusing the President of Caesarism. After Mr. Roosevelt won the election, Mr. Lewis resigned as head of what was then the Congress of Industrial Organizations, and Philip Murray, a Lewis lieutenant, took over. In 1942, however, Mr. Lewis broke with Mr. Murray, his "former friend," and the mine union left the CIO.

Mr. Lewis's period of greatest national influence, waning since 1940, concluded at that point. But from 1935 to 1942, when he symbolized the CIO, his name brought millions into the ranks of organized labor. Its magical incantation seemed to these workers to offer the promise of higher wages, better working conditions, union recognition. The name stirred hopes among those who toiled in textile mills, in rubber and tire factories, on the docks, in brass foundries, in ship building, in glass works, in garment and glove shops, and even on the farms.

Mr. Lewis, at that time, was larger than life. But his charisma was diminished after he quit the CIO.

Four years later he and his union were back in the AFL, but their stay lasted less than two years. Again there was a battle of words, this time over a provision of the Taft-Hartley Act requiring union officials to swear they were not Communists. The AFL was willing to comply with the act, Mr. Lewis was not. To him the law was "damnable, vicious, unwholesome, and a slave statute." As for the AFL, it has "no head, its neck just growed and haired over." The mine union then went its independent way.

Meantime, Mr. Lewis was tangling with the government. A series of wartime strikes won substantial wage increases, including portal-to-portal (or underground travel-time) pay for the miners.

Then in the spring of 1946 he called a soft-coal strike in a bid for royalties on each ton of coal mined, the money to go into the union's health and welfare fund. President Truman ordered the mines seized, and the strike ended on May 29 with a wage increase and a royalty arrangement. A hard-coal strike followed almost immediately, but it ended quickly on just about the same terms as were obtained in the bituminous fields.

Peace, however, was short-lived. In November Mr. Lewis denounced the contract under which the government had been running the mines. Quickly, on motion of the government, Federal Judge T. Alan Goldsborough issued an order restraining Mr. Lewis from maintaining the contract-termination notice. President Truman ordered the Justice Department to seek a contempt citation if Mr. Lewis disobeyed the court. And when the union chief made no move to halt the walkout, the judge found him and the union guilty of civil and criminal contempt. A fine of $10,000 was imposed on Mr. Lewis and $3.5 million on the union, despite his oration to the court.

Three days later, Mr. Lewis sent the miners back to work pending an appeal of the contempt ruling to the Supreme Court. In a seven-to-two decision in March 1947, that tribunal upheld the contempt judgment and the fine against Mr. Lewis. The fine against the union was reduced, however, to $700,000, with $2.8 million more to be assessed if a strike occurred during the government's operation of the mines. Mr. Lewis complied with the court and purged himself and the union of contempt.

In 1948, after the government had returned the mines to the operators, Mr. Lewis was once again in court. The miners were idle in a pension dispute, and Judge Goldsborough ordered Mr. Lewis and the union to end the walkout. He declined and was fined $20,000 and the union $1.4 million. The fines were eventually paid.

At the mine union convention in 1948, Mr. Lewis stormed against Mr. Truman for persecuting the union. "He is a man totally unfitted for the position," Mr. Lewis said of the President. "His principles are elastic. He is careless with the truth. He is a malignant, scheming sort of individual who is dangerous not only to the United Mine Workers but dangerous to the United States of America."

He added that Mr. Truman had been "too cowardly" to put him in jail.

The two men composed their differences before the end of Mr. Truman's tenure, and in 1952 the President reversed a ruling of his Wage Stabilization Board to permit a wage increase that Mr. Lewis had negotiated for the miners.

As a result of the royalty fees that Mr. Lewis negotiated with the mine operators, his union initiated a pension program in 1948. This became a model for other unions. He also built a number of hospitals in the coal areas, but these were less successful than the welfare and pension arrangement. Some were obliged to close and others were sold.

By his flair for dramatizing the problems of his miners Mr. Lewis also won a long struggle for federal mine inspection in 1952. When 119 miners perished in the West Frankfort, Illinois, mine explosion in 1951, he flew to the scene, inspected the shafts, and assailed Congress for failing to enact safety legislation. In dramatic testimony before a

Senate subcommittee, he called on Congress to give the federal government power to close unsafe mines.

The Federal Mine Safety Law was enacted. It set up a board of review of which the union's safety director was a member. To ensure its passage, Mr. Lewis called a ten-day "memorial" stoppage.

In 1953 Mr. Lewis was powerful enough to block President Dwight D. Eisenhower's choice of J. B. Lyon as director of the Bureau of Mines. The fight brought out that Mr. Lyon had a five-thousand-dollar-a-year pension from the Anaconda Copper Mining Company, had no experience in coal mining, and was opposed to the safety law.

In the fifties coal lost its dominance as a fuel. Oil and gas became competitive. To meet the crisis Mr. Lewis cooperated with the mine operators in introducing mechanization into coal production. This made it possible in 1952, for example, for 375,000 bituminous miners to produce more coal than double that number could have dug thirty years before.

He also convinced the operators that it was wise to close uneconomic mines and pay high wages in the efficient ones. This was done quietly, in contrast to his former tactics, and by 1955 the miners' daily scale was $20.25—well above the standard in other mass industries. When he stepped down as union chief in 1960 the scale was $24.25 a day. By that time the welfare and pension fund had collected $1.3 billion, had a reserve of $130 million, and had aided more than a million persons. Miners were enabled to retire at sixty with a pension of $100 a month. In 1960, a total of 70,000 were receiving these retirement benefits.

In the last years of the fifties Mr. Lewis clamped down on unauthorized strikes. Laying down the law at the union convention of 1956, he warned fractious miners that "you'll be fully conscious that I'm breathing down your necks" if they struck.

When he announced late in 1959 that he was preparing to retire, the operators expressed regret. They praised him both for his "outstanding ability" and as "an extraordinarily fine person."

In his farewell address to his union he said: "The years have been long and the individual burdens oppressive, yet progress has been great.

"At first, your wages were low, your hours long, your labor perilous, your health disregarded, your children without opportunity, your union weak, your fellow citizens and public representatives indifferent to your wrongs.

"Today, because of your fortitude and your deep loyalty to your union, your wages are the highest in the land, your working hours the lowest, your safety more assured, your health more guarded, your old age protected, your children equal in opportunity with their generation, and your union strong with material resources."

He retired on an annual pension of fifty thousand dollars and was voted the title of president emeritus. He remained chairman of the welfare and retirement fund to his death.

He lived alone, except for a housekeeper, in the boyhood home of Robert E. Lee. His wife died in 1942 and his daughter Kathryn died in 1962. A son John, a physician, lives in nearby Baltimore.

WESTBROOK PEGLER

Westbrook Pegler died in Tucson, Arizona, on June 24, 1969, at the age of seventy-four. Possessed of one of the most vituperative typewriters in the business, the columnist lived off his hates. And more than most, he shared his dislikes with his readers, which gave him a certain fascination for me.

IN TWENTY-NINE years as a newspaper columnist—from 1933 to 1962— Westbrook Pegler established a reputation as the master of the vituperative epithet. There was scarcly a public figure who sooner or later was not included in his pantheon of malign and malicious individuals.

He roared in print against President Franklin D. Roosevelt, referring to him as a "feeble-minded fuehrer" and as "Moosejaw," and saying: "It is regrettable that Giuseppe Zangara hit the wrong man when he shot at Roosevelt in Miami."

Mr. Pegler had in mind an assassination attempt in 1933, in which Mayor Anton Cermak of Chicago was killed.

Mrs. Roosevelt was labeled "La Boca Grande," the big mouth, and, after her husband's death in 1945, she was consistently called "the widow Roosevelt."

To Mr. Pegler, President Harry S Truman was "a thin-lipped hater," an abuse that Mr. Truman returned in kind by describing the columnist as "a guttersnipe."

For eleven years, until 1944, Mr. Pegler's column, "Fair Enough," appeared in the New York *World-Telegram*, a Scripps-Howard paper, and newspapers throughout the country to which it was syndicated. His articles in 1940 exposing labor union racketeering won him a Pulitzer Prize.

These articles dealt with, among others, George Scalise, president of the Building Service Employes International Union in New York. In the resulting official scrutiny of his affairs, Scalise was sent to Sing Sing prison for ten to twenty years for forgery and embezzlement. Scalise complained that he had been "Peglerized."

At the same time, in California, Willie Bioff, a movie union leader and convicted procurer, and other corrupt unionists were sent to jail after Mr. Pegler's newspaper exposures of their activities.

James Westbrook Pegler came of a newspaper family. He was born August 2, 1894, in Minneapolis, the son of Arthur James Pegler, who was credited with being an originator of the staccato "Hearst style" of writing a news article. The elder Pegler was later dismissed for a time from the Hearst organization for remarking that a Hearst newspaper resembled "a screaming woman running down the street with her throat cut."

Young Pegler entered the newspaper business in 1910 as a ten-dollar-a-week employee of the United Press in Chicago. "Bud," as he was called in those days, was described as "a raw kid, as freckled as a guinea egg."

His career was interrupted for two years of high school, before the United Press sent him first to St. Louis and then to Texas as a bureau manager. In 1916, he joined the press agency's staff in London as a foreign correspondent.

When the United States entered World War I, Mr. Pegler enlisted in the Navy and served until the close of the conflict. On his return to the United States, he became a sportswriter for U.P. because, he said, he had noticed that "the big salaries in newspapers usually were paid to sports men." And, at the urging of Floyd Gibbons, the war correspondent, he changed his byline from J. W. Pegler to Westbrook Pegler.

As a sportswriter, Mr. Pegler developed a tough and rowdy way of presenting events, much in contrast to the prevailing style of coverage. It made him stand out, as did his choice of funny or fantastic events to describe.

In 1925, Mr. Pegler went to work for the Chicago *Tribune*, writing, for $250 a week, a daily sports story that was syndicated around the country. On dull days he wrote about other topics, and this edged him by degrees into becoming a columnist of national affairs.

His first column, in December 1933, created a sensation for its defense of lynching. "As one member of the rabble," it began, "I will admit that I said, 'Fine, that is swell,' when the papers came up that day, telling of the lynching of two men who killed the young fellow in California, and that I haven't changed my mind yet for all the storm of rightmindedness which has blown up since."

He survived the resulting public criticism, although he began to lose the friendship of many of his newspaper friends, including Heywood Broun, a fellow columnist, who called Mr. Pegler "the light-heavyweight champion of the upperdog."

In the early days of the New Deal, Mr. Pegler was a supporter of President Roosevelt, but his attitude changed after 1936 to one of excoriation. Mr. Roosevelt was assailed for his proposal to increase the size of the Supreme Court, for welfare legislation, for his appointees, and then for a host of other actions.

Other New and Fair Dealers came out of Mr. Pegler's typewriter no less scathed. Vice-President Henry A. Wallace was "Old Bubblehead"; Assistant Secretary of State A. A. Berle Jr. was a "blood-thirsty bull twirp"; Justice Felix Frankfurter of the Supreme Court was a "fatuous windbag"; Fiorello H. La Guardia, the reform Mayor of New York, was "the little padrone of the Bolsheviki."

Not even J. Edgar Hoover, director of the Federal Bureau of Investigation, was immune. "A nightclub fly-cop" was how Mr. Pegler characterized him.

Those on the periphery of public life also felt the rasp of the columnist's displeasure. Elsa Maxwell, the party-giver, came to be called "a professional magpie," and Walter Winchell, a fellow columnist, was dismissed as "a gents-room journalist."

Mr. Pegler's style was free-swinging. He pictured himself as the average man, quick to wrath and slow to cool off. For this purpose he invented "George Spelvin, American," into whose mouth he placed a good deal of his lurid prose. One example was this attack on Harold L. Ickes, the New Deal Secretary of the Interior: "Hey, Ickes, you penny-ante moocher, tell us about the two times you put yourself away in the Naval Hospital in Washington for three dollars a day all contrary to law, and you a rich guy able to pay your way in regular hospitals as all other sick civilians have to do. Why you cheap sponger, you couldn't rent a hall room in a pitcher-and-bowl fleabag in Washington for three bucks a day. You know who paid the overhead on your hospital bargain, don't you? Well, I did! And George Spelvin. We paid it."

Mr. Pegler's irascibility was aroused not only by persons and institutions he considered malevolent, subversive, Communist, or traitorous, but also by natural phenomena that caused him discomfort. In this vein, he once fulminated against a rainstorm that kept him housebound in Connecticut for several days.

Switching to the Hearst-owned King Features Syndicate in 1944, Mr. Pegler changed the name of his column to "As Pegler Sees It." At one time it appeared in 186 papers, but by 1962 the total was down to 140.

Toward the end, Mr. Pegler was being edited in ways he disliked. The word "Ford's" was removed from "Ford's Fund for the Republic." An attack on former President Dwight D. Eisenhower and Henry R. Luce of *Time* magazine was killed as was a column that began, "There is something wormy about our State Department."

Mr. Pegler also attacked members of the Hearst organization by name, including William Randolph Hearst Jr.; Frank Conniff, the national editor, and Bob Considine, the reporter and columnist. This was evidently too much, for Mr. Pegler's contract was terminated on the ground that "too many irreconcilable differences on vital matters have existed between the parties to continue a workable relationship."

The break apparently came when some of Mr. Pegler's unflattering references to the Kennedy administration were blue-penciled. In a speech in 1962 to a Christian Crusade meeting in Tulsa, Oklahoma, Mr. Pegler told the ultraconservative organization: "Much of our daily press is now under a coercion as nasty and snarling and menacing as Hitler's was in the first year of his reign. I will not speak of other newspapers, but of recent alarming experiences in the Hearst organization.

"I received insolent, arrogant warnings from King Features that nothing unfavorable to the Kennedy administration or offensive to any member of the Kennedy family will be allowed out of New York where the censors sit."

Earlier, however, Mr. Pegler had caused the Hearst organization embarrassment and the loss of money in a libel suit brought by Quentin Reynolds, the writer and an old friend. In 1949 Mr. Pegler wrote, among other things, that Mr. Reynolds had "a yellow streak for all to see" and that he had once been seen "nuding along a road with a wench in the raw." He also implied that the former war correspondent held leftist political views.

In the resulting trial, in which Louis Nizer represented Mr. Reynolds, Mr. Pegler conceded that 130 statements he had made about Mr. Reynolds were not the truth. Mr. Reynolds was awarded $175,001 in damages against the columnist, the Hearst Corporation, and Hearst Consolidated Publications.

At one point during the trial in 1954 Mr. Nizer stepped up to Mr. Pegler on the witness stand to show him a document. "Stand down there where you belong," ordered Mr. Pegler, pointing to the counsel tables.

"Please, Mr. Pegler," Federal Judge Edward Weinfeld interposed, "I'm running this courtroom. Don't tell counsel where to go."

After the trial Mr. Pegler's influence tended to wane. He also moved perceptibly to the right. Following his break with King Features, he wrote a monthly article for two years for *American Opinion*, the organ of the John Birch Society.

In one article, according to Oliver Pilat, who wrote a critical biography of Mr. Pegler, the columnist "developed an entirely new contention that Americans with Jewish names who came from countries like Russia and Poland were instinctively sympathetic to Communism, however outwardly respectable they appeared."

Mr. Pegler gave up writing for the Birch publication when it rejected a piece he wrote about Chief Justice Earl Warren in 1964.

Mr. Pegler was quite candid about his hates, which multiplied with the years. "For myself, I will say that my hates always occupied my mind much more actively and have given me greater spiritual satisfaction," he once remarked.

Nonetheless, he could and did turn out an occasional humorous column, or one that was a deft piece of reminiscence or one that created an emotional impact for its hard-boiled treatment of a sentimental subject. Or he could be self-critical. One New Year's Day column, for instance, consisted of "I will never mix gin, beer, and whiskey again" repeated fifty times.

At the start of his career as a columnist Mr. Pegler was a tall, slim, handsome man. But with the years he put on weight and extra chins and a fierce mien. He also developed a brusqueness of manner that put off those who sought to befriend him.

Mr. Pegler married three times. He met his first wife, Mrs. Julia Harpman Pegler, when she was a reporter for the New York *Daily News*. Their marriage in 1922 culminated a two-year romance. She died in Rome in 1955 at the age of sixty-one. During most of their married life, the Peglers lived in New York or Connecticut.

He married Mrs. Pearl W. Doane in 1959. They were divorced shortly afterward. His third wife was Maud Towart of Cannes, France, whom he married in 1961 after he moved to Tucson. Mr. Pegler had no children.

SIDNEY J. WEINBERG

Sidney J. Weinberg died in New York on July 23, 1969, at the age of seventy-seven. A kewpie doll of a man with an extraordinarily fast mind for figures, he typified Wall Street to itself and to that part of the country involved in finance. He was not a national name (how many investment bankers are these days?), but he was a powerful insider and richly entitled to the obit space he got.

A TART-TONGUED man whose formal education ended with eighth grade, Sidney J. Weinberg was one of the most sought-after wizards in the intricate world of corporate financing and merging.

Partner in Goldman, Sachs & Co., one of Wall Street's leading investment banking houses, Mr. Weinberg was an acknowledged oracle— in such demand that at one time he sat on thirty-one boards of directors, most of them the bluest of the blue-chip companies.

While he was earning the sobriquet "Mr. Wall Street," he was also serving as an unofficial adviser to five Presidents. Franklin D. Roosevelt nicknamed him "The Politician" as a tribute to his knack for getting things done. Mr. Weinberg also counseled Harry S Truman, Dwight D. Eisenhower, John F. Kennedy, and Lyndon B. Johnson.

The most succinct (and probably one of the most accurate) testimonial to Mr. Weinberg's abilities was written when he was sixteen years old and leaving Public School 13 in Brooklyn.

"To whom it may concern," his teacher's letter read:

"It gives me great pleasure to testify to the business ability of the bearer, Sidney Weinberg.

"He is happy when he is busy, and being always ready and willing to oblige, we believe he will give satisfaction to anyone who may need his services."

Typically, Mr. Weinberg not only was busy but also gave satisfaction in two notable Wall Street deals. One was the sale in 1956 of $650 million worth of Ford Motor Company stock for the Ford Foundation.

It was the largest corporate-financing project in history up to that time. The sale, arranged in the greatest secrecy, took more than two years to bring off, and it earned its architect a fee estimated at $1 million. Describing Mr. Weinberg's feat in the *New Yorker* in 1966, E. J. Kahn Jr. wrote:

"Although others naturally had a hand in the proceedings, the immense chore of reorganizing the Ford Company's entire financial setup was left pretty much up to him. The big problem was to get all hands to agree on how much money the Ford family should get for transferring part of their voting rights in the company to the shares the Foundation wanted to sell.

"Although the Foundation owned more than 88 percent of all Ford shares, with Ford directors, officers, and employees owning nearly 2 percent more, these shares were all of the nonvoting variety; every bit of the voting power, which meant direction of the company's affairs, was vested in the remaining 10 percent, and this was owned by the Ford family.

"The New York Stock Exchange would not accept Ford stock for trading unless it had voting power, and voting power was just what the Foundation's trustees were powerless to convey without the cooperation of the Fords.

"As Weinberg set about his assignment, he could see that any plan he devised would have to be acceptable to the Ford family, to the Foundation's trustees, to the New York Stock Exchange, and to the Internal Revenue Service. The last party was a far from inconsiderable one, since if it should rule that whatever benefits the Ford family got out of the deal weren't tax-free, the Fords wouldn't be interested, and if the Foundation's tax-exempt status should be questioned, it wouldn't be interested.

"Weinberg prepared some fifty-odd reorganization plans; under the one that was finally approved by all parties, the Ford family increased its equity in the company by 1.74 percent—which, reckoned in terms of the stock's value on the day it was marketed, amounted to a paper gain of nearly $60 million."

Of all the securities packages that he had a hand in marketing, Mr. Weinberg was proudest of his Ford accomplishments. Afterward, he joined the company's board and at one time held three thousand shares of its stock.

His second outstanding financing success occurred in 1958, when he was the underwriter for $350 million of Sears, Roebuck debentures. The largest company debt offering to that time, it was floated in a bond market so soft that some financiers doubted that the issue would sell at all. Mr. Weinberg, however, judged the acquisitive temper of the market correctly by offering the debentures at a price to yield 4.75 percent, slightly above comparable offerings.

Mr. Weinberg's securities flotations, his directorships (they totaled thirty-five over a lifetime), his network of friendships, and his intimate government jobs) made him one of the most powerful men in Wall links with Washington (he saw to it that some of his friends got high Street.

He was not, however, the richest by any means. Many of his financing fees went to Goldman, Sachs. About his personal fortune, he was close-mouthed.

Mr. Weinberg hustled his way to eminence from slum beginnings. The third of eleven children of Pincus Weinberg, Sidney James was born on October 12, 1891, in the Red Hook section of Brooklyn. His father was a wholesale liquor dealer of such modest means that his son was obliged to fend for himself as soon as he was graduated from grammar school.

By that time, however, he was already somewhat familiar with Wall Street, having been a summer runner at thirteen for a brokerage house. This career was cut short because he got similar jobs with two other brokers, and when his triplicity was discovered all three employers discharged him.

After graduation, the young man worked briefly as "a flower and feather horse," a boy who delivered millinery goods, for two dollars a week. But when the Panic of 1907 broke, he realized that there was more money to be made—as much as five dollars a day—standing on line for depositors in the run on the Trust Company of America.

In November of that year, after taking a course in penmanship, the youth joined the financial community for life by getting a job as assistant to the janitor at Goldman, Sachs, then at 43 Exchange Place. Mr. Weinberg liked to recall that he canvassed the building from the top down, inquiring of each company if it wanted a boy, until he was hired.

Then a pioneer in financing industrial corporations, Goldman, Sachs seemed ill suited to a lowly employee who delighted in putting tacks on the chairs of company clerks. Mr. Weinberg, however, had other qualities, which started to come to light in 1909 through chance.

One day he was told to deliver a flagstaff to the home of Paul Sachs, one of the partners. After taking the eight-foot pole uptown in a trolley car, young Weinberg knocked at Mr. Sachs's door and was greeted by the partner himself. Demonstrating a knack for becoming friendly with men in a position to help him, the youth impressed Mr. Sachs with his energy and his brightness. Mr. Sachs urged him to persevere in Wall Street and to go to night school.

Nonetheless, his promotions were slow, and he resigned in 1917 to enlist in the Navy. Although he was underweight and nearsighted and stood only five feet four inches tall, he persuaded the recruiting officer to accept him as an assistant cook, a rating of which he was ever after proud.

After a few weeks the Navy felt it could dispense with his cookery and shifted him to Intelligence, where his talents as an organizer and his innate gregariousness were utilized in inspecting cargoes at the port of Norfolk, Virginia.

Returning to civilian life, Mr. Weinberg was re-employed by Goldman, Sachs as a trader in the bond department. In a short time, he was doing most of the work on one corporate-financing job after another. He was so astute in his pricing recommendations that he was given participation in the profits. That started at one eighth of 1 percent, and by 1930, when he became a senior partner, it reached 33⅓ percent.

In April 1925, Mr. Weinberg bought a seat on the New York Stock Exchange for $104,000. Twenty months later he became a partner in his firm, making a $100,000 capital contribution to it.

Mr. Weinberg always stressed that the money came from his own income. "It was my money, which I earned," he said proudly in an interview two years ago. "None of it was from trading."

"I never traded," he added. "I'm an investment banker. I don't shoot craps. If I had been a speculator and taken advantage of what I knew, I could have five times as much as I have today."

Nonetheless, he grew so accustomed to money in the millions that he once told a visitor, "Money? Keeps coming in all the time, and hardly means anything at all."

The investment banker had a close call in the financial crash of 1929 and the Depression. This came about through the Goldman, Sachs Trading Corporation, an investment trust that Goldman, Sachs set up in 1928 and of which Mr. Weinberg was the treasurer.

The trading company was brought to market at $104 a share. Its price soared to $326 and then it tumbled in the crash to $1.75, wiping out hundreds of investors in the process.

One of the losers was Eddie Cantor, the comedian, who made Goldman, Sachs the butt of some of his most biting humor. In one joke, Mr. Cantor would show up with a stooge who tried to squeeze juice from a dry lemon. "Who are you?" the comedian would ask, and the stooge, quick as a flash, would respond, "The margin clerk for Goldman, Sachs." It was a sure laugh-getter.

Mr. Cantor compounded his wit by suing Goldman, Sachs for

$100,000; it was one of a score of legal actions that the company had to contest. The partners also had to confront their own losses, an aggregate of $12 million.

Ultimately, Mr. Weinberg was able to work the company's way out of the fiasco and liquidate the investment trust by selling its assets to Floyd Odlum's Atlas Corporation, which later sold them at a profit.

Mr. Weinberg's explanation for his association with the trust was simple. "I just wasn't very bright," he said. He offered the same explanation a few years later, when the president of McKesson & Robbins, a drug house on whose board Mr. Weinberg was sitting, was found to have defrauded the company of $21 million.

Mr. Weinberg's triumphs far outnumbered his lapses of judgment. In fact, his success as a corporate financier was credited in the 1930's and 1940's with having helped to restore investor confidence in Wall Street.

Part of this was said to be Mr. Weinberg's presence on company boards. Save for the hoodwinking to which he was subjected by the McKesson & Robbins president, Mr. Weinberg was an extraordinarily keen-minded director. He could be counted upon to have a mastery of the company he served and a keen eye for its stockholders' welfare.

One example of this was described in Mr. Kahn's article. "In the winter of 1954," he wrote, "when the Lambert Company (Listerine), of which he was then a director, was considering an invitation to merge with Warner-Hudnut (Sloan's Liniment and cosmetics), his fellow officials in the concern voted to leave all the negotiations up to him.

"The merger went through, resulting in a new firm called the Warner-Lambert Pharmaceutical Company, but not before Weinberg worked out a deal highly advantageous to his side: each share of Warner-Hudnut, which had been worth $36 when the bargaining began, could be exchanged for one share in the new company, but so could each share of Lambert, which had been worth only $28."

Something of a wag, Mr. Weinberg was not always reverent toward industrialists and corporations. Citing Mr. Weinberg's sense of humor, Mr. Kahn's *New Yorker* article related this incident:

"Shortly after he was elected a director of General Electric, he was called upon by Philip D. Reed, the chairman of its board, to address a flock of company officials at a banquet in the Waldorf-Astoria.

"In presenting Weinberg, Reed said that he was sure that the new director would have some interesting and penetrating remarks to make about GE, and that he hoped that Mr. Weinberg felt, as he felt, that GE was the greatest outfit in the greatest industry in the greatest country in the world.

"Weinberg rose—or, at any rate, got to his feet. 'I'll string along

·with your chairman about this being the greatest country,' he began. 'And I guess I'll even buy that about the electrical industry being a pretty fair industry. But as to GE's being the greatest business in the field, I'm damned if I will commit myself until I've had a look-see.'

"Then he sat down to vehement applause, which was probably occasioned not only by his brevity but by his brashness."

Mr. Weinberg's plain talk was no bar to his directorships. Among the thirty-five concerns in whose board rooms he sat—in addition to General Electric, Sears, Roebuck, and Ford—were National Dairy Products (now Kraftco), B. F. Goodrich, Continental Can, General Foods, McKesson & Robbins, Cluett Peabody, Corinthian Broadcasting and General Cigar. At his death he was a director of only two companies— Ford and Corinthian.

Mr. Weinberg was fanatically loyal to his companies' products. When he was living in Scarsdale, New York, from 1923 until a couple of years ago, when he moved into the Sherry-Netherland, his house was stuffed with Kraft cheese (to which he professed himself extremely partial) as well as with hundreds of other boons of his directorships. He even switched to Ford-made cars when he became a Ford director.

An "independent Democrat" and "practical liberal," Mr. Weinberg entered politics in 1932 by working for Mr. Roosevelt's election. Almost immediately he began an intimate association with the White House that continued until this year.

At President Roosevelt's suggestion in 1933 he organized the Business Council, through which businessmen could present their views to the government.

He was assistant director of the War Production Board in World War II and special assistant in the Office of Defense Mobilization in the Korean conflict. He was also chairman of the balance of payments advisory committee of the Commerce Department and a member of a Treasury Department liaison committee.

In 1936, after helping finance Mr. Roosevelt's second campaign, Mr. Weinberg was offered the ambassadorship to the Soviet Union. He turned it down after his wife said she was unwilling to have their two sons tutored abroad. Mr. Weinberg also told his friends that he had declined "because I don't speak Russian, so who the hell could I talk to over there?"

Mr. Weinberg detoured from the New and Fair Deals in 1952 to help raise $1.7 million for General Eisenhower's campaign. His fund-raising technique, mostly personal solicitation in his rasping voice, was abrupt. According to his friend John Hay Whitney, the financier and newspaper and radio proprietor, "Sidney is the best money-getter I've ever seen. He'll go to one of his innumerable board meetings—General Foods, General Electric, or General Whatnot—and make no bones about telling everybody there what he wants. Then he'd say, 'Come on, boys, where is it?'—and up it comes."

Mr. Weinberg's influence in the two Eisenhower administrations was conceded to be enormous. He was also a power at the White House with President Kennedy, who called on him for advice on tax proposals and for help in putting together Comsat, the Communications Satellite Corporation.

In 1964 he helped form a Johnson-for-President group and later recommended John T. Connor and Henry H. Fowler to the President. Mr. Connor became Secretary of Commerce and Mr. Fowler Secretary of the Treasury. Mr. Weinberg's only campaign loser was Hubert H. Humphrey, for whom he raised money in 1968.

MIES VAN DER ROHE

Mies van der Rohe died in Chicago on August 17, 1969, at the age of eighty-three. More than to any other architect of our time, we owe to Mies the glassy skyscrapers and sleek-walled buildings of twentieth-century cities. His style, which was widely (if not always well) copied, was the product of a mind that knew exactly what it was doing.

LUDWIG MIES VAN DER ROHE, a man without any academic architectural training, was one of the great artist-architect-philosophers of his age, acclaimed as a genius for his uncompromisingly spare design, his fastidiousness, and his innovations.

Along with Frank Lloyd Wright and Le Corbusier, the German-born master builder who was universally known as Mies (pronounced mees) fashioned scores of structures expressing the spirit of the industrial twentieth century.

"Architecture is the will of an epoch translated into space," he remarked in a talkative moment. And pressed to explain his own paradigmatic role—a matter on which he was shy, as he was on most others—he said: "I have tried to make an architecture for a technological society. I have wanted to keep everything reasonable and clear—to have an architecture that anybody can do."

A building, he was convinced, should be "a clear and true statement of its times"—cathedrals for an age of pathos, glass and metal cages for an age of advanced industrialism.

He thought the George Washington Bridge in New York an outstanding example of a structure expressing its period, and he used to go to admire it whenever he visited the city. "It is the most modern building in the city," he remarked in 1963. He was fond of the bridge because he considered it beautifully proportioned and because it did not conceal its structure. Mies liked to see the steel, the brick, the concrete of buildings show themselves rather than be concealed by ornamentation. A twentieth-century industrial building had to be pithy, he believed.

Mies's stature rested not only on his lean yet sensuous business and residential buildings but also on the profound influence he exerted on his colleagues and on public taste. As the number of his structures multiplied in the years since World War II and as their stunning individuality became apparent, critical appreciation flowed to him in torrents, and his designs and models drew throngs to museums where they were exhibited. It became a status symbol to live in a Mies house, work in a Mies building—or even to visit one.

The Mies name had already been established among architects long before he came to the United States in 1937. In 1919 and 1921 in Berlin he designed two steel skyscrapers sheathed in glass from street to roof. Although never built, the designs are now accepted as the origin of today's glass-and-metal skyscrapers.

In 1922 he introduced the concept of ribbon windows, uninterrupted bands of glass between the finished faces of concrete slabs, in a design for a German office building. It has since become the basis for many commercial structures.

Mies, in 1924, produced plans for a concrete villa that is now regarded as the forerunner of the California ranch house. He is also said to have previsioned the return of the inner patio of Roman times in an exhibition house built in 1931; to have started the idea of space dividers, the use of cabinets or screens instead of walls to break up interiors; and to have originated the glass house, with windows and glass sliding panels extending from floor to ceiling that permit outside greenery to form the visual boundaries of a room.

Apart from simplicity of form, what struck students of Mies's buildings was their painstaking craftsmanship, their attention to detail. "God is in the details," he liked to say. In this respect the buildings reflected the man, for Mies was fussy about himself. A large, lusty man with the massive head of a Dutch burgher topping a five-foot, ten-inch frame, he dressed in exquisitely hand-stitched suits of conservative hue, dined extravagantly well on *haute cuisine*, sipped the correct wines from the proper goblets, and chain-smoked hand-rolled cigars.

For a man so modern in his conceptions, he had more than a touch of old-fashionedness. It showed up in such things as the gold chain across his waistcoat to which was attached his pocket timepiece. Rather than live in a contemporary building or one of his own houses (he briefly contemplated moving to a Mies apartment but feared fellow tenants might badger him), he made his home in a high-ceilinged, five-room suite on the third floor of an old-fashioned apartment house on Chicago's North Side. The thick-walled rooms were large and they included, predictably, a full kitchen with an ancient gas range for his cook.

The apartment contained armless chairs and furniture of his own design as well as sofas and wing chairs—in which he preferred to sit. The walls were stark white; but the apartment had a glowing warmth, given off by the Klees, Braques, and Schwitterses that dotted its walls. Paul Klee was a close friend, and Mies's collection of Klees was among the finest in private hands.

Mies's chairs were almost as well known as his buildings, and they were just as spare. He designed his first chair, known as the MR chair, in 1927. It had a caned seat and back and its frame was tubular steel. There followed the Tugendhat chair, an armless affair of leather and steel that resembled a square S; the Brno chair with a steel frame and leather upholstery that looked like a curved S; and the Barcelona chair, an elegant armless leather and steel design in which the legs formed an X. The bottoms of all these chairs were uniformly wide, a circumstance that puzzled furniture experts until one of them asked Mies for an explanation. It was simple, he said, he had designed them with his own comfort in mind.

Mies did not receive wide public recognition in the United States until he was over fifty. Up to 1937 he lived in Germany, where he was born, at Aachen, on March 27, 1886. Emigrating to Chicago, he had to wait for the postwar building boom before many of his designs were translated into actuality. At his death examples of his work were in Chicago, Pittsburgh, Des Moines, Baltimore, Detroit, Newark, New York, Houston, Washington, Mexico City, Montreal, Toronto, and West Berlin. All his buildings were dissimilar, although the same basic principles were employed in each.

These principles centered on a Gothic demand for order, logic, and clarity. "The long path through function to creative work has only a single goal," he said, "to create order out of the desperate confusion of our time."

One Mies structure, counted among his outstanding ones, is the thirty-eight-story dark-bronze and pinkish-gray glass Seagram Building on Park Avenue between 52nd and 53rd Streets. Called by appreciative critics the city's most tranquil tower and "the most beautiful curtain-walled building in America," it emphasizes pure line, fine materials, and meticulous detailing outside and in. (Mies designed the room numbers, doorknobs, elevator buttons, bathroom fixtures, and mail chutes as well as the furniture.)

The building's grace is enhanced by its being set in a half-acre fountained plaza of pink granite. It was begun in 1955 and completed two years later at a cost of $35 million. It was, at the time, the city's most costly office building.

Not everyone who gazed upon it or watched its extruded bronze age was convinced of its beauty. Acerbic nonarchitectural critics pointed out that the tower rises 520 feet without setbacks and that it is unornamented. It is too sparse, they said. One likened it to an upended glass coffin.

Those who worked in the building were put off at first by its floor-to-ceiling windows and the illusion of giving off into space that they created; but once they became adjusted to the sensation they did not mind looking out the windows.

The Seagram Building ranked third in Mies's offhand list of his six favorites, chosen to illustrate his most notable concept—"Less is more." (By this Delphic utterance he meant achieving the maximum effect with the minimum of means.)

First on the list was the Illinois Institute of Technology's Crown Hall. This is a single glass-walled room measuring 120 feet by 220 feet and spanned by four huge trusses. The structure appears to do no more than to enclose space, a feeling reinforced by its interior movable partitions. It was one of twenty buildings that Mies designed for the school's hundred-acre campus on Chicago's South Side. Crown Hall is as good an example as any of Mies's "skin-and-bones architecture," a phrase he once used to describe his point of view.

The Chicago Federal Center, Mies's largest complex of high- and low-rise buildings, was his second favorite. He considered its symmetry symbolic of his lifelong battle against disorder.

Another Chicago creation was fourth—two twenty-six-story apartment house towers at 860 and 880 Lake Shore Drive that overlook Lake Michigan. The façades are all glass. Tenants had to accept the neutral gray curtains that were uniform throughout the buildings and that provided the only means of seeking privacy and excluding light. No other curtains or blinds were permitted lest they mar the external appearance. He was also the architect of the Promontory Apartments in Chicago, in which he used brick and glass in an exposed frame.

Mies's fifth favorite was a project for a Chicago convention hall, a place for fifty thousand persons to gather in unobstructed space under a trussed roof 720 feet square. The project, however, never materialized.

The final pet on the architect's list was the since-destroyed German Pavilion at the 1929 International Exposition at Barcelona. It was, one critic said, "a jewel-case structure employing the open planning first developed by Frank Lloyd Wright that combined the richness of bronze, chrome, steel, and glass with free-standing walls."

In addition to the Seagram Building, the architect was represented in the New York area by Pavilion Apartments and Colonnade Apartments, both in Colonnade Park, Newark. He also devised a master plan for a twenty-one-acre development in New Haven, Connecticut.

Mies's most recent building, the National Gallery in Berlin, opened last September. It is a templelike glass box set atop a larger semi-basement, and serves as a museum.

Although many accolades were bestowed on Mies for these and other works, there were also brickbats. "Unsparing," "grim," the work of "barren intellectualism," and "brutal in its destruction of individual possessions and the individual," were some of the terms his detractors used. "Less is less," they also said, turning his aphorism against him.

Ludwig Mies, who added the "van der Rohe" from his mother's name because of its sonority, learned the basics of architecture from his father, a German master mason and stonecutter, and from studying the medieval churches in his native Aachen (Aix-la-Chapelle).

At times, friends recalled, he would describe with unrestrained enthusiasm the quality of brick and stone, its texture, pattern, and color. "Now a brick, that's really something," he once said. "That's really building, not paper architecture.'

For him the material was always the beginning. He used to talk of primitive building methods, where he saw the "wisdom of whole generations" stored in every stroke of an ax, every bite of a chisel. For his students in this country and in Germany it meant that they had to learn the fundamentals of building before they could start to consider questions of design. He taught them how to build, first with wood, then stone, then brick, and finally with concrete and steel.

Each material had its specific characteristics that had to be understood. "New materials are not necessarily superior," he would say. "Each material is only what we make it."

At Aachen, Mies attended trade school and became a draftsman's apprentice before setting off for Berlin at the age of nineteen to become an apprentice to Bruno Paul, Germany's leading furniture designer. Two years later he built his first house, a wooden structure on a sloping site in suburban Berlin. Its style was eighteenth-century.

In 1909 Mies apprenticed himself to Peter Behrens, then the foremost progressive architect in Germany, who had also taught Le Corbusier and Walter Gropius. Mies was put in charge of Behrens' German Embassy in St. Petersburg, Russia.

Going to the Netherlands in 1912, he designed a house for Mrs. H. E. L. J. Kröller, owner of the renowned Kröller-Muller collection of modern paintings, near the Hague. He set up a full-scale canvas and wood mockup on the site to ensure perfection, but the house was never built.

Mies returned to Berlin in 1913 and opened his own office, but with the outbreak of the war in 1914 his life was dislocated for four years in the German army, during which he built bridges and roads in the Balkans. After the war, with his own style coming into definition, he directed the architectural activities of the Novembergruppe, an organization formed to propagandize modern art, and became one of the few progressive architects of the time to employ brick.

Often he would go to the kilns to select one by one the bricks he wanted. He used them for the monument (now destroyed) to Karl Liebknecht and Rosa Luxemburg, the German Communist leaders; for suburban villas for wealthy businessmen; and for low-cost housing for the city of Berlin.

From 1926 to 1932 he was first vice-president of the Deutscher Werkbund, formed to integrate art and industry in design. He directed the group's second exposition, the Weissenhof housing project erected in Stuttgart in 1927. In addition to Mies, houses designed by Gropius, Le Corbusier, Oud, Stam, Behrens, Hilberseimer, Pölzig, and Tauts were represented. Mies's contribution was a four-story apartment building built around a steel skeleton—the basic principle for all the architect's American apartment buildings. (Ludwig Hilberseimer, then and later, was one of Mies's intimate friends; he taught for many years in Chicago.)

The peak achievements of Mies's European career were the German Pavilion he designed for the Barcelona exposition of 1929 and the Tugendhat house in Brno, Czechoslovakia, in 1930. A. James Speyer, a critic for *Art News*, extolled them both as "among the most important buildings of contemporary architecture and the most beautiful of our generation." The pavilion consisted of a rectangular slab roof supported by steel columns, beneath which free-standing planes of Roman travertine, marble, onyx, and glass of various hues were so placed as to create the feeling of space beyond. The Tugendhat house permitted space to flow in a similar fashion.

In 1930 Mies took over direction of the Bauhaus, a laboratory of architecture and design in Dessau, Germany. It was closed three years later after the Nazis attacked the architect as "degenerate" and "un-German."

At the urging of Philip C. Johnson, the New York architect and a close friend, Mies emigrated to the United States to head the School of Architecture at the Armour (now Illinois) Institute of Technology in Chicago. He retired from the post in 1958.

He designed a new plant for the institute, but only a dozen of the research, laboratory, and residence buildings of the twenty from his drawing board were completed. Crown Hall was among them.

As a teacher Mies did not deliver formal lectures, but worked, seminar fashion, with groups of ten or twelve students. His method of teaching, according to a former student, was "almost tacit." "He was never wildly physically active, and he did not do much talking," this student recalled, adding that Mies, sitting Buddhalike, would frequently puff through a whole cigar before commenting on a student sketch. Abandoning the Beaux Arts System based on competition for prizes, Mies sternly told his students, "First you have to learn something; then you can go out and do it."

He was not one to tolerate self-expression among his students. One of them once asked him about it. Silently he handed the student a pencil and paper and told her to write her name. This done, he said, "That's for self-expression. Now we get to work."

Another former student thought of Mies as "a great teacher because he subjects himself to an extraordinary discipline in thinking and in his way of working, and because what he is teaching is very clear to him."

Mies himself was quite confident of his influence. "I don't know how many students we have had," he said a couple of years ago, "but you need only ten to change the cultural climate if they are good."

In the years that Mies was with the institute and since, he was a constantly busy designer. Ideas and projects streamed from his Chicago office, some of them never built but all of them provocative.

Nevertheless, he worked slowly, using sketch pads to draft his ideas. The result was not a rough drawing but a precise delineation, with each detail filled in. In his later years, when he was slowed by arthritis, he worked mostly at home. He would frequently sit so wrapped in thought that he neglected to answer the telephone. He was also unresponsive to letters.

Despite a seclusiveness during the day, Mies liked company in the evening, especially that of old friends. Talking in German-accented English, he could be the life of a party. His shyness was with strangers, and then it was painful, for he could usually find nothing to say. They came away persuaded that he was unpersonable.

Mies was well-to-do, but not wealthy. He received the usual architect's fee of 6 percent of the gross cost of a building, but he was not a very careful manager of his income, according to his friends. He was considered generous with his office staff and on spending for designs that were unlikely to see the light of day.

The architect received three noteworthy honors—the Presidential Freedom Medal and the gold medals of the Royal Institute of British Architects and of the American Institute of Architects. He was also a member of the National Institute of Arts and Letters.

DREW PEARSON

Drew Pearson, the syndicated columnist, died in Washington on September 1, 1969, at the age of seventy-one. Most newspapermen, and even most columnists, are not public personalities. Mr. Pearson was an exception, and this made him interesting to write about.

FEW OF THE 50 million daily readers of "Washington Merry-Go-Round" were noncommittal about its principal author, Drew Pearson. Some considered him a talented practitioner of one of the loftiest forms of journalism—scourging the venal and corrupt in public life. Others abominated him as a skilled exponent of one of the basest forms of journalism —assassinating the character of selfless public servants through falsehood and distortion.

Either way, Mr. Pearson was one of the country's most influential political columnists for more than thirty-five years. "Nobody comes even close to competing with the Pearson product, which is a unique blend of carnival pitch, news, synthetic philosophy, and rumor," Robert G. Sherrill, another Washington writer, said earlier this year.

One reason for Mr. Pearson's stature, even among his colleagues, was that he had excellent sources of information in the government. Another reason was that he was fearless (although he was also opinionated and self-assured). A third reason was that he compiled an impressive record of exposing wrongdoing (although he was often faulted for his inaccuracies).

Disclosures in Mr. Pearson's column led, in 1967, to Senate censure of Thomas J. Dodd, Democrat of Connecticut, for conduct "contrary to accepted morals" that tended to bring the Senate into disrepute. Mr. Dodd, a Senate committee found, had diverted to his own use at least $116,083 from testimonial dinners and campaign contributions. Other disclosures concerned Adam Clayton Powell, Democrat of Manhattan, who was ousted from the House of Representatives for financial misdeeds.

In addition, according to William L. Rivers' *The Opinionmakers*, Mr.

Pearson's persistent muckrakings "have sent four members of Congress to jail, defeated countless others, and caused the dismissal of scores of government officials." "His digging," the book continued, "covers a wide range—from evidence that Congressman Andrew May of Kentucky took a bribe to evidence that a State Department official leaked documents to the Senate." To whatever malefactor or misfeasance he addressed himself, the columnist exhibited a zeal quite at variance with his mildness of manner and softness of speech.

Mr. Pearson had a lot of fun as a watchdog of virtue, but he was also a serious reformer. "My chief motive," he told *The Nation* last July, "is to try to make the government a little cleaner, a little more efficient, and I would say also, in foreign affairs, to try to work for peace." His approach to politics, though, was personal.

"I've always tried to emphasize the personal side of Washington," he said. "I think it's helped make my broader points about clean government more effective, and it doesn't put people to sleep as fast as some of my thumb-sucking colleagues do."

Mr. Pearson made some notable enemies. One of them was Senator Robert F. Kennedy, who was annoyed when the "Merry-Go-Round" charged that he, as Attorney General, had authorized electronic surveillance of the Reverend Dr. Martin Luther King, Jr.'s, telephones. J. Edgar Hoover, director of the Federal Bureau of Investigation, was another target who did not relish Mr. Pearson's attentions.

Indeed, the columnist took on all comers. Senator George A. Smathers, Democrat of Florida, was not far from the mark several years ago when he said that he joined "two Presidents [Franklin D. Roosevelt and Harry S Truman], twenty-seven Senators, and eighty-three Congressmen in describing Drew Pearson as an unmitigated liar."

For his part, the columnist once said proudly, "I suppose I've got more enemies per square inch on Capitol Hill than any place else in the world."

Actually, Mr. Roosevelt called him "a chronic liar" after Mr. Pearson had said Secretary of State Cordell Hull hoped World War II would bleed the Soviet Union white. Mr. Truman's epithet was "SOB" for his criticism of Major General Harry S. Vaughan, a White House military aide. In addition, Mr. Truman declined to invite him to the White House perhaps less for what he said about General Vaughan than for a column the President thought critical of his wife.

The most eloquent diatribes against Mr. Pearson, however, probably came from Senator Kenneth McKellar of Tennessee and Eleanor (Cissy) Patterson, publisher of the Washington *Times-Herald* and once Mr. Pearson's mother-in-law.

The Democratic Senator, after Mr. Pearson had accused him of attacking another Senator with a pocketknife, excoriated the columnist for an hour as "an ignorant liar, a pusillanimous liar, a peewee liar," and "a revolving, constitutional, unmitigated, infamous liar."

Mrs. Patterson, in the fury that followed Mr. Pearson's decision to switch his column to the Washington *Post*, denounced him in a full-page editorial as, among other things, "one of the weirdest specimens of humanity since Nemo, the Turtle Boy" and "the Quaker Oat [an allusion to his religion] who became a sour mash in Washington."

Not only invective but violence was aroused by Mr. Pearson. Once he was assaulted by a lobbyist for Generalissimo Francisco Franco, the Spanish dictator. Another time Senator Joseph R. McCarthy, the Wisconsin Republican, "sidled up to me [in Washington's Sulgrave Club], pinned my arms to my sides, and proceeded to use his knee in the accepted manner of the waterfront.'

Beyond such attacks, the columnist was sued "maybe fifty times," mostly without success (the losers included Senator Dodd), and he, in turn, sued (and lost) a number of times. One of the largest suits against the columnist, for $1.75 million, was filed by General of the Army Douglas MacArthur, who was accused of lobbying for his own promotion. The 1934 suit was dropped.

In at least two instances the columnist went out of his way to affect an election outcome. Once was in the late 1930's when "I did my best to defeat [Senator Millard] Tydings [in Maryland]." Mr. Tydings, according to Mr. Pearson, had attacked his father, who had been appointed Governor of the Virgin Islands by President Herbert Hoover. President Roosevelt so approved Mr. Pearson's activities, the columnist said, that he cleared Maryland appointments with Mr. Pearson rather than the Senator.

Another instance was in 1948, when Mr. Pearson hired a New Mexico radio network to attack and help defeat Major General Patrick J. Hurley, who was running for the Senate. Years before, General Hurley, then Secretary of War, had publicly cursed the columnist for disclosing that he rehearsed ballroom entrances before a mirror.

Although Mr. Pearson said that he didn't "enjoy collecting scalps," he was proud to have made the enemies he did. He was also proud of the reforms he believed he had a hand in, such as the establishment of basic ethical standards for members of Congress. And he was especially proud of the Friendship Train, which he organized and espoused. The train collected stores of American food for France, Italy, Germany, Austria, and Greece after World War II.

Mr. Pearson was a good deal less pugnacious in person than in print.

Dressed in sports shirts and tweedy jackets, he did not resemble a moralizing, fire-eating journalist. A British woman, meeting him at a Washington party, turned to a friend and asked, "What sort of a city is this where a scandal columnist looks like a country squire?"

His background had, in fact, a quality of gentility. Andrew Russell Pearson was born December 13, 1897, in Evanston, Illinois, the son of Paul Martin Pearson, a college speech teacher, and Edna Wolfe Pearson. He went to Phillips Exeter Academy in New Hampshire and then to Swarthmore College, graduating in 1919.

Bent on a diplomatic career, he went to Europe, where he sidetracked his ambition to become director of relief in the Balkans for the British Red Cross. Returning to this country in 1921, he taught industrial geography for a year at the University of Pennsylvania.

Then he signed as a seaman on the *President Madison* out of Seattle and headed for the Orient. After knocking about the Far East, he went to Australia and New Zealand for six months, lecturing in both countries. He traveled on to Britain by way of India and filed dispatches to Australian newspapers.

For the next ten years (with a year out in 1924 to teach geography at Columbia University), Mr. Pearson was a peripatetic newspaperman. He was in Europe and the Far East, mostly as a freelancer, until he joined the staff of the Baltimore *Sun* in 1929 and later headed its Washington bureau. By this time he had married Countess Felicia Gizycka, daughter of Cissy Patterson.

Mr. Pearson and his wife, who had one daughter, Ellen, were subsequently divorced, and in 1936 he married Luvie Moore. She had a son, Tyler Abell, by a previous marriage.

In the capital, Mr. Pearson became acquainted with Robert S. Allen, chief of the Washington bureau of the *Christian Science Monitor*. The two fell to discussing how they could use all the inside material they had gathered on the Hoover administration, which their papers declined to publish. Mr. Pearson was convinced that "even the so-called liberal papers are increasingly controlled by their cash registers and that one of the few outlets to free journalism is through the medium of books."

The result was the publication in 1931 of *Washington Merry-Go-Round*, full of information "the capital loves to whisper but hates to see in print." The authorship of the book was anonymous, as it was of *More Merry-Go-Round* in 1932. But this did not affect the books' sales, which totaled the then astounding figure of two hundred thousand copies.

Eventually, though, the authorship mystery was penetrated, and Mr. Pearson and Mr. Allen lost their jobs. Out of that circumstance, their column was born in December 1932. Distributed then by United Features, it started out with about a dozen papers and rose to 350 by 1941 and to about 600 in 1969.

For a while Mr. Pearson and Mr. Allen worked nineteen hours a day, turning out seven columns a week. They also collaborated, in the middle thirties, on a comic strip called *Hap Hazard*, which featured a Washington correspondent, and *News for Americans*, a radio program. In addition they wrote two more books, *Nine Old Men*, and *Nine Old Men at the Crossroads*, both muckraking accounts of the United States Supreme Court and the very aged Justices who then sat on it.

Mr. Allen withdrew from the partnership in 1942 to go on active duty with the army. Mr. Pearson carried on alone, using a small staff to gather and check material. About ten years ago he was joined by Jack Anderson, who shared the column's byline. Mr. Pearson, however, was his own best reporter, making the rounds of government offices and taking an active part in the capital's social life. He sometimes addressed a column to one of his grandsons, Drew Arnold.

Moreover, tips and news often came to the columnist without solicitation. "When you are known to be a critic of a certain public figure," Mr. Pearson explained, "news about him comes toward you like lightning toward a lightning rod." This, in essence, was how the column acquired its information about Senator Dodd and gained the cooperation of members of his staff, including James P. Boyd, Jr., who supplied the column with copies of compromising documents.

For many years Mr. Pearson conducted a weekly radio show. In its early versions in the 1950's he featured what he called "my predictions of things to come." An independent check over a six-month period indicated that 60 percent of these forecasts were correct, but it was pointed out that some of the predictions were obvious or inevitable.

Mr. Pearson wrote his radio program and most of his column in a cluttered study of his Georgetown home, a stately yellow brick house. His journalism earned him most of his two-hundred-thousand-dollar yearly gross.

He also sold muck and manure. The manure derived from a herd of two hundred cattle on his Maryland farm and from the Chicago stockyards. Its brand name was "Drew Pearson's Best Manure" and it was advertised as "better than in the column."

Although Mr. Pearson often disclosed stories damaging to individual members of Congress, he believed that "the great majority of Senators and Representatives are honorable men, but too often they let themselves be victimized by a system that puts almost irresistible pressure on men in high places. who will do almost anything they can get away with to stay there."

This somewhat dubious accolade was one of the themes of *The Case Against Congress*, which Mr. Pearson wrote with Mr. Anderson in 1968. In the same year he was listed as the author of a novel, *The Senator*. Investigation disclosed, however, that Mr. Pearson relied very heavily on Gerald Green, author of *The Last Angry Man*, for editorial assistance. Ken McCormick, senior editor at Doubleday, the book's publisher, said the book "was completely written by Green." Mr. Green called it "truly a collaborative effort." Mr. Pearson said Mr. Green "helped me." Whatever the arrangement, the novel did not reap critical praise.

Reflecting on his career a couple of years ago, Mr. Pearson felt that the good he had accomplished far outweighed the harm. He looked on the attacks as "part of the business," and added: "I'd rather be liked than not, but I can understand why some people don't like me."

HO CHI MINH

Ho Chi Minh died in Hanoi on September 3, 1969, at the age of seventy-nine. The North Vietnamese leader, who was also a hero to thousands in South Vietnam, was a figure of world stature whose life was a demonstration of how an ideal—in his case national freedom— can seize a man and become his whole life.

AMONG twentieth-century statesmen, Ho Chi Minh was remarkable both for the tenacity and patience with which he pursued his goal of Vietnamese independence and for his success in blending Communism with nationalism.

From his youth Ho espoused freedom for the French colony of Vietnam. He persevered through years when his chances of attaining his objective were so minuscule as to seem ridiculous. Ultimately, he organized the defeat of the French in 1954 in the historic battle of Dienbienphu. This battle, a triumph of guerrilla strategy, came nine years after he was named President of the Democratic Republic of Vietnam.

After the supposedly temporary division of Vietnam at the 17th parallel by the Geneva Agreement of 1954 and after that division became hardened by United States support of Ngo Dinh Diem in the South, Ho led his countrymen in the North against the onslaughts of American military might. In the war, Ho's capital of Hanoi, among other cities, was reportedly bombed by American planes.

At the same time Ho was an inspiration for the National Liberation Front and its guerrilla arm, the Viet Cong, which operated in South Vietnam in the long, bloody, and costly conflict against the Saigon regime and its American allies.

In the war, in which the United States became increasingly involved, especially after 1964, Ho maintained an exquisite balance in his relations with the Soviet Union and the People's Republic of China. These Communist countries, at ideological sword's points, were Ho's principal suppliers of foodstuffs and war goods. It was a measure of his diplomacy that he kept on friendly terms with each.

To the 19 million people north of the 17th parallel and to other millions below it, the small, frail aged-ivorylike figure of Ho, with his long ascetic face, straggly goatee, sunken cheeks, and luminous eyes, was a patriarch, the George Washington of his nation. Although his name was not attached to public squares, buildings, factories, airports, or monuments, his magnetism was undoubted, as was the affection that the average citizen had for him.

He was universally called "Uncle Ho," a sobriquet also used in the North Vietnamese press. Before the exigencies of war confined him to official duties, Ho regularly visited villages and towns. Simply clad, he was especially fond of dropping into schools and chatting with the children. Westerners who knew Ho were convinced that, whatever his guile in larger political matters, there was no pose in his expressions of feeling for the common people.

Indeed, Ho's personal popularity was such that it was generally conceded, even by his political foes, that Vietnam would have been unified under his leadership, had the countrywide elections, pledged at Geneva, taken place. As it was, major segments of South Vietnam were effectively controlled by the National Liberation Front despite the presence of hundreds of thousands of American troops.

Intelligent, resourceful, dedicated, Ho created a favorable impression on many of those who dealt with him. One such was Harry Ashmore of the Center for Democratic Studies and former editor of the *Arkansas Gazette*. Mr. Ashmore and William C. Baggs, editor of the Miami *News*, were among the last Americans to talk with Ho at length when they visited Hanoi in early 1967. The chief of state conversed with the two men in the Presidential Palace (the former Governor General's residence), in the servants' quarters, in which he lived.

"Ho was a courtly, urbane, highly sophisticated man with a gentle manner and without personal venom," Mr. Ashmore recalled in a recent interview. At the meeting Ho was dressed in his characteristic high-necked white pajama type of garment, called a *cu-nao*, and he wore open-toed rubber sandals. He chain-smoked cigarettes, American-made Salems.

Their hour-long conversation started out in Vietnamese, Mr. Ashmore said, but soon shifted to English. Ho astonished Mr. Ashmore by his adeptness in English, which was one of several languages—the principal others were French and Russian—in which he was fluent.

At one point Ho reminded Mr. Ashmore and Mr. Baggs that he had once been in the United States. "I think I know the American people," Ho said, "and I don't understand how they can support their involvement in this war. Is the Statue of Liberty standing on her head?"

This was a rhetorical question that Ho also posed to other Americans in an effort to point up what to his mind was an inconsistency: a colonial people who had gained independence in a revolution were fighting to suppress the independence of another colonial people.

Ho's knowledge of American history was keen, and he put it to advantage in the summer of 1945 when he was writing the Declaration of Independence of the Democratic Republic of Vietnam. He remembered much of the wording of the American Declaration of Independence, but not its precise verbiage. From an American military mission then working with him he tried in vain to obtain a copy of the document, and when none could supply it Ho paraphrased it out of his recollection.

Thus his Declaration begins, "All men are created equal; they are endowed by their Creator with certain unalienable Rights; among these are Life, Liberty, and the pursuit of Happiness." After explaining that this meant that "all the peoples on the earth are equal from birth, all the peoples have a right to live, to be happy and free," Ho went on to enumerate, in the manner of the American Declaration, the grievances of his people and to proclaim their independence.

Apart from Americans, Ho struck a spark with many others who came in contact with him over the years. "Extraordinarily likable and friendly" was the description of Jawaharlal Nehru, the Indian leader. Paul Mus, the French orientalist who conducted delicate talks with him in 1946 and 1947, found Ho an "intransigent and incorruptible revolutionary, à la Saint-Just."

A French naval commander who observed the slender Vietnamese for the three weeks he was a ship's passenger concluded that Ho was an "intelligent and charming man who is also a passionate idealist entirely devoted to the cause he has espoused" and a man with "naïve faith in the politico-social slogans of our times and, generally, in everything that is printed."

Ho was an enormously pragmatic Communist, a doer rather than a theoretician. His speeches and articles were brought together in a four-volume Selected Works of Ho Chi Minh issued in Hanoi between 1960 and 1962. The late Bernard B. Fall, an American authority on Vietnam, published a collection of these in English in 1967 under the title Ho Chi Minh on Revolution. They are simply and clearly worded documents, most of them agitational or polemical in nature and hardly likely to add to the body of Marxist doctrine.

Like Mao Tse-tung, a fellow Communist leader, Ho composed poetry, some of it considered quite affecting. One of his poems, written when he was a prisoner of the Chinese Nationalists in 1942–43, is called *Autumn Night* and reads in translation:

In front of the gate, the guard stands with his rifle.
Above, untidy clouds are carrying away the moon.
The bedbugs are swarming around like army tanks on maneuvers,
While the mosquitoes form squadrons, attacking like fighter planes.
My heart travels a thousand li toward my native land.
My dream intertwines with sadness like a skein of a thousand threads.
Innocent, I have now endured a whole year in prison.
Using my tears for ink, I turn my thoughts into verses.

Ho's rise to power and world eminence was not a fully documented story. On the contrary, its details at some crucial points are imprecise. This led at one time to the suspicion that there were two Hos, a notion that was discounted by the French Sûreté when they compared photographs of the early and the late Ho.

One explanation for the confusion is that Ho used about a dozen aliases, of which Ho Chi Minh (Ho, the Shedder of Light) was but one. Another was Ho's own reluctance to disclose biographical information. "You know, I am an old man, and an old man likes to hold on to his little mysteries," he told Mr. Fall. He continued, with a twinkle, "Wait until I'm dead. Then you can write about me all you want."

Nonetheless, Mr. Fall reported, before he left Hanoi he received a brief, unsigned summary of Ho's life "obviously delivered on the old man's instructions."

Despite Ho's apparent self-effacement, he did have a touch of personal vanity. Mr. Fall recalled having shown the Vietnamese leader a sketch of him by Mrs. Fall. "Yes, that is very good. That looks very much like me," Ho said. He took a bouquet of flowers from a nearby table and, handing it to Mr. Fall, said: "Tell her for me that the drawing is very good and give her the bouquet and kiss her on both cheeks for me."

Although there is some uncertainty over Ho's birth date, the most reliable evidence indicates he was born May 19, 1890, in Kimlien, a village in Nghe-An Province in central Vietnam. Many sources give his true name as Nguyen Ai-Quoc, or Nguyen the Patriot. However, Wilfred Burchett, the Australian-born correspondent who knew Ho well, believes (and it is now generally accepted) that Ho's birth name was Nguyen Van Thanh, or Nguyen Who Will Be Victorious.

He was said to be the youngest of three children. His elder brother died in 1950 and his sister in 1953. Ho's father, who lived into the 1930's, was only slightly better off than the rice peasants of the area, but he was apparently a man of some determination, for by rote learning he passed mandarinal examinations that gave him a job in the imperial administration just when the French were taking over.

An ardent nationalist, Ho's father refused to learn French, the language of the conquerors of his country, and joined anti-French secret societies. Young Ho got his first underground experience as his father's messenger in an anti-French network. Shortly, the father lost his government job and became a healer, dispensing traditional oriental potions.

Ho's mother was believed to have been of peasant origin, but he never spoke of her.

Ho received his basic education from his father and from the village school, going on to a few years of high school at the Lycée Quoc-Hoc in the old imperial capital of Hué. This institution, founded by the father of Ngo Dinh Diem, was designed to perpetuate Vietnamese national traditions. It had a distinguished roster of graduates that included Vo Nguyen Giap, the brilliant guerrilla general, and Pham Van Dong, the current Premier of North Vietnam.

Ho left the school in 1910 without a diploma and taught, briefly, at a private institution in a South Annam fishing town. It was while he was there, according to now accepted sources, that he decided to go to Europe. As a step toward that goal, he went in the summer of 1911 to a trade school in Saigon, where he learned the duties of a kitchen boy and pastry cook's helper, skills in demand by Europeans of that day.

His training, incidentally, gave Ho a gourmet's palate, which he liked to indulge, and an ability to whip up a tasty dish, which he delighted to do when he could.

For the immediate moment, though, his training enabled him to sign aboard the *Latouche-Treville* as a kitchen boy, a job so menial that he worked under the alias Ba. In his travels, he visited Marseilles and ports in Africa and North America. Explaining the crucial significance of these voyages for Ho's education as a revolutionary, Mr. Fall wrote in *The Two Vietnams:* "His contacts with the white colonizers on their home grounds shattered any of his illusions as to their 'superiority,' and his association with sailors from Brittany, Cornwall, and the Frisian Islands—as illiterate and superstitious as the most backward Vietnamese rice farmer—did the rest.

"Ho still likes to tell the story of the arrival of his ship at an African port where, he claims, natives were compelled to jump into the shark-infested waters to secure the moorings of the vessels and were killed by the sharks under the indifferent eyes of passengers and crew.

"But his contacts with Europe also brought him the revelation of his own personal worth and dignity; when he went ashore in Europe in a Western suit, whites, for the first time in his life, addressed him as 'monsieur,' instead of using the deprecating 'tu,' reserved in France for children but used in Indochina by Frenchmen when addressing natives, no matter how educated."

In his years at sea, Ho read widely—Shakespeare, Tolstoy, Marx, Zola. He was even then, according to later accounts, an ascetic and something of a Puritan, who was offended when prostitutes clambered aboard his ship in Marseilles. "Why don't the French civilize their own people before they pretend to civilize us?" he is said to have remarked.

(Ho, incidentally, is believed to have been a bachelor, although the record on this point is far from clear.)

With the advent of World War I, Ho went to live in London, where he worked as a snow shoveler and as a cook's helper under Escoffier, the master chef, at the Carlton Hotel. Escoffier, it is said, promoted Ho to a job in the pastry kitchen and wanted to teach him the art of cuisine. However that may be, the twenty-four-year-old Vietnamese was more interested in politics. He joined the Overseas Workers Association, composed mostly of Asians, and agitated, among other things, for Irish independence.

Sometime during the war, Ho gave up the Carlton's kitchen for the sea and journeyed to the United States. He is believed to have lived in Harlem for a while. Ho himself often referred to his American visit, although he was hazy about the details. According to his close associate, Pham Van Dong, what impressed Ho in the United States were "the barbarities and ugliness of American capitalism, the Ku Klux Klan mobs, the lynching of Negroes."

Out of Ho's American experiences came a pamphlet, issued in Moscow in 1924, called *La Race Noire* (The Black Race), which assailed racial practices in America and Europe.

About 1918 Ho returned to France and lived in a tiny flat in the Montmartre section of Paris, eking out a living by retouching photos under the name of Nguyen Ai-Quoc. He subsisted on a diet of rice, sausage, and fish as he made friends in the French Socialist Party and among the thousands of Vietnamese exiles in the city.

At the Versailles Peace Conference of 1919, Ho emerged as a self-appointed spokesman for his native land. Seeing in Woodrow Wilson's proposal for self-determination of the peoples the possibility of Vietnam's independence, Ho, dressed in a hired black suit and bowler hat, traveled to the Palace of Versailles to present his case. He was, of course, not received, although he offered a program for Viëtnam. Its proposals did not include independence, but basic freedoms and equality between the French rulers and the native population.

Whatever hopes Ho may have held for French liberation of Vietnam were destroyed in his mind by the failure of the Versailles Conference to settle colonial issues. His faith was now transferred to Socialist action. Indeed, his first recorded speech was at a congress of the French Socialist party in 1920, and it was a plea, not for world revolution but "against the imperialists who have committed abhorrent crimes on my native land." He bid the party "act practically to support the oppressed natives."

At this congress Ho became, fatefully, a founding member of the French Communist Party because he considered that the Socialists were equivocating on the colonial issue whereas the Communists were willing to promote national liberation.

"I don't understand a thing about strategy, tactics, and all the other big words you use," he told the delegates, "but I understand well one single thing: the Third International concerns itself a great deal with the colonial question. Its delegates promise to help the oppressed colonial peoples to regain their liberty and independence. The adherents of the Second International have not said a word about the fate of the colonial areas."

A similar pragmatism was evident in an article Ho wrote in 1960, "The Path Which Led Me to Leninism," that traced the roots of his Communism. In it he said: "At first patriotism, not yet Communism, led me to have confidence in Lenin, in the Third International. Step by step, along the struggle, by studying Marxism-Leninism parallel with participation in practical activities, I gradually came upon the fact that only Socialism and Communism can liberate the oppressed nations and the working people throughout the world from slavery."

With his decision to join the Communists, Ho's career took a marked turn. For one thing, he became the French party's resident expert on colonial affairs and edited *La Paria* (The Outcast), the weekly paper of the Intercolonial Union, which he was instrumental in founding in 1921. This group was a conglomeration of restless Algerian, Senegalese, West Indian, and Asian exiles in Paris who were united by a fervid nationalism and, to a lesser extent, by a common commitment to Communism.

For another thing, the fragile-looking Ho became an orator of sorts, traveling about France to speak to throngs of Vietnamese soldiers and war workers who were awaiting repatriation. It was a stimulating departure for a book-oriented revolutionary.

And for a third thing, Ho gravitated to Moscow, then the nerve center of world Communism. He went there first in 1922 for the Fourth Comintern Congress, where he met Lenin and became a member of the Comintern's Southeast Asia Bureau. By all accounts, Ho was vocal and energetic, helping to organize the Krestintern, or Peasant International, for revolutionary work among colonial peoples, and meeting all the reigning Communists.

After a brief sojourn in France, Ho was back in Moscow, his base for many years thereafter. He attended the University of the Toilers of the East, receiving formal training in Marxism and the techniques of agitation and propaganda. Then (and later) he steered clear of intraparty doctrinal disputes, which probably saved his life in the Stalin purges of the thirties.

Following his studies in Moscow, Ho was dispatched to Canton, China, in 1925 as an interpreter for Michael Borodin, one of the leaders of the Soviet mission to help Chiang Kai-shek, then in Communist favor as an heir of Sun Yat-sen. Once in Canton, Ho set about to spread the spirit of revolution in the Far East. He organized Vietnam refugees into the Vietnam Revolutionary Youth Association and set up the League of Oppressed Peoples of Asia, which soon became the South Seas Communist Party, the forerunner of various national Communist groups including Ho's own Indochinese Communist Party of 1930.

For two years, until July 1927, when Chiang turned on his Communist allies, Ho sent apt Vietnamese to Chiang's military school at Whampoa while conducting a crash training course in political agitation for his compatriots. Some of the best of them he sent to Moscow for more advanced schooling.

One of Ho's students and a graduate from Whampoa was Pham Van Dong, who remained loyal to his preceptor. But there were those who faltered and many of them, it is said, were picked up and liquidated by French colonial agents in Vietnam. Ho's critics have charged that this was his way of dealing with defectors.

Following the Chiang-Communist break, Ho fled to Moscow by way of the Gobi. His life immediately thereafter is not clear, but it is believed that he lived in Berlin for a time (he spoke some German and seemed to know the geography of Berlin) and traveled in Belgium, Switzerland, and Italy, using a variety of aliases and passports.

After 1928 Ho turned up in eastern Thailand, disguised as a shaven-headed Buddhist monk. He traveled among Vietnamese exiles and organized political groups and published newspapers that were smuggled over the border into Vietnam.

In 1930, on advice from the Comintern, Ho was instrumental in settling the vexatious disputes that had arisen among Communists in

Indochina and in organizing the Indochinese Communist Party, which later became the Vietnamese Communist Party and, still later, the Vietnamese Workers Party.

In that same year a peasant rebellion erupted in Vietnam, which the Communists backed. On its suppression by the French, Ho was sentenced to death in absentia. At the time he was in a British jail in Hong Kong, having been arrested there in 1931 for subversive activities. The French sought his extradition, but Ho argued that he was a political refugee and not subject to extradition. The case, which was handled in London by Sir Stafford Cripps in a plea to the Privy Council, was decided for Ho. He was released, and fled Hong Kong in disguise (this time as a Chinese merchant) and made his way back to Moscow.

There he attended Communist schools—the Institute for National and Colonial Questions and the celebrated Lenin School. He was, however, back in China in 1938, now as a communications operator with Mao Tse-tung's renowned Eighth Route Army. Subsequently, he found his way south and entered Vietnam in 1940 for the first time in thirty years.

The timing was a master stroke, for the Japanese, virtually unopposed, had taken effective control of the Indochina Peninsula and the French administrators, most of them Vichy adherents, agreed to cooperate with the Japanese. With great daring and imagination, Ho took advantage of World War II to piece together a coalition of Vietnamese nationalists and Communists into what was called the Viet Minh, or Independence Front.

The Viet Minh created a ten-thousand-man guerrilla force, "Men in Black," that battled the Japanese in the jungles with notable success.

Ho's actions projected him onto the world scene as the leading Vietnamese nationalist and as an ally of the United States against the Japanese. "I was a Communist," he said then, "but I am no longer one. I am a member of the Vietnamese family, nothing else."

In 1942 Ho was sent to Kunming, China, for military training, reportedly at the request of his American military aides. He was arrested there by Chiang Kai-shek's men and jailed until September 1943, when he was released, it has been said, by American request.

On his release, according to Mr. Fall, Ho cooperated with a Chinese Nationalist general in forming a wide Vietnamese freedom group. One result of this was that in 1944 Ho accepted a portfolio in the Provisional Republican Government of Vietnam. That government was largely a paper affair, but it permitted Ho to court vigorously the American Office of Strategic Services. Thus when Ho's Viet Minh took over Hanoi in 1945, senior American military officials were in his entourage. It was in this period that he took the name of Ho Chi Minh.

With the end of World War II, Ho proclaimed the independence of Vietnam, but it took nine years for his declaration to become an effective fact. First, under the Big Three Agreement of Potsdam, the Nationalist Chinese occupied Hanoi and the northern sector of Vietnam. Second, the French (in British ships) arrived to reclaim Saigon and the southern segment of the country. And third, Ho's nationalist coalition was strained under pressure of these events.

Forming a new guerrilla force around the Viet Minh, Ho and his colleagues, according to most accounts, dealt summarily with dissidents unwilling to fight in Ho's fashion for independence. Assassinations were frequently reported. Meantime, as the Chinese withdrew from the North and the French advanced from the South, Ho negotiated with the French to save his nationalist regime.

In a compromise that Ho worked out in Paris in 1946, he agreed to let the Democratic Republic of Vietnam become a part of the French Union as a free state within the Indochina federation. The French recognized Ho as chief of state and promised a plebiscite in the South on the question of a unified Vietnam under Ho.

By the start of 1947, the agreement had broken down, and Ho's men were fighting the French army. The Viet Minh guerrillas held the jungles and the villages, the French the cities. For seven years the war raged as Ho's forces gathered strength, squeezing the French more and more. For most of this time Ho was diplomatically isolated, for he was not recognized by Communist China nor by the Soviet Union until his victory over the French was virtually assured.

In an effort to shore up their political forces, the French resurrected Bao Dai, the Japanese puppet who held title as Emperor. Corrupt and pleasure-loving, he soon moved with his mistresses to France, leaving a weak and splintered regime in Saigon.

This, of course, proved no support for the French army, which was also sapped by General Giap's guerrilla tactics. Finally, on May 8, 1954, the French were decisively defeated at Dienbienphu. The Indochina War ended officially in July at a cost to the French of 172,000 casualties and to the Viet Minh of perhaps three times that many.

The cease-fire accord was negotiated on July 21, 1954, in Geneva, and it represented far less than Ho's hopes. But by that time the United States was involved in Vietnam on the French side through $800 million a year in economic aid. Fear of Communist expansion in Asia dominated Washington, with Vice-President Richard M. Nixon saying, "If, to avoid further Communist expansion in Asia, we must take the risk of putting our boys in, I think the Executive Branch has to do it."

The Geneva Accord, however, divided Vietnam at the 17th parallel, creating a North and a South Vietnam. It removed the French from the peninsula and provided for all-Vietnam elections in 1956, the winner to take all the country.

Although a party to the Geneva Accord, the United States declined to sign it. On this ground, South Vietnam refused to hold the elections. Meantime, the United States built up its military mission in Saigon and its support of the Ngo Dinh Diem regime there as a counter to continued guerrilla activity of the National Liberation Front, which became pronounced after 1956.

The front, technically independent of Ho Chi Minh in the North, increased its sway into the 1960's. It supplied itself from captured American arms and from matériel that came through from the North. Beginning in 1964, thousands of American troops were poured into South Vietnam to battle the Viet Cong and then to bomb North Vietnam.

Various attempts were made to end the war, which by 1967 was clearly a conflict between the United States and the people of South Vietnam and Ho's Democratic Republic of North Vietnam.

On several occasions Ho was said to be willing to discuss a settlement if the United States would halt its bombing of the North and deal also with the Viet Cong or the National Liberation Front as a party to the war. But nothing came of these overtures on either side.

Throughout, Ho was serenely confident of victory. In 1962, when the war was still a localized conflict between the South Vietnamese forces and 11,000 American advisers and a smaller guerrilla force, Ho told a French visitor: "It took us eight years of bitter fighting to defeat you French, and you knew the country and had some old friendships here. Now the South Vietnamese regime is well armed and helped by the Americans.

"The Americans are much stronger than the French, though they know us less well. So it perhaps may take ten years to do it, but our heroic compatriots in the South will defeat them in the end."

Ho was still confident in January 1967, when he talked with Mr. Ashmore and Mr. Baggs. "We have been fighting for our independence for more than 25 years," he told them, "and of course we cherish peace, but we will never surrender our independence to purchase a peace with the United States or any party."

At the close of his conversation, he clenched his right fist and said emotionally, "You must know of our resolution. Not even your nuclear weapons would force us to surrender after so long and violent a struggle for the independence of our country."

JOSEPH P. KENNEDY

Joseph P. Kennedy died at Hyannis Port, Massachusetts, on November 18, 1969, at the age of eighty-one. A man of enormous drive who accepted nothing short of success, he was redeemingly candid about himself and his aspirations. He was a classic example of upward mobility, and my obit sought to give him his due.

WITH SINGLE-MINDED perseverance Joseph Patrick Kennedy devoted himself to founding a family political dynasty. To this purpose he committed his extraordinary skill for making money, his far-reaching business and political friendships, and his unquestioned position as a paterfamilias.

In pursuing his goal (in which pride of name was a conspicuous part) he amassed a tremendous fortune, perhaps $500 million, and with it a reputation for financial shrewdness. In the end, however, he discounted his riches, saying: "The measure of a man's success is not the money he's made. It's the kind of family he's raised."

And after the election of his son to the presidency in 1960 he put it this way: "I have a strong idea that there is no other success for a father and a mother except to feel that they have made some contribution to the development of their children."

Mr. Kennedy was forthright about his own contribution. He had nurtured his eldest son, Joseph, Jr., for a political career that he hoped would culminate in the White House; but the young man was killed in World War II. He then turned his attention to John, his second son.

"I got Jack into politics, I was the one," Mr. Kennedy said in 1957 of his son, then a United States Senator who hoped to become President. "I told him Joe was dead and that it was his responsibility to run for Congress. He didn't want to. He felt he didn't have the ability and he still feels that way. But I told him he had to."

"It was like being drafted," John F. Kennedy said later. "My father wanted his eldest son in politics. 'Wanted' isn't the right word. He demanded it. You know my father."

Later, with John in the White House and Robert, another son, appointed Attorney General, Mr. Kennedy insisted that Edward M., his youngest son, have his share of public office, a Senatorship from Massachusetts.

The elder Kennedy laid down the law in a conversation with the President and the Attorney General: "You boys have what you want and everybody worked to help you get it. Now it's Teddy's turn. I'm going to see that he gets what he wants."

And Edward got the Senate seat that he wanted in 1962 but without the active participation of his father, who had been partly paralyzed by a stroke in December 1961.

Mr. Kennedy's pride in his sons was immense. John's election to the presidency—he was the first Roman Catholic to sit in the White House—gave his father unexampled satisfaction. The beam of Mr. Kennedy's face in photographs at the time reflected the sweet triumph he felt.

Afterward, when his son was assassinated in November 1963, Mr. Kennedy was a frail invalid, yet he met the tragedy with stoic fortitude, concealing his intense grief in silence. For the fulfillment of his family ambitions, he would have to look to Edward and to Robert, the elder surviving son, in whose election to the Senate from New York in 1964 Mr. Kennedy found pleasure.

But tragedy continued to stalk the Kennedys. On June 5, 1968, only minutes after he had won the California primary for the Democratic presidential nomination, Robert Kennedy was shot by an assassin in a Los Angeles hotel. He died the next day.

Mr. Kennedy had nine children. Three of his four sons predeceased him, as did a daughter, Kathleen, who was killed in an air accident in 1948. Rosemary, another daughter, has been in an institution since the 1940's as mentally retarded.

Of the three other daughters, Jean was married to Stephen Smith, later active in the Kennedy financial dealings; Eunice was married to Sargent Shriver, manager of the Kennedys' Merchandise Mart in Chicago and later director of the Peace Corps and the Office of Economic Opportunity and Ambassador to France; and Patricia was married to Peter Lawford, the British actor. The Lawfords were divorced in February 1966.

Mr. Kennedy's success as a dynast was equaled by that in the realm of finance. He enjoyed making money, and was very good at it indeed. He coined millions in stock speculation, the movies, liquor importing, real estate, oil ventures, and corporate reorganization. Sharp and shrewd, he was not primarily interested in industry and production, but rather in stocks and securities. Of these he was an astute analyst, so keen, in fact, that he developed a prescience of what the stock market would do. His exquisite sense of timing gave him an edge over many other speculators.

In explaining Mr. Kennedy's success in the stock market, Richard J. Whalen wrote in *The Founding Father*: "He mixed well in all kinds of company, against every background. He was equally at ease with hard-eyed manipulators like [Ben] Smith and Wall Street patricians like Jeremiah Milbank, with corporation bosses as different as Paramount's [Adolph] Zukor and GE's Owen D. Young, with bantering newspapermen and press lords like William Randolph Hearst, Colonel Robert R. McCormick, and Joseph M. Patterson. He could enjoy the companionship of celebrities at the Ziegfeld Roof and of roistering theatrical unknowns at Bertolotti's in Greenwich Village. Kennedy moved through many worlds, and only the keenest observer would detect the profound detachment of this gregarious man who belonged to no world but his own."

Although Mr. Kennedy was, in his heyday, a hail-fellow-well-met with important friends in key corporate and financial and political positions, he was not accepted socially by the entrenched families He was blackballed when he sought membership in the Cohasset Country Club in Massachusetts, which was run by Boston's old families. In New York he fared a little better, but he and his family were never really taken into the city's society. In Hollywood, where he passed time in the late 1920's, his status was higher, but he was still uncomfortable.

Mr. Kennedy resented the doors closed against him, and he eventually took opulent refuge in Palm Beach, Cap d'Antibes on the French Riviera, and Cape Cod.

Mr. Kennedy's eagerness to make money was so strong that many observers considered him brusque and unfeeling in his use of economic power. As an example, his critics cite the fact that, shortly after buying control of the Keith-Albee-Orpheum theater chain in 1928, Mr. Kennedy responded to a business suggestion from E. F. Albee, the chain's titular president, by telling him: "Didn't you know, Ed? You're washed up, you're through."

At one time Mr. Kennedy had political ambitions for himself. He served with distinction as first chairman of the Securities and Exchange Commission, and he supported President Franklin D. Roosevelt when other business leaders reviled him.

Mr. Kennedy was named Ambassador to Britain in 1938 and served through 1940. There, during the crisis over Czechoslovakia at Munich, he made known his support of Prime Minister Neville Chamberlain's appeasement policy. "It is true," Mr. Kennedy said then, "that the democratic and dictator countries have important and fundamental divergencies of outlook. But there is simply no sense, common or otherwise, in letting these differences grow into unrelenting antagonism. After all, we have to live together in the same world, whether we like it or not."

War, in Mr. Kennedy's view, was a fearsome catastrophe. "Joe thought war was irrational and debasing," a confidant said. "War destroyed capital. What could be worse than that?"

In 1940, after war had broken out, Mr. Kennedy explained his view in a letter to a friend in the United States: "I always believed that if England stayed out of war it would be better for the United States and for that reason I was a great believer in appeasement. I felt that if war came, that was the beginning of the end for everybody, provided it lasted for two or three years. I see no reason yet for changing my mind one bit."

Meanwhile, Mr. Kennedy expressed somewhat similar views in public in the United States. "As you love America," he told one Boston audience in 1939, "don't let anything that comes out of any country in the world make you believe you can make a situation one whit better by getting into the war. There is no place in this fight for us."

These remarks caused Mr. Kennedy to lose prestige abroad and at home, for in the climate of those times his isolationism was severely criticized. He had seemingly misjudged the thrust of events and in doing so he voiced opinions that proved to be political liabilities not only to himself but also to his son John. After John Kennedy began his rise in politics, his father's isolationism was kept in the background lest it be misunderstood.

At the time there were whispers that Mr. Kennedy was anti-Semitic. These reports were based in part on Mr. Kennedy's habit of referring in conversation to Jews as "sheenies" and "kikes." (He was, it was pointed out in his defense, equally inelegant about Italians—he called them "wops"—and the Irish who were "micks" to him.) In part, the whispers were also based on documents in the Nazi archives, among them dispatches from Herbert von Dirksen, the German envoy in London. In one message allegedly covering a long talk with Ambassador Kennedy, von Dirksen wrote: "The Ambassador then touched upon the Jewish question. In this connection it was not so much the fact that we wanted to get rid of the Jews that was so harmful to us, but rather the loud clamor with which we accomplished this purpose." Mr. Kennedy denied the authenticity of the interview and said that the views attributed to him were "complete poppycock." He often publicly criticized Hitler's persecution of the Jews in later years.

Joseph P. Kennedy's independence and his fierce will to succeed were bred into him as a child. His father, Patrick J. Kennedy, was born in an East Boston slum, but he became a "lace-curtain" Irishman, with a comfortable income derived from ownership of saloons, a wholesale liquor business, and an interest in a bank. He was determined that his son, who was born on September 6, 1888, should rise high in the world.

With this in mind, he sent Joseph to Boston Latin School and to Harvard, schools that few Boston Irish Catholics attended in those years. There the young man experienced the hauteur of the established families. He got to know the well-connected at Harvard (his class was 1912) but he was not a member of the best clubs. (Mr. Kennedy's connections with Harvard were never enthusiastic, and they became positively frigid when he was turned down for an honorary degree later in life.)

In addition to giving his son educational advantages that most Roman Catholic boys of his day did not enjoy, Patrick Kennedy endowed Joseph with a political heritage that was to come in handy for Joseph's sons. Patrick was a power in Boston politics, serving five terms as a State Representative and one as a State Senator. He was also a member of the famous Board of Strategy, the inner circle of Boston Irish ward leaders.

Quiet-spoken, Patrick Kennedy had little in common temperamentally with the ebullient John F. (Honey Fitz) Fitzgerald, the maternal grandfather of the thirty-fifth President. In fact, Pat Kennedy found Honey Fitz, who served three terms in Congress and was Mayor of Boston, a barely tolerable buffoon, much given to singing *Sweet Adeline*.

But the families were on social terms, and in 1914, Joseph P. Kennedy married Rose Fitzgerald, daughter of Honey Fitz.

Joseph was at that time a lanky youth with pale-blue eyes and sandy-red hair who had showed business acumen by earning five thousand dollars as entrepreneur of a tourist-bus enterprise during summer vacations at Harvard.

He told friends that he would be a millionaire before he was thirty-five. Within two years of his graduation he was president of a bank, the Columbia Trust Company, in which his father was a director. He and Mrs. Kennedy moved to Brookline, then a moderately fashionable suburb of Boston. The family expanded rapidly—five babies in six years, nine in all.

John F. Kennedy, their second child, was born in the Brookline house on May 29, 1917. Shortly after his birth, the father accepted Charles M. Schwab's offer of a wartime executive job at the Bethlehem Steel Company's big Fore River plant in Quincy, Massachusetts.

At the end of World War I, he joined an investment banking firm in Boston. He foresaw the beginning of a wild financial boom and soon he was in Wall Street, trying his luck as a lone-wolf operator.

During the 1920's Mr. Kennedy dabbled in show business. He bought a chain of New England movie houses, got control of a small producing company, and finally flourished as a board chairman, special adviser, or reorganizer of five film, vaudeville, and radio companies: Paramount, Pathé, First National, Keith-Albee-Orpheum, and the Radio Corporation of America. He is said to have made $5 million in three years in the motion-picture business.

In pursuit of his motion-picture ventures, Mr. Kennedy spent a considerable time on the West Coast, leaving the day-to-day rearing of the family to his wife. It was she who ruled the children in her husband's name and saw to it that, absent though he was, he retained their respect.

Among the movie stars Mr. Kennedy backed was Gloria Swanson, whose banker, adviser, and close friend he was for several years. The end of their relationship was abrupt. "I questioned his judgment," Miss Swanson recalled. "He did not like to be questioned." Earlier, however, she had named her adopted son for him.

All the while Mr. Kennedy was managing Miss Swanson's fortunes and making money in Hollywood, he was busy in Wall Street. When the crash came in 1929 he was largely out of the market, having taken his winnings early and in cash. "Only a fool," he said at the time, "holds out for the top dollar." He also made money in the crash itself by selling stocks short.

Meanwhile, by 1926, Mr. Kennedy's varied business interests were concentrated so exclusively in New York that he decided to uproot his family from the Boston scene. The move was made in style—a private railroad car brought the family from Brookline to their new home in the Riverdale section of the Bronx.

Later the family moved to Bronxville, New York, where Mr. Kennedy had purchased an eleven-bedroom red-brick mansion surrounded by spacious lawns. This was the family homestead until World War II.

Mr. Kennedy had announced his intention of settling a $1 million trust fund on each of the children. He said he wanted them to be able to look him in the eye and tell him to go to hell. Yet, with all this outward show of encouraging independence, he somehow managed to instill in the children a fierce kind of tribal loyalty.

Mr. Kennedy entered national politics in 1932. Through dealings with William Randolph Hearst, the publisher, he was of significant help in obtaining the Democratic presidential nomination for Mr. Roosevelt. Moreover, he gave $25,000 to his campaign fund, lent it $50,000, and raised $100,000 for it from friends.

He had a hope of being named Secretary of the Treasury, but President Roosevelt chose him as the first chairman of the Securities and Exchange Commission. In this post he was responsible for writing the stern regulations that outlawed wild buying on margin and that protected investors from sharp Wall Street practices.

Just before taking the government job, Mr. Kennedy made a million dollars or more by cornering the important franchise for several Scotch whiskies and a British gin. With repeal imminent, he obtained a government permit to import thousands of cases of his whisky and gin for medicinal purposes. Kennedy warehouses were bulging and ready to flow when repeal came. The franchise had cost $118,000. Mr. Kennedy sold it thirteen years later for $8.5 million.

Just before his appointment to the SEC, Mr. Kennedy was questioned by President Roosevelt in the presence of Raymond Moley, a New Deal adviser. In the conversation, Mr. Moley told Mr. Kennedy that "if anything in your career in business could injure the President, this is the time to spill it."

In his book, *After Seven Years*, Mr. Moley recalled what happened next: "Kennedy reacted precisely as I thought he would. With a burst of profanity he defied anyone to question his devotion to the public interest or to point to a single shady act in his whole life. The President did not need to worry about that, he said. What was more, he would give his critics—and here again the profanity flowed freely—an administration of the SEC that would be a credit to the country, the President, himself, and his family—clear down to the ninth child."

And, indeed, liberals who had protested Mr. Kennedy's appointment were obliged to concede that he did a splendid job at the commission. He was a good administrator—conscientious, outspoken, thorough.

He resigned in 1935, but was recalled to Washington as chairman of the Maritime Commission, a post in which he served with distinction in an attempt to reorganize the nation's merchant navy.

In 1936, when many business leaders were joining the Liberty League to battle the New Deal, Mr. Kennedy supported Mr. Roosevelt's second-term bid, writing an effective tract, *I'm for Roosevelt*, that argued that the New Deal was saving the capitalist economic structure.

His reward this time was the post of Ambassador to the Court of St. James's. He was to represent the United States in London at one of the most crucial periods of Anglo-American relations—1938 through the outbreak of World War II and until his resignation in the fall of 1940.

Mr. Kennedy's honeymoon with the British press was short-lived. A chill also quickly developed between the Ambassador and the White House. In London Mr. Kennedy had become a close and frequently consulted friend of Prime Minister Chamberlain and other leading appeasers of Hitler in the government—Sir Horace Wilson and Sir John Simon. Like them, he felt that Munich assured "peace in our time."

He made a widely quoted speech at the British Navy League dinner in 1938 in which he said that the world was big enough for the democracies and the dictatorships, and there was no reason why they couldn't get along together without war.

President Roosevelt had not yet taken an open stand against the Munich agreement, but he found Mr. Kennedy's words hard to swallow. Shortly after the Navy League speech, the Ambassador was in the news again with a plan to remove six hundred thousand Nazi-persecuted Jews from Germany and resettle them in sparsely populated parts of the world. In Washington, President Roosevelt and Secretary of State Cordell Hull, clearly annoyed, said they knew nothing of the Kennedy plan.

The war years were grim for the Kennedys. Mr. Kennedy's eldest son and namesake went to war as a Navy pilot, and was killed when his plane exploded over the English Channel on August 12, 1944. His death cut off a political career that had begun in 1940 when he was a twenty-five-year-old delegate to the Democratic National Convention.

Mr. Kennedy was emotionally shattered, for at that time his son John, also a Navy lieutenant, was in Chelsea Naval Hospital, Boston, recovering from severe injuries suffered when a Japanese destroyer rammed his PT boat in the Solomon Islands. Only a few weeks after the death of Joseph, Jr., Mr. Kennedy lost his son-in-law, the Marquess of Hartington, the husband of Kathleen. He was killed while leading an infantry charge in Normandy. (Four years later Kathleen was killed in a plane crash in France.)

After the war, Mr. Kennedy increased his fortune by Texas oil investments and the purchase of real estate in New York, Palm Beach, and Chicago. He bought Chicago's Merchandise Mart, the world's largest commercial building, from Marshall Field in 1945 for $12.5 million, putting up only $800,000 in cash, and promptly mortgaged it for $18 million.

By the end of 1945 Mr. Kennedy owned real estate in New York having an assessed valuation of $15 million. His transactions were spectacular. He bought a property at 51st Street and Lexington Avenue for $600,000 and sold it for $3,970,000; another at 46th Street and Lexington for $1.7 million, selling it for $4,975,000, and another at 59th and Lexington for $1.9 million, which skyrocketed in value to more than $5.5 million.

As fast as he moved into real estate, Mr. Kennedy got his money out by mortgaging his properties to the hilt. Much of the money he made went into oil ventures offering depletion allowances for tax purposes. He joined syndicates backing wildcat wells, and although his luck ran hot and cold he managed to earn high profits.

Meanwhile, in 1946, John F. Kennedy was persuaded to get into politics. A family council decided that he should make his debut in a race for the House of Representatives from the 11th Massachusetts District, which embraced Harvard, slum areas, and middle-class Irish and Italian wards in Boston.

At the time, the elder Kennedys were not legal residents of Massachusetts and John was not a registered Democrat, a qualification he met as the deadline was about to expire. The primary in June 1946 was crucial since the district was solidly Democratic. Ten aspirants sought the nomination, but only one had Joseph P. Kennedy for a father, whose command post was a suite in Boston's Ritz-Carlton Hotel. "I just called people," Mr. Kennedy said modestly in after years. "I got in touch with people I knew. I have a lot of contacts."

Describing Mr. Kennedy's role in that campaign, Mr. Whalen wrote in *The Founding Father:* "The telephone was the instrument and symbol of Kennedy's power. That a man with his enormous wealth enjoyed influence was not unusual; but the scope of his influence was extraordinary. He knew precisely whom to call to move the levers of local political power.

"Jack's campaign had two separate and distinct sides. On display before the voters was the candidate, surrounded by clean-cut, youthful volunteer workers, the total effect being one of wholesome amateurism. At work on the hidden side of the campaign were the professional politicians whom Joe Kennedy had quietly recruited. In his hotel suite and other private meeting places, they sat with their hats on and cigars aglow, a hard-eyed, cynical band, brainstorming strategy."

The result was that John Kennedy's district was saturated with his name, and he himself went from door to door soliciting votes. His brothers and sisters also pitched in. Joseph Kennedy did not believe in leaving politics to chance. His son won easily; his father's cash outlay, according to Mr. Whalen, was fifty thousand dollars. Once in office, Representative Kennedy was re-elected handily in 1948 and 1950.

As early as 1949, however, John (and his father) had an eye on Henry Cabot Lodge's Senate seat, which would be up for contest in

1952. Every weekend John was in Massachusetts on speaking engagements in preparation for that campaign. "We're going to sell Jack like soap flakes," his father said.

And again in 1952 Mr. Kennedy moved into the Ritz-Carlton, recruited campaign personnel, and worked out of the public view. How much he spent was never disclosed, but the cost of the Kennedy campaign was estimated to exceed five hundred thousand dollars.

The campaign against Mr. Lodge and his defeat had overtones for Mr. Kennedy. In 1916, Mr. Lodge's grandfather had barely beaten Mr. Fitzgerald, Mrs. Joseph Kennedy's father. Moreover, since 1936, Mr. Lodge, the quintessence of Brahminism, had defeated James M. Curley, Joseph Casey, and David I. Walsh, three popular Irish politicians who had sought the Senatorship.

A few weeks before the election the Boston *Post* switched support from Mr. Lodge to his opponent. Six years later a House investigating committee discovered that Joseph Kennedy had lent John Fox, owner of the *Post*, five hundred thousand dollars. The loan was made after the election and Mr. Kennedy insisted that it was "simply a commercial transaction."

This was a time when Senator Joseph R. McCarthy, Republican of Wisconsin, was at the height of his power in Washington. Mr. Kennedy contributed to Mr. McCarthy's campaign. It was later alleged that one purpose of Mr. Kennedy's contribution was to keep the Wisconsin Senator from coming into Massachusetts and campaigning in behalf of Mr. Lodge. Whatever the truth of this, the fact was that Mr. McCarthy stayed out of Massachusetts. And John F. Kennedy suppressed any urge he might have had to attack Mr. McCarthy.

But when he ran for President in 1960 his father was a definite albatross. At the Democratic convention in Los Angeles, supporters of Adlai E. Stevenson charged that Joseph P. Kennedy had attempted to buy the nomination for his son and had tried to influence delegates, notably from New York and New Jersey. Mrs. Franklin D. Roosevelt, who had never liked Joseph Kennedy, wondered about the father's influence on the son.

And just a few hours before John F. Kennedy won the nomination, Senator Lyndon B. Johnson of Texas, a leading contender for the nomination, made a bitter attack on his father. "I was never any Chamberlain umbrella policy man," Senator Johnson said. "I never thought Hitler was right."

If the Johnson slur angered Senator Kennedy, political expediency dictated an overnight healing of wounds. Next day he said he wanted Senator Johnson as running mate and, to the astonishment of many,

Mr. Johnson accepted. He succeeded President Kennedy after his assassination in 1963.

The idea that Senator Kennedy seldom, if ever, agreed with "Old Joe" on political issues was carefully nurtured by the Democrats in the campaign and by the candidate himself. "Dad is a financial genius, all right," his son once said, "but in politics he is something else."

Joseph Kennedy was more than three thousand miles from American shores, in a villa at Cap d'Antibes, when his son won the nomination. He stayed there most of the summer. He was back in his rambling beachfront home at Hyannis Port, Massachusetts, on Cape Cod, in time for the election.

"I just think it's time for seventy-two-year-old men like me to step aside and let the young people take over," he told a correspondent who hunted him out on the Riviera. Rose, his wife, had another explanation: "He has been rather a controversial figure all his life and he thinks it's easier for his sons if he doesn't appear on the scene."

He surfaced quickly when the election had been won. Shortly after Richard M. Nixon, the Republican candidate, had conceded, the Kennedys gathered for news photographers at Hyannis Port. The photos included a beaming Joseph Kennedy, sitting at the right of the new President.

Subsequently, until his crippling stroke, Mr. Kennedy was prominent in photos and articles on the activities of the First Family at the White House, Palm Beach, and Cape Cod. After his stroke, Mr. Kennedy lived in virtual seclusion either at Palm Beach or in Hyannis Port.

THEODOR REIK

Dr. Theodor Reik died in New York on December 31, 1969, at the age of eighty-one. One of the first students of Sigmund Freud, he was a talented contributor to psychoanalytic theory and practice. I had spent an afternoon with him shortly before his death and was impressed, despite his illness and fading faculties, by the degree of brilliance that remained.

IN 1910 AN impoverished twenty-two-year-old psychology student at the University of Vienna met Sigmund Freud, then fifty-four and a teacher of neurology at the school, who had just published *The Interpretation of Dreams*. Theodor Reik, the gifted young man, and the founder of psychoanalysis struck up an immediate and devoted friendship, which lasted until Freud's death in 1939.

One result of this personal and professional bond was that Dr. Reik became a pupil, protégé, expounder, and defender of Freud. More, in his own right, he became one of the titans of psychoanalysis, a master of theory and technique who made important contributions to the development of both.

Of his fundamental contributions, elaborated in fifty books, three were considered especially significant: the importance of creative intuition in analysis; the role of masochism in human relations; and the relation of love to sex.

Listening with the Third Ear, one of Dr. Reik's most widely read and admired books, summed up his view that there is an essential interaction in psychoanalysis between the unconscious of the patient and his analyst; and that the analyst, by using creative intuition—"the third ear"—can sense the unspoken and unconscious thoughts of his patient and turn them to therapeutic benefit.

In *Masochism and Modern Man*, which Dr. Reik said was his masterwork, he proposed that the masochist is basically a pleasure-seeking person. Masochism, he argued, is a revelation of universal need;

and the masochist "degrades and humiliates and often ingratiates himself [for] only one aim: to be loved.

"He is not only willing but eager to sacrifice everything else, to take abuse and punishment of every kind if he can only gain this end," he wrote.

Social masochism, he believed, is an important sociological and historical phenomenon. One instance he gave was that of the Christian martyrs, who sought "victory through defeat."

As for sex, Dr. Reik denied in *The Psychology of Sex Relations* that all neuroses have a sexual origin; neuroses, he suggested, come about because of a weakness in the ego. "A neurosis is an emotional disturbance caused by a shake-up of the self-trust and self-confidence of a person," he wrote. Love, for its part, is not an offshoot of the sex drive, but rather "a rival of it, fighting it and finally uniting with it."

He gave this definition of love: "All love is founded on a dissatisfaction with oneself. It is an attempt to escape from oneself in search of a better, an ideal self. The lover imagines that he has found it in his object. Is love thus an illusion? Of course it is, but that is not the most significant thing about it. Illusions are also psychical realities. Freud called religion an illusion, but he did not deny that it was a great educational factor in the history of mankind. We attend a theatrical performance and give ourselves up voluntarily to an illusion. We don't like to be deprived of the illusion while the performance lasts or to be reminded that Lady Macbeth is really Peggy Smith and King Duncan a certain Harry Brown. We enjoy the illusion and follow the scenes on the stage with an interest as genuine and emotions as strong as if we were here concerned with 'real life.' Love is an attempt to change a piece of a dream-world into reality."

Dr. Reik was among the most readable writers on psychoanalysis, aphoristic, witty, free of technical jargon. "It would be superfluous to tell woman that the proper study of mankind is man. She will never be interested in anything else," he once said.

Some of his other observations were these:

¶ "I have come across some women in analytic practice who lacked the faculty of being catty. They were either emotionally perverted, masochistic, homosexual, or neurotic."

¶ "Suffering, consciously experienced and mastered, teaches us wisdom."

¶ "No one should ever have a guilt feeling about his thoughts. If you stand before Tiffany's window and want to steal some of its contents, there's no reason for a guilt feeling. The more guilty your thoughts make you feel, the more likely you are to commit a crime."

¶"To express unafraid and unashamed what one really thinks and feels is one of the great consolations of life."

¶"No one is as stubborn and successful in having bad luck as the masochist."

¶"Women in general want to be loved for what they are and men for what they accomplish. The first for their looks and charm, the latter for their actions."

¶"Beware of bachelors who have an idealistic view of noble, chaste womanhood. Young women should prefer the company of declared woman-haters. They always marry."

Dr. Reik was not only a prolific writer in German and English, but he was also a dedicated analyst, with a reputation for gentleness and generosity toward his patients. His English was authentically Viennese, and his manner was courtly with a touch of shyness to it. Like his preceptor, he placed his patients on a couch, which he once figured he had had reupholstered every five years.

In his earlier years Dr. Reik was clean-shaven, but in his late sixties he grew a beard, and it gave his face a remarkable resemblance to Freud's. Indeed, when he stood against a background of photographs of Freud in his study he seemed to merge with the pictures and become one with his mentor.

Theodor Reik was born in Vienna on May 12, 1888, the son of Max and Caroline Reik. His father was a civil servant, who died when Theodor was in his teens. At the University of Vienna, which he entered when he was eighteen, he studied literature and psychology, and he took his doctorate in psychology in 1912, the first ever awarded in that subject by the university. His thesis dealt psychoanalytically with Flaubert's *Temptation of St. Anthony*.

Freud recognized Dr. Reik's talent for psychoanalysis almost immediately and persuaded him to undertake writing and research rather than spend time becoming a medical doctor. At the same time Freud supported his protégé while he was being analyzed in Berlin by Karl Abraham, who waived his fee.

"It was a stroke of luck that I met Freud," Dr. Reik recalled in after years. "When I went to his office I had my heart beating like a young girl. After dinner Freud was accustomed to take a long walk. I knew what streets he would walk along and I would wait along his way so that I could accompany him. I was very poor, so he gave me from his pocket a certain amount."

Freud did more than keep his friend alive: he obtained for him membership in the Vienna Psychoanalytic Society. And after World

War I, in which Dr. Reik served with distinction, he was elected secretary of the organization.

From 1918 to 1928 Dr. Reik practiced in Vienna. He was also a member of a select group that met with Freud on Wednesday evenings. In this period he wrote extensively and importantly on crime. According to Joseph M. Natterson, a biographer, "These papers include many interesting clinical examples of case material and technical problems in psychoanalytic treatment, but the major concept is that unconscious guilt motivates both the crime itself and the criminal's need to be caught and punished."

Moving to Berlin in 1928, Dr. Reik set up practice and taught at the Berlin Institute until the advent of Hitlerism obliged him to move to The Hague. In these years he pioneered an attack on the view that the unconscious can be made to yield to an orderly, methodical approach. "Reik boldly asserted that psychoanalysis is not, and perhaps never will be, ready for such a systematic approach and that, in fact, such an approach can have the paradoxical effect of vitiating the psychoanalytical experience," Dr. Natterson asserted, adding: "According to Reik, the essence of the psychoanalytic experience is that it is an unconscious duet between patient and analyst. The important insights arise from this unconscious interplay as surprises to both the analyst and patient, and reliance on consciously held theoretical asumptions by the analyst serve to interfere with, rather than implement, the arrival at the appropriate truths."

In 1938, with the Nazi German threat hanging over the Netherlands, Dr. Reik fled to the United States with eight dollars in his pocket. He had hoped to be received with some acclaim by his colleagues here, but he was snooted instead because he was not a physician. Indeed, he was denied membership by the New York Psychoanalytic Society. Subsequently, he helped to found a more tolerant organization, the National Psychological Association for Psychoanalysis.

In addition to treating private patients, he set up a clinic for those who could not afford the high fees of most analysts. Known as the Theodor Reik Clinic, it was housed at 158 East 38th Street. There Dr. Reik modified that intensive, six-day-a-week therapy that was the custom of many therapists. Instead, patients were seen in fifty-minute sessions, once, twice, or possibly thrice weekly, according to need.

As Dr. Reik pursued his own work here and as his books were published, esteem for him grew. And when he was sixty-five a group of his colleagues, friends, and pupils issued *Explorations in Psychoanalysis*, a tribute to his work. Assessing Dr. Reik at that point, Dr. Robert Lindner wrote: "Theodor Reik is an anachronism in the twentieth century, wherein most men are cast in a mass mold. A soaring and inquisitive soul, fiercely independent, proudly skeptical, he calls to mind certain Renaissance figures whose genius has been to fructify whatever their minds have touched.

"Possessed of a wide-roving intellect, unafraid, and denying that there are any limits to inquiry, he belongs among the pioneers of the conquering human spirit who dare beyond the perimeters of complacency into the uncharted wilderness."

Later came recognition of Dr. Reik's skills as a writer, among them one from Professor John Dollard of Yale, who considered him "undoubtedly the best living writer about psychoanalysis."

Dr. Reik continued to see patients, to teach, and to write into the mid-sixties, but he was too modest and too diffident to capitalize on his fame. Indeed, he suffered public neglect, spending the last years of his life in a nondescript apartment on West 86th Street. Illness robbed his brilliant mind of its coherence, but he struggled to be pleasant with visitors and to tell anecdotes about his life.

His office-study contained a desk, a couch and chairs—all ancient and without any special style. One wall was covered with photographs of Freud; and on another wall were pictures of Gustav Mahler, Arthur Schnitzler, Anatole France, Richard Beerhofmann and Feodor Dostoyevsky. There was also, atop a bookcase, Nietzsche's death mask and a miniature reproduction of Michelangelo's *Moses*.

Dr. Reik was married twice. His first wife died in the mid-thirties, when the couple were living in the Netherlands. His second wife, the former Marija Cubelic, died in 1959 after a long illness. He had three children: a son, Arthur, by his first marriage; and two daughters, Irene and Miriam, by his second marriage.

In his life Dr. Reik was often beset by those who believed that psychoanalysts overrated their skills and could not be called scientists.

"No, no, no! That is not so," he always retorted to such charges, "because I have seen hundreds of patients and the laws of human dynamics are as exceptionless as the laws of physics and chemistry."

DAVID O. MCKAY

David O. McKay died in Salt Lake City on January 18, 1970, at the age of ninety-six. The Mormon leader was an extraordinary man, little known to most Americans yet a world figure with whose life readers should be acquainted. My obit, which involved a trip to Salt Lake City, was an attempt to cast some light on both Mr. McKay and his church.

As Prophet, Seer, and Revelator of the Church of Jesus Christ of Latter-day Saints, David Oman McKay was the supreme spiritual leader of almost three million Mormons around the world. He was the ninth head of a church organized by Joseph Smith and five other men at Fayette (now Waterloo), New York, on April 6, 1830.

During Mr. McKay's administration, which began on April 9, 1951, when he was seventy-seven years old, the Mormon Church experienced its greatest growth both in membership and in influence. Much of this was attributable to the ceaseless exertions of Mr. McKay, the warmth and humanity of his personality, and the breadth of his approach to religion. He captured the esteem and affection not only of his own people, but also of people of other faiths. In the opinion of many discerning Mormons he had more genuine magnetism than any of their leaders but Joseph Smith.

A man of simple eloquence, quite in contrast to the thundering of Brigham Young or the dryness of his immediate predecessors, Mr. McKay personified missionary suasion. He appealed to the heart, offering hope and salvation to those who sought the solace of his faith. Indeed, many Mormons, asked to characterize Mr. McKay's chief contribution to the church, called him "the missionary president."

Before he became president, Mr. McKay was active in the mission field; and from 1951 until he was nearly ninety-five he traveled the world in support of missions. The doubling of the church membership in this period reflected his zeal. Much of this astonishing growth was outside the United States—in Europe, Latin America, New Zealand, and the South Seas. The expansion tended to universalize the Mormon church, changing it from a small, Utah-centered group to a large and respected global institution.

In an interview for this article in the fall of 1968, Mr. McKay himself ranked as his greatest accomplishment "the making of the church a worldwide organization." This had been brought about, he said, by, among other things, "visits to every foreign mission; meeting leaders of nations, ambassadors, and other government officials; personally greeting all members of the church and investigators; holding meetings in every mission; and stimulating the work of local members and missionaries."

Mr. McKay met the church's growth by providing temples for its new members. Five were built in his presidency—in Britain, Switzerland, New Zealand, Los Angeles, and Oakland—bringing the total to thirteen. Previously there had been eight temples—four in Utah, including the spired granite structure in Salt Lake City, and one each in Arizona, Idaho, Canada, and Hawaii.

These temples, not to be confused with the thousands of houses of worship, are of central importance in the Mormon religion, for in them must be performed such sacred ordinances as endowment (a pledging of oneself to the church) and sealing in marriage. The temples built under Mr. McKay's direction served further to extrovert the church, since it was no longer necessary for Mormons to travel to the United States or Canada to participate in the highest rites of their faith. The church headquarters remained anchored in Salt Lake City, of course; but the outlook from Temple Square was no longer so completely parochial.

In the process of universalizing and humanizing his church, Mr. McKay managed to mute many of its past frictions with the Roman Catholic and Protestant communities. His approach was personal rather than theological, broad rather than sectarian. Reflecting this was his reply to a question about the most important moment of his life. It was: "The feeling of such peace and satisfaction and love for all God's children, which comes late in life after more than eighty years of work in the church and travels among people of all lands. My one great desire for them is that they may have peace and happiness in this world and the world to come."

Apart from having a personality that radiated confidence and good will, Mr. McKay was able to exercise his leadership through his unusual position in the church, at whose apex he stood. His authority derived from a revelation to Joseph Smith in 1843, in which God pronounced that "there is never but one on earth at a time" on whom the full power of the Holy Spirit is conferred, and that one is the head of the Mormon church.

Faithful Mormons believed that Mr. McKay was a prophet of God, a man whose words and actions were divinely inspired and a man, moreover, capable of receiving revelations. At least one prophecy was credited to Mr. McKay. As related by Alvin R. Dyer, one of his Counselors, Mr. McKay said in 1960, "The time has come for many thousands of people in Europe to accept the teachings of the church."

"And," Mr. Dyer reported in an interview in 1968, "in two years fifty thousand persons joined the church. This was in direct fulfillment of Mr. McKay's prophecy."

Although no written revelations such as those produced by Joseph Smith and Brigham Young were attributed to Mr. McKay, church leaders said that revelations took place every day. "The direction of God's people is dependent on relevation," Mr. Dyer asserted. He ascribed to revelation decisions to build temples, to revise the church welfare plan, and to reinstitute a program to strengthen family bonds. Other revelations, said Joseph Fielding Smith, another Counselor, had to do with church assignments "according to the will of the Lord."

Mr. Dyer expressed the view that revelations through Mr. McKay, although not reduced to writing, were perfectly valid. Divine inspiration, he remarked, could take many forms. He recalled several temple meetings on church matters in which Mr. McKay had buttressed his presentations by adding, "Thus sayeth the Lord."

Mr. McKay's patriarchal authority, which was reinforced by tradition, extended from the spiritual into the temporal realm. In both areas he was accounted by many Mormons a liberal, at least in the first years of his administration. One instance of his liberalism was a positive attitude toward Negroes, according to Dr. Sterling G. McMurrin, a Mormon and head of the graduate school at the University of Utah.

Basing its position on an obscure passage in the Book of Abraham, written by Joseph Smith, the Mormon Church, while accepting Negroes as communicants, bars them from the priesthood, to which all other Mormon men are eligible. This discrimination has disturbed many Mormons, especially in the intellectual community, who have sought to accommodate the church to the twentieth century.

Dr. McMurrin was among those who discussed the problem with Mr. McKay in 1954. Recalling the conversation in 1968, the educator quoted the Mormon leader as declaring that "there is no doctrine that holds Negroes under a divine curse," but that rather it was a matter of practice, "which we expect to change."

The change did not materialize. Dr. McMurrin explained this by saying that Mr. McKay, for all his humaneness, did not think in terms of laying out rules for the Mormon institution. "He was not sophisticated about social forces," Dr. McMurrin said. He added that as Mr. McKay aged he was more and more surrounded by conventional and conservative advisers.

In his robust years Mr. McKay was a firm, even stubborn, executive who sometimes ignored his Counselors, albeit after patiently listening to their advice. Six feet one inch tall and weighing two hundred well-proportioned pounds, he was an imposing figure. His eyes were hazel, and they seemed to many to be extraordinarily penetrating. "He could look right through you," it was said.

He gave off an air of command that called implicitly for obedience. "Never give an order that's not obeyed, or cannot be obeyed," he once explained to his children. "And if you give an order, be certain that it's followed through."

His general manner, however, was more genial than stern, his smile more ready than his frown. He was prepared to overlook some of the rigidities of church practice. New converts, for example, were not required absolutely to give up smoking; he tolerated coffee-drinking in Mormons who felt they needed the stimulant; he encouraged freedom of speech and opinion in church circles; and he was accessible to almost anyone who wanted to talk with him.

Mr. McKay put in a formidable working day. Rising usually at 4 A.M., he was in his sparsely furnished office on the first floor of the gray granite church headquarters building at 5:30. He sat in a plain leather swivel chair, and his desk was an oblong, glass-covered table, at which he received visitors. With an interruption for lunch (his preference was a beefsteak, rare) and a short nap, he dispatched religious and temporal business until early evening. He dined with his wife and some church official or a member of his family and retired early.

The range of business that passed through his hands was enormous —from the selection and assignment of church personnel to the location of a federal office building in Salt Lake City; from decisions on church investments to religious education; from the affairs of the church-owned Beneficial Life Insurance Company to those of the church-operated Hotel Utah; from bills before the Utah Legislature to a speech at a church conference.

Miss Clare Middlemiss, his secretary for more than thirty years, kept a daily diary that ultimately filled a large bookcase. One entry from January 25, 1957, related Mr. McKay's concern lest Mormons not take polio vaccine. "I have learned," he wrote, "that some of our church officials are advising members not to take the polio vaccine and to rely

wholly on faith. I made it clear that the Lord expects us to do everything we can to take advantage of all the improvements and discoveries
[of medicine] and only when we have done all we can do we go to
the Lord and rely upon His help."

Other diary entries recorded conversations with legislators over public
policy and requests of Mr. McKay "to pass the word" on the church's
stand on various proposals. In Utah, with 70 percent of the population
Mormon, the church position carried preponderant weight. Although
Mr. McKay was not a heavy-handed theocrat, he did flex the church's
muscle on such issues as opposition to liberal liquor statutes and support
of so-called right-to-work laws.

A plan to sell whiskey by the drink was easily defeated in a Utah
referendum after Mr. McKay had inveighed against it. Utah also banned
the union shop. This was an extension of Mormon belief in the doctrine
of free agency, by which man is considered to have a choice whether to
accept God's teachings. Applied in the temporal sphere, the belief
militates against compulsory union membership, an ingredient of the
union shop. Critics of Mormon policy in this area have said that the
union shop ban reflects the church's close alliance with conservative
business interests. Critics have also charged that the ban is responsible
in part for low wages in the state. Utah, they point out, is thirty-sixth
in the Union in per capita income. Its figure of $2,604 (in 1968) com-
pares with $3,969 for Connecticut, which ranks first, and with $1,896 for
Mississippi, which ranks fiftieth.

Mr. McKay's church was itself enormously wealthy. Its income was,
however, a closely guarded secret, although some estimates put it at $1
million a day. Some of the money came from investments as diverse as
a cattle ranch in Florida and an equity in the Los Angeles *Times*. Some
came from its members, who gave 10 percent of their gross income to
the church. Not all Mormons tithed, of course; but for most it was a
sacred obligation, the fulfillment of which was essential for admission
to a temple.

If church income was high, so was its outgo, for Mr. McKay and his
colleagues spent generously on missions, on education, and on buildings,
while taking nothing for themselves in salary. Mr. McKay, for example,
received his expenses and that was all.

The tradition of selfless sacrifice for the church was one into which
Mr. McKay was born.

His ancestry was Scotch-Welsh, and his paternal grandparents,
William and Ellen Oman McKay, were among the first in the British
Isles to be converted to Mormonism by missionaries dispatched from
Salt Lake City. In 1849, and for almost a century thereafter, the church

sought to strengthen itself in the United States by encouraging converts to immigrate to Utah and its vicinity. Converts were obtained then by "tracting" (a more sophisticated system was instituted by Mr. McKay), which involved knocking on doors and proselytizing anybody who seemed willing.

William McKay and his wife and their four children came to the United States in 1856, selling all their possessions to pay for the trip. After reaching the Mormon settlement in Iowa, they walked a thousand miles across the plains and mountains to Ogden, Utah.

Also converts, David O. McKay's maternal grandparents, Thomas and Margaret Evans, came from South Wales and settled in Ogden. William's son David married Thomas's daughter Jeanette, and their first son was David Oman McKay, born on a farm in Huntsville, near Ogden, on September 8, 1873. This was four years before the death of Brigham Young.

The farm, which Mr. McKay maintained until his death, shaped his early years, gave him a lasting interest in horsemanship (he was an excellent rider) and outdoor life, and was the place he retired to meditate from time to time. The rural values of enterprise and hard work and cooperation were those he prized.

"The individual is the most important element in our society," he said time and again, adding: "There can be no progress without individual leadership. Too many say, 'Let the government help us,' but that's not the way mankind has progressed. Rather we progress by having leaders who start on new courses that men follow. We must strike out and be individuals. Everyone must be a free agent—to be able to think and choose for himself."

David had his introduction to responsibility and leadership as a boy of eight, when his father spent two years as a missionary in Britain and left the farm nominally in his eldest child's charge. (In Mormon households the father is the patriarch and in his absence the oldest male child carries the burden.) This habit of authority, learned young, persisted in Mr. McKay when it came to his own family. "Father expected us to obey, and we did," David Lawrence McKay, one of his sons, recalled in an interview in 1968. He added that although his father could be commanding he could also enter into his children's games, playing baseball with them and crokinole and rook, two parlor pastimes.

While herding cattle and performing other farm chores, David found time to read in the English classics, for which he developed a lifelong fondness and from which he could quote, even in old age, long swatches. Robert Burns was a favorite, as was Shakespeare.

The boy attended public schools in Huntsville and then Weber Stake

Academy (later Weber College), of which his father was a founder. He began a career as a teacher at the age of twenty as principal of the Huntsville grade school. A year later, to qualify for a state teaching certificate, he enrolled for three years at the University of Utah, where he played on its first football team, was president of his class, and was its valedictorian when he was graduated in 1897.

This period of Mr. McKay's life coincided with federal persecution of the Mormon church, which was begun with the Edmunds Act in 1882. The persecution was aimed both at the Mormon practice of plural marriage and at the economic and political theocracy that the church had built in Utah. Under the Edmunds Act and the Edmunds-Taylor Act of 1887, Mormon leaders were jailed and church property was seized.

John Taylor, the immediate successor to Brigham Young, spent most of his ten-year administration in hiding. Wilford Woodruff, the next prophet, acting in the face of virtual dispersal and breakup of the church, decided to submit to federal power in 1890. Gradually, some church property was returned, but by the time Utah was admitted to the Union in 1896 the church was at an ebb (its membership was around two hundred thousand) and it was searching out likely young men as missionaries and leaders.

At about the same time, Mr. McKay once recalled, he sought divine help for his own future by kneeling and asking God for a revelation that would guide his spiritual thoughts. His answer, he said, came while he was serving as a missionary in Scotland, a call he undertook upon graduation from the university. The answer was given by a Mormon official who assured him: "If you are faithful, you will yet stand in the leading councils of the church."

The missionary call was an event he still remembered at ninety-five, when he thought of it as an opportunity "to follow in my father's footsteps and go to Scotland to teach the beliefs and principles of the Gospel." Missionary work in those days was arduous and often perilous. Joseph Fielding Smith, who also served in the British Isles, recalled in a conversation in 1968, when he was ninety-three, that he had been stoned at least once on his tour of duty. And finding likely converts was a matter of chance.

Mr. McKay returned exhilarated to Utah in 1899 after having been president of the Glascow district of the British mission. He immediately began to teach English at Weber, becoming superintendent of the college in 1902. His experience as a teacher made him a stickler for grammatical exactitude in himself and others. It also helped him forge a bond with young people, in whose educational welfare he was profoundly interested for the rest of his life.

In April 1906, while still head of Weber, he was called to membership in the Council of Twelve Apostles, the church's governing body.
At thirty-two he was its youngest member. In Mormon practice, a call,
or an appointment, is regarded as a divine summons, which has priority
over any temporal business in which the Mormon may be engaged.

Once an Apostle, Mr, McKay rose steadily in the church organization. A member of the Deseret Sunday School Board, he was appointed
second assistant general superintendent of the churchwide Sunday school
and then a member of the church Board of Education. Increasing responsibilities obliged him to resign his job at Weber in 1908 to devote
his full energies to religious affairs. For fifteen years his chief task was
in the field of church education, but he also took part in the work
of the Ogden Betterment League and the Red Cross.

Mr. McKay's career took a dramatic turn in late 1920, when he set
off on a thirteen-month tour of all the church's foreign missions, except
that in South Africa. The 62,500-mile trip, the most extensive of any
Mormon leader up to that time, opened his eyes to the world outside
Utah and laid the groundwork for his global religious outlook.

Almost immediately on his return to Salt Lake City he was dispatched to Liverpool for two years to head the church's European
missions. Once back in Salt Lake City, he was given general responsibility for the worldwide missions, a post in which he traveled extensively. Then, in 1934, he was named Second Counselor in the First
Presidency, the highest executive body in the church. The church leader
was then Heber J. Grant, and when he died in 1945 Mr. McKay was
continued as a Counselor by George Albert Smith, Mr. Grant's successor.

At various times during his membership in the First Presidency Mr.
McKay filled civic posts—he was chairman of the Utah State Centennial
Commission and the Utah Council of Child Health and Protection; he
served as regent of the University of Utah, trustee of the State Agricultural College, and trustee of Brigham Young University, a church-
operated institution.

The serenity of Mr. McKay's tenure as a Counselor was broken in
1945, when his favorite niece, Fawn McKay Brodie, published *No Man
Knows My History*, a biography of Joseph Smith. The Mormon leadership considered that the book, by the daughter of an Assistant Apostle,
cast some reflections on the founder of their religion, and Mrs. Brodie
was ordered to show cause why she should not be excommunicated. She
ignored the request. Her relations with her uncle, already strained
because she had married out of the faith, were virtually broken.

How much Mr. McKay was involved in Mrs. Brodie's disfellowship
was never made clear. Observers noted, however, that in his adminis-

tration no such penalty was imposed on Mrs. Juanita Brooks, a Mormon historian who wrote a book that rattled some church skeletons. Moreover, when there was a move to excommunicate Dr. McMurrin a few years ago, Mr. McKay had it quashed.

Mr. McKay came to the church presidency on the death of Mr. Smith in April 1951. As the eldest Apostle in point of service, he was "sustained," or accepted, as the Mormon prophet by a church conference then in progress.

The first years of his administration were marked by a strong surge in missionary work. In a decade the number of missionaries was quadrupled to about 12,000, and the number of annual converts rose from 12,000 to 180,000. Apart from Europe, a traditional source, conversions were accelerated in Latin America and the South Seas. Whenever converts were made the church provided schools and recreation facilities. Mr. McKay's active guidance in these projects was apparent, for he traveled everywhere in an effort to stimulate church growth—a total of three hundred thousand miles, he calculated.

At the same time Mr. McKay impressed his personality on the church by a nondogmatic approach to religious and civil affairs. On occasion he overrode his more conservative counselors in taking the church out of some political disputes. He seemed to want to play down the church as an obvious arbiter at the ballot box.

In the early 1960's the church leadership was troubled by the John Birch Society, whose ultraconservative views appealed to many Mormons, among them Ezra Taft Benson, an Apostle and Secretary of Agriculture in the Eisenhower Cabinet. When in 1963 Mr. Benson outspokenly endorsed the aims of the society he was sent to Europe for two years to head the church missionary effort. "David O. McKay sent him out of the country," according to Wallace Turner in *The Mormon Establishment*. If Mr. Benson harbored any indignation over his "exile," he did not show it publicly. In fact, in an interview in 1968, he praised Mr. McKay as "a true man of God."

Mr. McKay's liberalism, according to many observers, was a heartfelt feeling and it was against the grain of many of the aged church leaders, for whom authoritarianism was a righteous practice. In his later years, perhaps from 1965 onward, these observers said, Mr. McKay tended more toward tradition than he formerly had.

Until illness enfeebled him Mr. McKay was a familiar figure in Salt Lake City. He greeted friends on the streets; he mingled with church members at conferences; he seemed never too busy for a brief chat. He was, according to one Mormon who did not always agree with him, "the loving father of his people."

In addition to his role in opening the church to the world and in liberalizing some of its practices, Mr. McKay played a strong part in a program to fortify family bonds. He sought to have families gather one night each week, with the father in charge, for a discussion of spiritual problems, for it was his conviction that the family was the basic unit of society and of the church.

His own family life was close. His wife was Emma Ray Riggs, whom he married in 1901 and who was living at his death. They had seven children, of whom six survive: David Lawrence McKay, Dr. Llewelyn R. McKay, Mrs. Eugene Blood, Mrs. Emma Rae Ashton, Dr. Edward R. McKay, and Robert R. McKay.

BERTRAND RUSSELL

Bertrand Russell died at his home in Wales on February 2, 1970, at the age of ninety-seven. In almost everything he did he stirred dusts of criticism, yet he managed to be right so often—and he lived so long— that his life was a feast for any obit writer.

"THREE PASSIONS, simple but overwhelmingly strong, have governed my life: the longing for love, the search for knowledge, and unbearable pity for the suffering of mankind."

In those words Bertrand Arthur William Russell, the third Earl Russell, described the motive forces of his extraordinarily long, provocative, and complex life. But only one yearning, that for love, was fully satisfied, he said, and only when he was eighty and married his fourth wife, Edith Finch, then a fifty-two-year-old American.

Of his search for knowledge, he reflected, "a little of this, but not much, I have achieved."

And as for pity: "Echoes of cries of pain reverberate in my heart. Children in famine, victims tortured by oppressors, helpless old people a hated burden for their sons, and a whole world of loneliness, poverty, and pain make a mockery of what human life should be. I long to alleviate this evil, but I cannot, and I too suffer."

Russell's self-assessment scanted his lifelong passionate skepticism, which provided the basis for his intellectual stature. Possessing a mind of dazzling brilliance, he made significant contributions to mathematics and philosophy for which, alone, he would have been renowned. Two works, *The Principles of Mathematics* and *Principia Mathematica*, both published before World War I, helped to determine the direction of modern philosophy. Russell's name, as a result, was linked with those of such titans of thought as Alfred North Whitehead and Ludwig Wittgenstein.

Largely for his role as a philosopher, Russell received the Nobel Prize for Literature in 1950. A year earlier, he had been named by King George

VI to the Order of Merit, whose British membership is limited to twenty-four persons. These honors cast into strange relief the fact that in 1940 a New York State Supreme Court justice ruled him unfit to teach at City College.

Unlike some generative thinkers, Russell epitomized the philosopher as a public figure. He was the Voltaire of his time, but lacking in the Sage of Fernay's malice. From the beginning to the end of his active life, Russell engaged himself with faunlike zest in the great issues of the day—pacifism, rights for women, civil liberty, trial marriage, new methods of education, Communism, the nuclear peril, and war and peace —for he was at bottom a moralist and a humanist. He set forth his views on moral and ethical matters in such limpidly written books as *Marriage and Morals, Education and the Social Order,* and *Human Society in Ethics and Politics.*

He posed awkward questions and gave answers that some regarded as less than commonsensical. However, from his first imprisonment (as a pacifist in World War I) to his last huzza of dissent (as a Zola-like accuser of the United States for its involvement in Vietnam) he scorned easy popularity and comfortable platitudes. He was, indeed, untamable, for he had a profound faith in the ultimate triumph of rationality, which he was certain he represented in an undidactic fashion.

"I don't think, taking it generally, that I have a dogmatic temperament," he insisted. "I am very skeptical about most things and I think that skepticism in me is deeper than positive statements. But, of course, if you get into propaganda you have to make positive statements."

His active involvement in causes (and the scores of positive declarations he made in their behalf) earned him a good deal of abuse and even ridicule. "England's wisest fool," was what his deriders said.

Some of the severest criticism was directed at Russell for his condemnation of United States policy in Vietnam and for his attempts to show this country guilty of crimes against humanity there. Oddly, the criticism came not only from war partisans but also from the Soviet Union—a professed ally of North Vietnam—which Russell believed lacked stanchness because it was under the thumb of the United States.

His vitriolic stand on Vietnam stemmed from concern over the possibility of a nuclear war. Although he had once suggested the threat of a preventive nuclear war to impose disarmament on the Soviet Union, his views sobered in the mid-fifties and through the Committee of 100 in Britain he strove to arouse mass opposition to atomic weaponry. For his part in a demonstration in London's Trafalgar Square in 1961 he went unrepentantly to jail. He was eighty-nine at the time.

Later, at the height of the Cuban missile crisis in 1962, he dispatched letters to President John F. Kennedy and Premier Nikita S. Khrushchev, bidding them hold summit talks to avert war. Although he was curtly rebuffed by Mr. Kennedy, Russell was convinced that he had been instrumental in settling the dispute peacefully. *Unarmed Victory*, published in 1963, contained this correspondence as well as letters he addressed to U Thant, Jawaharlal Nehru and Chou En-lai, among others, about the Chinese-Indian border conflict, for the settlement of which he also took some credit.

No Communist ("I dislike Communism because it is undemocratic and capitalism because it favors exploitation") Russell was a relentless critic of the Soviet Union until after the death of Stalin in 1953. He then softened his attitude because he considered the post-Stalin leadership more amenable to world peace.

In the Vietnam conflict he was certain that the United States acted from sinister economic and political motives—a grasping for Southeast Asian raw materials and an itching for war with China.

Russell took the position that the United States, "the excessive power in the world," had escalated a war for which it bore "total responsibility." He compared American actions to the German occupation of Czechoslovakia, French terror in Algiers, and Soviet suppressions in Hungary.

"Whatever happens," he told a visitor in his wafer-thin voice in the spring of 1967, "I cannot be a silent witness to murder or torture. Anyone who is a partner in this is a despicable individual. I am sorry I cannot be moderate about it. What I hope is that the Americans will arouse so much opposition that in their own minds they will start to think that it is not worth the trouble."

Convinced by data collected for him in Vietnam that the United States was committing war crimes, Russell organized and helped finance a mock trial of this country's leaders. The War Crimes Tribunal, presided over by Jean-Paul Sartre and Isaac Deutscher, met in Stockholm in May 1967, and issued a detailed indictment of United States military practices. Although the State Department discounted the testimony adduced by the tribunal, Russell was impressed by the evidence. The tribunal, in the end, caused only a minor stir, in part because the Communist press in Europe boycotted its proceedings.

Because of the stridency of his views, some charged that Russell was senile and a dupe of one of his secretaries, Ralph Schoenman, who was also for a time secretary of the Bertrand Russell Peace Foundation and active in the War Crimes Tribunal. Dispassionate reporters who traveled to Russell's home overlooking the winding Glaslyn River at Penrhyndeudraeth, Wales, found the frail philosopher very much alert. As to Mr.

Schoenman, he said, "You know, he is a rather rash young man, and I have to restrain him."

A gentle, even shy man, Russell was delightful as a conversationalist, companion, and friend. He was capable of a pyrotechnical display of wit, erudition, and curiosity, and he bubbled with anecdotes about the world's greats. Despite his title, he was "Bertie" to one and all. His charm, plus his assured position in the upper reaches of the British aristocracy, created for him a worldwide circle of friends. They were a heterogeneous lot, ranging over the years from Tennyson to Graham Greene to Mr. Sartre.

Friends included philosophers such as Whitehead and Wittgenstein; scientists such as Einstein, Niels Bohr, and Max Born; writers such as P. G. Wodehouse, Joseph Conrad, D. H. Lawrence, E. M. Forster, T. S. Eliot, Ezra Pound, George Bernard Shaw, Maxim Gorky, and H. G. Wells; and political figures such as Sydney and Beatrice Webb, Harold Laski, Lenin, and Trotsky. They numbered in the hundreds, and Russell maintained a lively correspondence with them. Someone calculated, in fact, that he wrote one letter for every thirty hours of his life.

As a young man, gaunt and black-haired, Russell favored a flowing mustache and high, starched collars. In his autumnal years his spareness became frailty and, mustache discarded, he resembled a frost-famished sparrow. His glittering eyes and half-smile, combined with a shock of white hair, gave him the appearance of a sage, at once remote and kindly. It was a visage cartoonists delighted to draw.

Although he wrote a book about the mysteries of relativity, he humorously admitted that he could not change a light bulb or understand the workings of an automobile engine. However, he had a reason for everything. William Jovanovich, the American publisher, recalled that as a Harvard student he ate in a cafeteria where the food was cheap and not very good.

"I would sit at a long public table where on many occasions also sat the philosopher Bertrand Russell," Mr. Jovanovich said. "One day I could not contain my curiosity. 'Mr. Russell,' I said, 'I know why I eat here. It is because I am poor. But why do you eat here?' 'Because,' he said, 'I am never interrupted.'"

In his last years Russell lived on liquids—a food concentrate, soups, puddings, tea, and seven double Red Hackle scotches a day—because an intestinal kink had been discovered when he was in his eighties and surgery was ruled inadvisable.

He told a visitor that he had started drinking scotch as a pacifist in World War I. "King George V took the pledge because he thought he could save money and use the money to kill Germans, so I drank," he explained with a twinkle.

Russell's eccentricity, or, as he would have it, his independence of mind, was familial. He was born at Ravenscroft, Monmouthshire, on May 18, 1872. He was the youngest of three children of Lord Amberley and the former Katharine Stanley, daughter of Baron Stanley of Alderley. His paternal grandfather was John Russell, the first Earl, who was twice Prime Minister and a leader in obtaining passage of the Reform Bill of 1832, which liberalized election to the House of Commons.

One of Bertrand's maternal uncles became a Roman Catholic and a bishop in partibus; another became a Moslem and made the pilgrimage to Mecca; a third was a combative agnostic. His mother campaigned for votes for women and was a friend of Mazzini, the Italian revolutionary. His father was a freethinker. Together they shocked society by arranging a ménage à trois with the tutor of their elder son, Frank.

Bertrand's mother died when he was two and his father about a year later. Lord Amberley left the guardianship of his sons (the third child, a daughter, had died) to the tutor and another man, both atheists. The guardianship was broken, however, by Lord John Russell, and Bertrand was reared, after his grandfather's death in 1878, by the Dowager Lady Russell, a woman of strict Puritan moral views.

In the first volume of *The Autobiography of Bertrand Russell*, published in 1967, the philosopher candidly disclosed his mixed feelings for his grandmother. He felt that she was overly protective; on the other hand, he admired (and profited from) one of her favorite Bible texts, "Thou shalt not follow a multitude to do evil."

Russell's childhood, as he recalled it, was a lonely one, for most of his companions were adults and he had a succession of German and Swiss governesses. He was rescued, however, by geometry.

"At the age of eleven I began Euclid, with my brother [seven years his senior] as my tutor," Russell wrote. "This was one of the great events of my life, as dazzling as first love. I had not imagined there was anything so delicious in the world. From that moment until Whitehead and I finished *Principia Mathematica*, when I was thirty-eight, mathematics was my chief interest and my chief source of happiness."

As an adolescent Russell read widely, advanced in mathematics and speculated about religion. At seventeen he became convinced that there was no life after death, "but I still believed in God because the 'First Cause' argument appeared to be irrefutable," he wrote, adding: "At the age of eighteen, however, I read [John Stuart] Mill's *Autobiography*, where I found a sentence to the effect that his father had taught him that the question 'Who made me?' cannot be answered since it immediately suggests the further question 'Who made God?' This led me to abandon the 'First Cause' argument and to become an atheist."

Russell's *Autobiography* recites in detail the painful intellectual struggle that he waged with himself over theology, in the course of which he wrote out in his journal the argumentation that led to his conclusions.

Entering Trinity College, Cambridge, at eighteen, Russell was soon in the company of its brightest minds—G. Lowes Dickinson, G. E. Moore, John Maynard Keynes, Lytton Strachey, Charles Sanger, Theodore Davies, John McTaggart, and Whitehead. Among them he became less and less solemn while continuing his devotion of philosophy and mathematics. "What I most desired," he said, "was to find some reason for supposing mathematics true."

Graduating with highest honors, he married Alys Pearsall Smith, a pretty American Quaker five years his senior. The marriage lasted from 1894 to 1921, but it was terminated in fact in 1901. "I went out bicycling one afternoon and, suddenly, as I was riding along a country road, I realized that I no longer loved Alys," he recalled. Subsequently, Russell had several love affairs, including a celebrated liaison with the flamboyant Lady Ottoline Morrell and another with Lady Constance Malleson. His second marriage, in 1921, was to Dora Winifred; his third was to Patricia Helen Spence in 1936; and his fourth, to Edith Finch, took place sixteen years later.

After Russell's first marriage he and his wife traveled on the Continent, where he studied economics and German Social Democracy, and thence to the United States, where he lectured on non-Euclidian geometry at Bryn Mawr College and Johns Hopkins University. Meanwhile, he became a Fellow at Trinity.

The year 1900 was one of the most important of Russell's life. In July he attended an International Congress of Philosophy in Paris and met Giuseppe Peano, an originator of symbolic logic. Russell devoured Peano's work. Recounting his exhilaration, he wrote: "For years I had been endeavoring to analyze the fundamental notions of mathematics, such as order and cardinal numbers. Suddenly, in the space of a few weeks, I discovered what appeared to be definite answers to the problems which had baffled me for years. And in the course of discovering these answers, I was introducing a new mathematical technique, by which regions formerly abandoned to vagueness of philosophers were conquered for the precision of exact formulae."

In October he sat down to write *The Principles of Mathematics*, putting down two hundred thousand words in three months. Its purpose was "first to show that all mathematics follows from symbolic logic, and, secondly, to discover, so far as possible, what are the principles of symbolic logic, itself." With its publication in 1902, he plunged into an eight-year task of elucidating the logical deduction of mathematics that became *Principia Mathematica*. Reducing abstractions to paper was a grueling intellectual task. "Every morning I would sit down before a blank sheet of paper," he said. "Throughout the day, with a brief interval for lunch, I would stare at the blank sheet. Often when evening came it was still blank."

As time went on and the agony of effort increased, Russell "often wondered whether I should ever come out of the other end of the tunnel in which I seemed to be." Several times he contemplated suicide, but he persevered. However, he said, "my intellect never quite recovered from the strain."

"I have been ever since definitely less capable of dealing with difficult abstractions than I was before," he said.

Principia Mathematica, one of the world's greatest rationalist works, cost Russell and Whitehead, his collaborator, fifty pounds each to publish. Despite its complexities, the book took the mystery out of mathematical knowledge and eliminated any connection that might have been supposed to exist between numbers and mysticism.

The Russell philosophy, which he called "logical atomism," freed logical analysis from the tyranny of ordinary grammar or syntax. One illustration of the point is his theory of descriptions, which he first developed in 1905, and which has to do with the problem of the meaning of existence. He explained it this way: "Suppose I say 'The golden mountain does not exist,' and suppose you ask 'What is the golden mountain?' It would seem that, if I say 'It is the golden mountain,' I am attributing some sort of existence to it.

"'The golden mountain does not exist' means there is no entity c such that 'x is golden and mountainous' is true when x is c, but not otherwise."

Thus, he argued, "existence" can only be asserted of descriptions.

In the years when Russell was writing his magisterial volumes, he continued his interest in social problems by participating in the woman suffrage movement and Fabian Society activities. World War I mobilized his concern for world affairs. A jingoist in the early stages of the Boer War, he later changed his mind and became an anti-imperialist; and in 1914 he was a pacifist, but not a pro-German. He wrote such books as *War—the Offspring of Fear, Principles of Social Recognition,* and *Justice in Wartime.*

"But of all the evils of war," he wrote, "the greatest is the purely spiritual evil: the hatred, the injustice, the repudiation of truth, the artificial conflict."

Russell was jailed for six months for his writings, spending his sentence writing and studying in a comfortable cell in Brixton Prison.

His pacifism alienated many of his friends, and in his loneliness he entered into an intense love affair with the actress Colette O'Niel. "Colette's love was a refuge to me, not from cruelty itself, which was inescapable, but from the agonizing pain of realizing that that is what men are," he recalled.

"I became for the first time deeply convinced that puritanism does not make for human happiness," he said. "I became convinced that most human beings are possessed by a profound unhappiness venting itself in destructive rages, and that only through the diffusion of instinctive joy can a good world be brought into being."

After the war, Russell visited the Soviet Union and met Lenin, Trotsky, and Gorky. He expressed sympathy for the aims espoused by Communists, but he also voiced misgivings about the Soviet regime.

In *The Practice and Theory of Bolshevism*, published in 1920, he wrote: "I am compelled to reject Bolshevism for two reasons: First, because the price mankind must pay to achieve Communism by Bolshevik methods is too terrible; and secondly because, even after paying the price, I do not believe the result would be what the Bolsheviks profess to desire."

In the twenties, after his second marriage, the Russells established an experimental school, the Beacon Hill School, to promote progressive education. Of the children there Russell wrote: "We allow them to be rude and use any language they like. If they want to call me or their teachers fools, they call us fools. There is no check on irreverence toward elders or betters."

The school's concepts had a wide influence in Britain and the United States, where they were the foundation for scores of similar institutions and practices. However, Russell revised his views about Beacon Hill, saying in later years, "I feel several things were mistaken on the principles on which the school was conducted; young children in a group cannot be happy without a certain amount of order and routine."

In 1931 Russell became the third Earl Russell on the death of his brother, John Francis Stanley Russell, the second Earl. Two years later his wife, Dora, who had borne him two children, announced that her third child had been sired by another man. The couple's divorce suit was a nine days' wonder in the press. After the decree was granted, Russell married his secretary, and the couple had a child in 1937.

With the rise of Hitler, Russell opposed Nazi methods, but opposed any steps that might lead to war. His attitude changed in 1939 after the German invasion of Czechoslovakia and Poland. In *Unarmed Victory*, he explained his shift from pacifism: "I had hoped until after the time of Munich that the Nazis might be persuaded into not invading other countries. Their invasions proved that this hope was in vain, and at the same time evidence accumulated as to the utterly horrible character of their internal regime.

"The two factors led me reluctantly to the conviction that war against the Nazis was necessary."

Meantime, in 1938, Russell began an extended visit to the United States, teaching first at the University of Chicago and then at the University of California at Los Angeles. He also gave a lecture series at Harvard, and in 1949 he received an appointment to teach at tax-supported City College in New York.

The step loosed a storm of protest from politicians now forgotten and from the Right Reverend William T. Manning, a Bishop of the Episcopal Church in New York. The Bishop charged that Russell was "a recognized propagandist against religion and morality and who specifically defends adultery." The registrar of New York County suggested that the philosopher be "tarred and feathered and run out of the country." A city Councilman called him "a bum." Among other things that incensed critics was a sentence from *Education and the Social Order* that read: "I am sure that university life would be better, both intellectually and morally, if most university students had temporary childless marriages."

Amid guffaws from the intellectual community, state Supreme Court Justice John E. McGeehan vacated the appointment on the ground that Russell was an alien and an advocate of sexual immorality. He said Russell would be occupying "a chair of indecency" at City College.

For a brief time Russell found himself publicly taboo. "Owners of halls refused to let them if I was to lecture," he recalled in the third volume of his autobiography, "and if I had appeared anywhere in public, I should probably have been lynched by a Catholic mob, with the full approval of the police." Although he undoubtedly overstated the case, Russell did have trouble earning money for a while. He was rescued from this situation by Dr. Albert C. Barnes, the inventor of Argyrol and the millionaire art collector and creator of the Barnes Foundation, who gave him a five-year appointment to lecture at his foundation in Merion, Pennsylvania.

In the fall of 1940, he also gave the William James Lectures at Harvard, and over the next four years he spoke at various institutions and put the finishing touches on his *History of Western Philosophy*, the chief source of his income for many years.

Returning to Britain in 1944, he wrote and lectured; and, in 1948, gave the first Reith Lecture for the British Broadcasting Corporation. His reputation then, as in former years, was mixed. He was thought to be wise, yet he was ridiculed for uttering his maxims oracularly. He was recognized as a brilliant logician but a deficient politician—as when he wanted to take advantage of Western atomic superiority to bring the Soviet Union to heel.

Russell was lecturing at Princeton in 1950 when he was awarded the Nobel Prize "in recognition of his many-sided and significant writings, in which he appeared as a champion of humanity and freedom of thought."

Since the middle fifties Russell devoted most of his seemingly inexhaustible energies to a drive against nuclear war. In taking his stand, he proposed that Britain be neutral in the East-West conflict. He urged the withdrawal of United States nuclear weapons from British soil. "For my part, both as a patriot and as a friend of humanity," he said, "I would wish to see Britain officially neutral. The patriotic argument is very obvious to me. No sensible man would wish to see his country obliterated. And as things stand, so long as Britain remains allied to America, there is a serious threat of extermination without the slightest advantage either to America or to the Western way of life."

In furtherance of his views Russell took part in a sit-down demonstration in London and was arrested for breach of peace. The eighty-nine-year-old man was jailed for seven days in Brixton Prison after replying "No, I won't" to a magistrate's request that he pledge himself to good behavior.

Although some thought Russell meddled in the Cuban crisis in 1962, the main point of his activity, as conveyed in letters to world leaders, appeared to be that no national objective justified a crisis that might lead to world destruction. "If people could learn to view nuclear war as a common danger to our species," he wrote, "and not as a danger due solely to the wickedness of the oppressing group, it would be possible to negotiate agreements which would put an end to the common danger."

Russell's attitude toward the Vietnam conflict flowed from his desire to advance the cause of world peace, which he saw endangered by United States imperialism. He believed that a rebuff for the United States, indeed a military defeat, would dampen war fires.

Russell had a rather pixie sense of humor about himself and death, and in 1937 he composed his own obituary as he imagined it might appear in the *Times* of London. He disclosed his article in an interview in 1959, and it read in part:

"In his [Russell's] youth he did work of importance in mathematical logic, but his eccentric attitude toward the first World War revealed a lack of balanced judgment, which increasingly infected his later writings.

"His life, for all its waywardness, had a certain anachronistic consistency, reminiscent of that of the aristocratic rebels of the early nineteenth century. His principles were curious, but such as they were they governed his actions. In private life, he showed none of the acerbity which marred his writings but was a genial conversationalist, not devoid of human sympathy."

ALEXANDER KERENSKY

Alexander Kerensky died in New York on June 11, 1970, at the age of eighty-nine. The onetime leader of the Russian Provisional Government in 1917 was, by the time he died, a historical curiosity, an amber-preserved anachronism. I had talked with him on the fiftieth anniversary of "his" revolution and he was still fighting those struggles. My obit tried to catch him at his apogee and to relate, through him, an outline of the Russian Revolution.

FOR A BRIEF and meteoric moment, Alexander Fyodorovich Kerensky, thirty-six years old and a lawyer, was at the vortex of the Russian Revolution, the greatest historical event since the French Revolution. The complex political, social, and economic forces that generated that event overwhelmed him, and the power he exercised for little more than four months dribbled from his grasp, to be picked up and held onto by the Communists.

For the remainder of his life he was the epitome of failure in a revolution, a man scorned by the victors, an exile from his country who was a curiosity in his adopted land and who passed his time in fulminations against the Soviet state and attempts to justify his actions in the Provisional Government of 1917.

Fortuitously involved in the drama of the revolution, Kerensky seemed to many, in perspective, to deserve Leon Trotsky's verdict: "Kerensky was not a revolutionist; he merely hung around the revolution." Nevertheless, from July to November 1917, when he was head of the Provisional Government that followed some three hundred years of autocratic rule by the Romanov czars, the eyes of the world were upon him as the giant seeking to bring stability and a measure of democratic rule to the vast, multinational domain of Russia and her 170 million persons.

Described by a British writer in those months as "a frail young man with a sullen mouth, deadly serious and endowed with that gift of tongue which is bestowed only on prophets and world movers," Kerensky appeared to many of his countrymen and to many abroad to personify Carlyle's "Ablest Man," the hero of a "new" Russia. Yet so swiftly did the engines of revolution run that by late October he had fled Petrograd, then the capital of Russia, never to return as the man in charge. His historical moment had concluded.

The man who took his place and fashioned the world's first Communist revolution was Vladimir Ilyich Ulyanov, the hardy, professional Bolshevik leader known as Lenin. Like Kerensky, Lenin was a lawyer; but the supreme irony was that the two men shared the same birthplace, Simbirsk (now Ulyanovsk), a sleepy provincial town on the middle Volga; and that Kerensky's father was the director of the gymnasium from which young Lenin was graduated. (Indeed, Fyodor Kerensky had praised the youth's academic and personal record and had been close enough to the family to offer advice on his university education.) There is no evidence, however, that Kerensky met Lenin, eleven years his senior, in Simbirsk or later.

Lenin was harsh in his judgment of his benefactor's son. Kerensky, Lenin wrote during the revolution, was a "loudmouth," an "idiot," and "objectively" an agent of Russian bourgeois imperialism.

Kerensky's assessment of Lenin was scarcely less cordial. In *Russia and History's Turning Point*, published in 1965, the former Russian leader insisted that Lenin was a paid agent of the German General Staff who had thwarted the Provisional Government "with a stab in the back." "Lenin," he wrote, "had no moral or spiritual objection to promoting the defeat of his own country." He argued that "Lenin's chief aim [in 1917] was to overthrow the Provisional Government as an essential step toward the signing of a separate peace [with Germany]."

He denied that he was unaware of Communist peril, but in his summing up of events, in 1965, he contended that attacks from rightist military men and political leaders had undermined his government and had opened the way for Lenin's success. Kerensky put it this way: "I feel it is very important to the cause of freedom everywhere to ascribe the main reason for the defeat of Russian democracy [in 1917] to this attack from the right instead of to the foolish myth that Russian democracy was 'soft' and blind to the Bolshevik danger."

In 1917 Kerensky was a moderate Socialist, a member of the Social Revolutionary Party. He was, however, not doctrinaire, but fitted rather the description of him by George F. Kennan, an American authority on Russia, as "a Socialist of sorts." His political convictions were molded by his experience in the turbulence of Russia, starting with the Revolution of 1905.

Born April 22, 1881, to a family of some station (his father was a school superintendent and his mother was an army officer's daughter), Kerensky was reared with considerable privilege. In his youth he wanted to be a musician or an actor (he was then living in Tashkent), but when he entered the University of St. Petersburg in 1899 it was to study history, classical philology, and jurisprudence.

Introduced to politics as a university student, Kerensky was first drawn to the moderate agrarianism of the Narodnik (Populist) movement, and his sympathies for those oppressed by czarism were lively. Indeed, after being admitted to the bar in 1904 he began his professional career by giving free legal advice to poor urban workers in St. Petersburg.

He was quickly caught up in the Revolution of 1905. After the "Bloody Sunday" massacre in January of that year, when a workers' procession petitioning the Czar was cut down by troops, Kerensky was one of a committee that aided the massacre's victims and their families. His displeasure with the Czar evaporated in October, however, when Nicholas II proclaimed a moderate constitutional reform that included a Duma, or parliament. Writing in 1965 of his feelings on hearing the Czar's manifesto. Kerensky said: "I spent the rest of that night in a state of elation. The age-long bitter struggle of the people for freedom . . . seemed to be over. . . . A wave of warmth and gratitude went through my whole being, and my childhood adoration for the Czar revived."

His mood shifted, however, and the volatile young man volunteered to help assassinate Nicholas. His offer was rejected "because I had no experience of a revolutionary and could not therefore be relied on." After a brief imprisonment in 1906 (he was convicted of possessing revolutionary literature), he eschewed politics until he was elected to the fourth (and most spurious) of the Czar's Dumas in 1912.

In the interval he accumulated celebrity throughout Russia as an eloquent defense lawyer. He defended Estonian peasants charged with sacking a baronial estate; he was counsel to striking workers, mutinous soldiers, rebellious peasants, and revolutionary intellectuals.

Kerensky's most famous legal exploit occurred in 1913, when Mendel Beiliss, a Jew, was tried on charges of having committed a ritual murder of a Christian boy. Kerensky was one of the chief sponsors of a resolution of the St. Petersburg bar that assailed the trial as "a slanderous attack on the Jewish people." His action won him acclaim in the Jewish community and among enlightened Christians. Nonetheless, he was sentenced to eight months' detention in 1914 for his role in attacking the czarist judicial system.

Kerensky's election to the Duma, through whose creaking doors he was to enter history, was adventitious. "I had never given much thought to the future and I had no political plans," he wrote later. "My only desire, since the beginning of my political life, had been to serve my country. As a result I had been taken unawares when . . . asked . . . to consent to stand for election to the Fourth Duma as a Trudovik [semi-Liberal and semi-Populist] candidate."

In the Duma, Kerensky supported World War I and urged "a reconciliation between the Czar and the people." "I felt," he said, "that the battle we had been waging against the remnants of absolutism could now be postponed." (In after years, however, he contended that "the great war was absolutely contrary to the national interests and aims of Russia.")

In the course of the war czarist repression increased and Kerensky became progressively disenchanted with the regime. His speeches in the Duma took on greater passion. In one of them he said: "Have you fully understood [that] the historic task of the Russian people . . . is the abolition of the medieval regime immediately at any cost? If you refuse to listen to the warning voice, you, gentlemen, will meet facts instead of warnings. Behold the flashes of lightning that are already flaring here and there across the skies of the Russian Empire!"

Toward the beginning of 1917, reverses in battle against the Central Powers shook the already fragile Romanov court. Adding to discontent at the front was war-weariness at home, economic privation, industrial dislocation, and bureaucratic rigidity. Criticism of the Czar, his family, and his Ministers mounted daily; and reflecting this within the Duma was a bloc of liberal and left deputies that by the end of February controlled 240 of that body's 402 votes.

But what touched off the one-week rising that was the February Revolution was a strike of ninety thousand St. Petersburg workers that began February 23 and by the following day involved two hundred thousand workers. Sketching how this unrest was transformed into a revolution, Professor Adam B. Ulam, an authority on Russia, wrote in *The Bolsheviks:* "Strikes were followed by street manifestations and disorders. What transformed the riots into a revolution was the behavior of the garrison of Petrograd. Called upon to help the police quell the disorders, the soldiers refused, and in some cases fired upon the police.

". . . . The Czarist regime disintegrated. . . . Confronted by events it could not control or even understand, it simply stopped functioning. . . . What took its place were several authorities, which tried to discharge the task of governing the vast country, sometimes working together, sometimes at cross purposes, but increasingly powerless in the face of growing defeat and anarchy and finally conquered by them."

Initially, two improvised governments appeared in Petrograd, the capital. One represented the Duma, which, refusing to disband on the Czar's order, set up an emergency committee that formed the nucleus of the eleven-member Provisional Government. Headed by Prince Georgi Lvov, it included Kerensky as Minister of Justice.

Simultaneously, the city's workers organized the other improvised government, the Petrograd Soviet (Council) of the Workers' and Soldiers' Deputies. Its Provisional Executive Committee included Kerensky as one of its two vice-chairmen, and he acted as intermediary between the Provisional Government and the Petrograd soviet for some time. Both groups professed to speak and act in the name of all the Russian people.

With the almost immediate abdication of Czar Nicholas II, Kerensky became in fact, if not in name, a dominating figure in Russian affairs. His comparative youth, his talents as a popular declamatory orator, his seeming grasp of the popular mood, his quick mind brought him to the fore. "From the moment of the collapse of the monarchy . . . I found myself in the center of events," he recalled in 1965. "I was, in fact, their focal point, the center of the vortex of human passion and conflicting ambitions which raged around me."

In the first days of the Revolution there was a degree of harmony between the Provisional Government and the Petrograd soviet. In this period Kerensky was responsible for initiating such democratic reforms as freedom of speech, assembly, press, and religion, equal rights for women, and universal suffrage.

As significant as were these reforms, they did not go to the core of popular demands for peace and for breaking up the landed estates. Indeed, the first fragmentation of the Provisional Government's authority appeared when it decided to carry on the war. The second element sapping its precarious strength was the grass-roots democracy of the Petrograd soviet: it, more than the government, held the confidence of the workers; and it, more than the government, exercised effective control among the troops. The soviet's Order No. 1, for example, sought to make every military unit in Russia subject to it; and to an increasing degree troops harkened to the soviet.

In the convulsive events of February and March the Bolsheviks played a minor role. They had no representatives in the Provisional Government and only a few in the soviet. The Social Revolutionaries, of whom Kerensky was then one, and the Mensheviks (left-of-center Socialists) were in control of the soviet, while even more moderate elements composed the government.

This inherently unstable balance of forces was tipped leftward, starting in April, when Lenin returned to Petrograd from exile in Switzerland, and shortly after other Bolshevik leaders, including Stalin, were released from czarist detention.

Immediately, Lenin and his Bolsheviks began to put forward a Communist revolutionary program—seizure of land by the peasants, control of industry by the workers, cessation of the war, and concentration of state power in the soviets. Lenin's central slogan—"All power to the soviets!"—eventually caught the imagination of key sections of the public, especially as more soviets were established throughout Russia. And in the months that followed, Bolshevik influence in these soviets (and in the Petrograd soviet in particular) increased measurably.

Although Lenin was the furiously busy mastermind of the Bolsheviks, one personality stood out then as the embodiment of the revolution to come. Describing him and his role, Harvard's Professor Ulam has written: "In May there returned another political exile, Lev Trotsky. . . . With his arrival the tempo of Bolshevik activity quickened. . . . From the beginning, Trotsky, his old quarrel with Lenin laid aside, supplied the missing element in Bolshevism. He was unmatched as a revolutionary orator and agitator."

In May also there was a grave ministerial crisis in the Provisional Government when the Foreign Minister resigned at Kerensky's insistence. The issue was Pavel N. Milyukov's espousal of annexationist aims in the war. In the resulting shifts Kerensky became Minister of War and the Navy. The Cabinet, in which Kerensky was definitely the strongest man, still agreed to continue the war and called for "a general democratic peace."

To revive shattered discipline among the armed forces and to instill patriotism in the troops, Kerensky toured the battlefronts and exhorted the men to fight on. He would cry in his mighty voice: "The destinies of the country are in your hands, and she is in great danger. We have drunk liberty and we are slightly intoxicated. However, we do not need intoxication, but the greatest soberness and discipline. We must enter history so that on our graves it will be written: 'They died but they were never slaves.' "

But words were not enough. The massive offensive that Kerensky ordered late in June against German and Austrian forces ended in a disastrous defeat for the Russians within a few days. The only winners were the Bolsheviks, and their insistent appeals for peace and bread.

Nonetheless, there was a dramatic reversal of Kerensky's fortunes in mid-July, when a Bolshevik adventurist attempt to seize power in Petrograd was suppressed (although Kerensky barely escaped being captured) and a number of Communist leaders, Trotsky among them, were jailed.

The Provisional Government's ordeal in quelling the uprising intensified conflicts within the Ministry, and Prince Lvov, its nominal but shadowy Premier, resigned his office to Kerensky.

Through August apparent calm returned to the surface in Russia. Some discipline was restored in the armed forces, democratic reforms were pushed and the influence of the soviets seemed to be abating. With Lenin in Finland, the Bolsheviks appeared to be in retreat. A party congress, however, claimed a membership of 240,000, a startling increase from the 50,000 in April.

Taking advantage of the lull, Kerensky sought to give his government a wider constituency among the various segments of society by convoking a National State Conference in Moscow, by proclaiming Russia a republic, and by convening a preparliament, the Council of the Republic.

But the fatal shortcoming of all these exertions was that Kerensky and his colleagues held only the shadow of power in a succession of explosive events in which no single group or organization exercised continuing authority. Cessation of the war was the imperative that Kerensky and his associates declined to undertake.

Many historians consider that Kerensky lacked understanding of the basic revolutionary forces with which he was dealing and that his policy errors stemmed from intellectual shallowness. His worst error, in the opinion of many writers, was his appointment of General Lavr G. Kornilov as supreme commander of the army and his early championship of him. The general, according to a fellow officer, had "the heart of a lion and the brains of a sheep." He became disgruntled with Kerensky and lent himself to those who believed that a military dictatorship could save Russia from the muddle she was in.

In early September Kornilov marched on Petrograd in an attempt at a coup d'état. To counter this threat to the government, Kerensky was obliged to seek help from the left. Trotsky and other Communist leaders were released from prison as Kerensky appealed to the soviets and the populace of Petrograd to repulse Kornilov.

Lenin was quick to grasp and to exploit the Kornilov plot. Urging Bolsheviks to fight the general without building up Kerensky, he said, "We shall now show everybody the weakness of Kerensky." And instead of winning credit for saving Russian democracy, Kerensky emerged from the coup (which was easily quashed) as inept. He lost not only the confidence of the officer corps, many of whom backed Kornilov, but also the respect of the main revolutionary elements; for who had balked Kornilov but the soviets?

Kerensky himself regarded the Kornilov affair as decisive. He argued afterward that financiers, industrialists, and rightists had supported the general and that he also enjoyed the backing of the British and French.

Beset from the right and the left, Kerensky's government was virtually paralyzed. Two million army deserters symbolized both the sentiment for peace and the regime's lack of authority. Inflation was uncurbed in the cities, land reform was faltering in the countryside. The result was that Kerensky lost his meager credit with the Russians, and nothing he could do could prevent the ineluctable drift to the October Revolution.

As power filtered from Kerensky, the Petrograd soviet set up a Military Revolutionary Committee, whose actual leader was Trotsky. To the soviet and to this committee, power gravitated. This picture of Petrograd in those climactic days emerges in Professor Ulam's study: 'In any other place and time except the fantastic Petrograd of 1917 the setting up of the Military Revolutionary Committee and its subsequent countermanding of the government's orders would have been taken as the beginning of a mutiny. But in fact nobody got unusually excited. . . Kerensky's government continued in its peaceful coma."

The coup de grâce by which the Bolsheviks finished off Kerensky's government was executed with astonishing dispatch. Carefully planned by Lenin and Trotsky and their close associates, the seizure of power took about a day, and it was accomplished on October 25 by the Julian calendar, or November 7 by the Gregorian. Troops loyal to the Bolsheviks simply occupied the principal government buildings, virtually without opposition, and arrested the ministers. Kerensky fled.

Writing long after the event, he remained persuaded that the toppling of his government was the result of a conspiracy between Lenin and the German General Staff. "The Germans needed a coup d'état in Petrograd to stop Austria from signing a separate peace treaty. For Lenin, an immediate peace with Germany after his accession to power was the only way he could establish a dictatorship," Kerensky wrote in 1965 in *Russia and History's Turning Point*.

Then he added: "I am firmly convinced that the uprising of October 24–25 was deliberately timed to coincide with the serious crisis in Austro-German relations."

The final minutes of his regime, as he recited them later, were these: 'The night of October 24–25 was a time of tense expectation. We were waiting for troops to arrive from the front. They had been summoned by me in good time and were due in Petrograd on the morning of October 25. But instead of troops, all we got were telegrams and telephone messages saying that the railways were being sabotaged.

"By morning (October 25) the troops had not yet arrived. The central telephone exchange, post office, and most of the government offices were occupied by detachments of Red Guards. The building that housed the Council of the Republic . . . had also been occupied by Red sentries.

"The Winter Palace was cut off, and even telephone contact was broken. After a long meeting that lasted into the early hours of the morning, most of the members of the government had gone home to get some rest. Left alone together, [I. A.] Konovalov [Minister of Trade] and I walked over to the district military staff. . . .

"After a brief discussion it was decided that I should drive out at once to meet the troops. We were all quite sure that the paralysis of will that had seized democratic Petrograd would pass as soon as it was recognized that Lenin's plot was by no means a 'misunderstanding' but a perfidious blow that left Russia entirely at the mercy of the Germans."

Kerensky always maintained that he had rejected an offer to be driven out of Petrograd under the American flag and that he had ridden boldly in his own automobile. Many historians, however, dispute this. William Henry Chamberlain, writing in *The Russian Revolution* and citing the American Ambassador in Russia, said: "About ten in the morning [of October 25] Kerensky decided that his only hope was to make his way to the front and return at the head of reinforcements. One of his adjutants requisitioned a car which belonged to Secretary Whitehouse of the American Embassy; and Kerensky made off in this car, which carried the American flag and, aided by this disguise, slipped through the numerous Bolshevik patrols which were already active in the city."

Soviet historians have added that Kerensky was garbed in woman's attire.

In any event, Kerensky sought vainly to rally armed support for himself and his government, but within days his cause was crushed and he went into hiding. He emerged, briefly, in January 1918, when the Constituent Assembly was convened in Petrograd, and he offered to address it. His political friends, however, were against the plan. According to Kerensky, they told him: "The situation in Petrograd has changed radically. If you appear at the Assembly it will be the end of all of us."

Kerensky said that he contemplated suicide, but "I did not cross the Rubicon of death." Instead, in May 1918, he made his way out of Russia, departing Murmansk for London on a French cruiser. He was disguised as a Serbian officer.

In London he called on Prime Minister David Lloyd George and in Paris he saw Premier Georges Clemenceau, who, having pinned their hopes for upsetting the Bolsheviks on Admiral Alexander V. Kolchak, no longer had any use for the former Premier.

In exile Kerensky pursued as forlorn a cause. Until 1940 he lived mainly in Britain and France and made occasional lecture tours in the United States. In the thirties he edited an émigré paper in Paris, which he left in 1940 for the United States, where he wrote and lectured.

In 1956 he went to Stanford University in Palo Alto, California, where he studied and classified Russian documents at the Hoover Institute of War, Revolution and Peace. He also taught seminars at Stanford and appeared as guest lecturer at a number of colleges.

From the middle of the forties he lived as the house guest of Mrs. Kenneth F. Simpson, the widow of a New York Republican leader, in her spacious red-brick townhouse on East 91st Street. He occupied the fifth and top floor, where he also had a study. He was a familiar figure in the neighborhood. For years, before his sight faded, he walked five or six miles a day, and one of his favorite strolls was to walk around the Central Park reservoir.

Kerensky was easily identified in a gathering by his height (five feet ten inches), by his erect bearing, his piercing blue eyes, his deeply creased face and by his close-cropped white hair. He spoke heavily accented English and when he was agitated his syntax was difficult to follow; but when his attention was diverted from Russian politics, he was a witty raconteur.

Kerensky's final years were passed in the backwater reserved for men shunted aside by historical change. He spent much time attempting to defend his leadership of what he came to call "the Kerensky revolution." On its fiftieth anniversary in 1967 he asserted again that it had made Russia one of the freest countries in the world by establishing press, speech, and political liberties for all. He also insisted again that the Bolsheviks had come to power through a coup d'état.

He believed, though, that Russia had not developed a Socialist system, but rather state capitalism. He saw new freedoms emerging for the Russian people as a result, and he expressed a nostalgic desire to return to his native land if the authorities "will not silence me."

On his leadership, the verdict of even his non-Communist critics was not kind. For example, reviewing *Russia and History's Turning Point*, his last book and his most detailed apologia, the London *Times Literary Supplement* said: "Behind this tale of woe there looms, of course, the fundamental question of whether a bourgeois democracy could have been established in the Russia of 1917 or of subsequent years. Mr. Kerensky is convinced he would have established it if only he had not received so many 'stabs in the back' from Milyukov and Kornilov, from the industrialists and bankers, from Lenin and Trotsky, from the Mensheviks, from his closest political associates, and from the Allied embassies.

"But do not all these 'stabs in the back' add up to the conclusion that parliamentary democracy had no chance of survival in Russia's political and social climate?

"It was the height of naïveté [on Kerensky's part] to imagine that Russia, having in the middle of a war emerged from centuries of autocracy, with a shattered semifeudal structure, with a land-hungry peasantry, with an underdeveloped bourgeoisie, with the national minorities in uproar, and with a highly dynamic, Marxist-oriented, and ambitious working class, could be charmed into the mould of a constitutional monarchy or a liberal republic."